EAST INDIANS IN TRINIDAD

East Indians in Trinidad

A Study in Minority Politics

YOGENDRA K. MALIK

Published for the
Institute of Race Relations, London

OXFORD UNIVERSITY PRESS

LONDON   NEW YORK   TORONTO

1971

Oxford University Press, Ely House, London W.1

GLASGOW   NEW YORK   TORONTO   MELBOURNE   WELLINGTON
CAPE TOWN   SALISBURY   IBADAN   NAIROBI   DAR ES SALAAM   LUSAKA   ADDIS ABABA
BOMBAY   CALCUTTA   MADRAS   KARACHI   LAHORE   DACCA
KUALA LUMPUR   SINGAPORE   HONG KONG   TOKYO

ISBN 0 19 218198 X

Printed in Great Britain
by Butler & Tanner Ltd, Frome and London

Contents

Tables

Plates

Introduction and Acknowledgements

TRINIDAD is a small country consisting of two islands, Trinidad and Tobago, which are the southernmost territories of what was formerly known as the British West Indies. The two islands are situated in the Caribbean, off the coast of South America, near Venezuela. Trinidad, the larger of the two islands, has an area of 1,863 square miles and Tobago, an area of only 116 square miles. The country has a population of 827,957, out of which 33,333 live in Tobago. The islands are 'prosperous; and their standard of living is well above the West Indian average'.[1]

Trinidad is a new nation and lacks a national identity. Negroes and East Indians are the two main ethnic groups, represented by the People's National Movement (P.N.M.) for the Negroes, and the Democratic Labour Party (D.L.P.) for the East Indians. The population is mainly Negro.

The social and cultural life of the minority, the East Indians, who have been highly successful in raising their economic status, has been the subject of various anthropological and sociological studies. But their political organization remains uninvestigated. The purpose of this book is to determine to what degree East Indians have been successful in their political organization.

I have tried to trace the events leading to the formation and the development of the D.L.P., which started as a party of a minority ethnic group. Not only its leadership but its mass following come from East Indians. I have attempted to answer the question of how far the particularist and kinship-oriented social structure of East Indians has been responsible for the decline of cohesion, and many splits within the East Indian leadership of the D.L.P. The role of the East Indian family, kinship groups, and religious organizations such as the *Sanatan Dharma Maha Sabha*, the *Arya Samaj*, the Muslim League, and the *Sunnat-ul-Jamait* as agencies of political socialization and recruitment has also been examined. A closely-focused study of the political perception and the attitude of the East

[1] *The Times*, Supplement on Trinidad and Tobago (25 January 1966).

For a comparison of the national incomes, gross national products, and average annual growth rates of such representative West Indian countries as Barbados, Jamaica, and Trinidad, see Tables 180 and 183 of *The U.N. Statistical Year Book 1965* (New York, Statistical Office of the U.N., Department of Economic and Social Affairs, 1966).

Indian *élite* has been attempted and an effort has been made to interrelate the political failure of East Indians to their cultural and social exclusiveness.

We will see that the East Indian political leadership, because of its failure to rise above the narrow racial-ethnic loyalties, and because of its social origin, became a conservative and conformist force and was unable to change the ethnic orientation of the D.L.P. even though it made an effort to adopt an ideology. Environmental factors contributive to the failure of the D.L.P. such as the fear of Negro violence, the rise of a propertied East Indian middle class more interested in the maintenance of law and order than in capturing political power, and the government party's efforts to win over a section of East Indians have been examined.

This study was conducted at two levels. Field-work consisted of interviews and collection of material in Trinidad and Tobago. The study of documents, government publications, and newspapers was made at the library of the University of West Indies, Mona, Jamaica, the Archives of Trinidad in Port of Spain, and at the library of the University of Florida, Gainesville. I had the opportunity of living and discussing with Negro and East Indian families in Trinidad. This provided an opportunity to make close observations of the social and cultural backgrounds of the two groups and of their diverse attitudes.

Special focus is placed on the East Indian *élite*. The term *élite* here is used strictly in the sense of Harold Lasswell: 'The concept of the elite is classificatory and descriptive designating the holder of high position in a given society.'[1] Defining the concept, S. F. Nadel says that *élite* does not mean oligarchies. 'It is intended to refer to an objective empirical fact, namely the existence in many, perhaps most, societies, of a stratum of population which, for whatever reason, can claim a position of superiority and hence a corresponding measure of influence over the fate of the community.'[2]

The East Indian *élites* were selected on the basis of institutional leadership and reputation. First a list was compiled from the following sources: *The Year Book of Trinidad and Tobago, The Year*

[1] Harold Lasswell, *et al.*, *The Comparative Study of Elites: An Introduction and Bibliography* (Stanford, Stanford University Press, 1952), p. 2.

[2] S. F. Nadel, 'The Concept of Social Elite', *International Social Science Bulletin* (Vol. VIII, No. 3, 1956), p. 413.

Book of the West Indies, East Indian members of the Trinidad Parliament, members of the Chamber of Commerce and the Businessmen's Association, East Indian office-holders of the Trinidad and Tobago Bar Association, former Members of the Federal Parliament, and office-holders of East Indian social organizations, such as the *Sanatan Dharma Maha Sabha*, the Muslim League, the *Sunnat-ul-Jamait*, the *Arya Samaj*, the East Indian National Congress, the West India Club, the Himalaya Club, and the Indian Association.

This list included 130 persons. One hundred and eighteen were contacted, out of which eighty-nine were interviewed. The rest were unable to keep the appointments or could not meet the interview schedule due to one reason or another. Civil Servants constituted the largest group of those who refused to be interviewed. In fact, none of the Civil Servants originally contacted agreed to be interviewed. On the other hand, active politicians were most eager to co-operate. I failed to talk with only one of that group. The rest of the non-respondents were spread among the remaining occupational groups. The data should be interpreted with these limitations in mind.

A structured interview schedule (see Appendix) was used in sessions lasting from one to three hours. The six-page interview schedule consisted of a mixture of fixed responses and open-end questions. The respondents were also asked to name five top East Indian political, religious, business, and social leaders. The interviews were conducted in English, and took place in the homes of the respondents. The notes were taken during the interview. Non-scheduled information, given in the form of personal opinions or comments, was recorded on the back of the interview sheets. Most respondents volunteered answers to almost all the questions, but they were hesitant to comment on their income. The question concerning income was finally dropped.

Table I-1 shows the religious and educational background of the eighty-nine respondents.

Table I-2 gives an idea of the type and number of *élites* in the different occupational groups.

The most frequently mentioned five leaders of the East Indian community were selected mainly on the basis of the *élite* interviews. They were also thoroughly interviewed, some of them three or even four times. They were asked the questions on the standard

Table I-1 *Religious and Educational Background*

Religion	Level of Education			
	Primary or below	Secondary	University	Total
Hindu	13	14	12	39
Muslim	3	4	3	10
East Indian Christian	4	16	19	39
No religion	—	1	—	1
Total	20	35	34	89

interview schedule. They were also asked a series of non-structured open-end questions touching numerous issues. The supplementary interviews were conducted in informal sessions lasting two to three hours.

I had the opportunity of meeting, and discussing various current issues, with the top East Indian political leaders at many social gatherings such as East Indian weddings or religious celebrations. I also toured and visited almost the whole of the island to interview non-*élites* using a two-page questionnaire. Although the data gathered in these interviews were not suitable for statistical presentation, they were suggestive in many ways and have been

Table I-2 *Occupational Distribution of Élites Interviewed*

Occupation	Religion				
	Hindu	Muslim	Christian	No religion	Total
Political	7	1	6	—	14
Party and trade union officials	4	—	2	1	7
Leading businessmen	14	3	4	—	21
Leading professionals	3	3	18	—	24
Religious leaders	7	2	6	—	15
Social leaders	4	1	3	—	8
Total	39	10	39	1	89

used in order to supplement and support the *élite* data. This systematic collection and analysis of the questionnaire survey material has been complemented by library research and participatory observations.

Acknowledgements

I am indebted to various individuals and organizations for their co-operation and help in completing this study. A research grant from the Caribbean Research Center at the University of Florida, a Summer Fellowship awarded by the College of Arts and Sciences, supplemented by a research grant from the Asia Society in New York in 1965, enabled me to travel in the West Indies. I express my sincerest thanks to all these organizations.

In particular, I want to thank Professor Arnold J. Heidenheimer, who as a dissertation adviser, friend, and teacher, contributed to this work in more ways than can be reckoned. In addition, I have also benefited from the advice and comments of Professors Manning J. Dauer and Herbert Doherty, University of Florida, A. W. Singham, University of West Indies, K. Bahadoorsingh, Trinidad, Wendell Bell, Yale University, R. B. Henderson, Southwest Texas State University, Ivar Oxaal, University of Hull, William D. Muller, State University, New York, and Peter Nexdorff, University of Kentucky.

In Trinidad, I received full co-operation from numerous East Indian political, social, and business leaders, I would like to express my special thanks to H. P. Singh, S. N. Capildeo, Stephen C. Maharaj, L. F. Seukeran, Vernon Jamadar, A. C. Rienzi, and C. L. R. James who provided me with numerous opportunities for discussing personally the party politics of the island country.

I also thank the editors and the publishers of the *Western Political Quarterly* and the *Sociological Bulletin* for their permission to reprint and revise the articles originally published in their journals.

Last but not least, I must express my sincere thanks to my wife, Usha, who tirelessly helped me, not only in field research, but also in the typing and retyping of a number of drafts of the manuscript.

Yogendra K. Malik
University of Akron

1. Bhadase Sagan Maraj (extreme right), president general of the *Sanatan Dharma Maha Sabha* and former Leader of the Democratic Labour Party.

2. Vernon Jamadar, Leader of the Opposition and acting Leader of the D.L.P.

3. The late Dr. R. N. Capildeo, former Leader of the D.L.P.

4. Dr. Eric Williams, the Prime Minister
and Political Leader of the P.N.M.

I

The Pluralistic Social Structure of Trinidad

Multi-ethnic Societies and the Concept of Cultural Pluralism

THE organization of Trinidad society is highly complex. The deep cleavages existing between the different sections cannot be understood only by referring to its multi-ethnic character. Diversities are sharpened not only by the racial factors but also by cultural–institutional structures.

Such societies can be best analysed on the basis of 'cultural pluralism'. While studying the societies of Burma and the East Indies, J. S. Furnivall formulated the concept of a 'plural society', which he defines as a 'society . . . comprising two or more elements of social order, which live side by side, yet without mingling in one political unit. . . . In a plural society there is no common will, except possibly, in matters of supreme importance'.[1] In such societies people hold on to their distinctive cultures, languages, and beliefs. There is little intermixing across racial lines. Even economic activities are divided on ethnic lines. The different sections are held together by a political structure superimposed by a colonial power.[2] Distinct from the Western societies, the plural societies are not based upon common values and they lack consensual basis.

With special reference to the Caribbean countries, the term 'plural society' as a conceptual framework has been further developed and refined by M. G. Smith.[3] He accepts institutions

[1] J. S. Furnivall, *Netherland Indies* (London, Cambridge University Press, 1939), p. 446.
[2] J. S. Furnivall, *Colonial Policy and Practice* (London, Cambridge University Press, 1948), p. 304.
[3] M. G. Smith, 'Social and Cultural Pluralism', *Annals of the New York Academy of Sciences* (Vol. 83, January 1960), p. 767. For a further analysis of his concept of 'social and cultural pluralism', see his *The Plural Society in the British West Indies* (Berkeley, University of California Press, 1965). For detailed comments on his concept, see different articles written by the West Indian experts in Vera Rubin (ed.), *Annals of the New York Academy of Sciences* (Vol. 83, January 1960); R. T. Smith, 'Review of Social and Cultural Pluralism in the Caribbean Societies', *American Anthropologist* (Vol. 63, 1961), pp. 155–7; H. I. McKenzie,

such as family, kinship, and caste as the core of a culture and be-lieves that culturally distinguishable societies could be differenti-ated from each other on the basis of their institutional structure. Thus a homogeneous society is characterized by 'a single set of institutions' and in such societies the population has a uniform social structure, common values, and action patterns. On the other hand, in a plural society there exist 'two or more different cultural traditions'.[1] The people differ in their basic institutions such as religion, marriage, and property and they practise a different system 'of beliefs and values'.[2] M. G. Smith does not believe that 'culture' and 'ethnicity' are synonymous. The people of different racial origins may have a common culture.[3] But I believe that cultural institutional structure is only one dimension of human relations in a multi-ethnic society, the other dimension is ethnicity. Because in plural societies such as Guyana and Trinidad 'social cum biological mingling' between East Indians and Negroes is extremely limited, relations across the ethnic lines are not only disapproved of on cultural bases but on ethnic bases. In the recent histories of these societies tension in the relations between different ethnic groups has occurred on ethnic rather than merely on cultural lines. Hoetink, a Dutch sociologist, who has also studied the Caribbean societies, recognizes the importance of this fact and gives equal weight to race and culture. He calls such societies 'segmented', which he defines as a 'society which at its moment of origin consists of at least two groups of people of different races and cultures, each having its own social institutions and social struc-ture; each of these groups, which I shall call segments having its own rank in the social structure; and society as a whole being governed by one of the segments'.[4] His definition of a 'segmented'

'The Plural Society Debate, Some Comments on Recent Contributions', *Social and Economic Studies* (Vol. 15, 1966), pp. 53–60; Leo A. Despres, 'The Implications of Nationalist Politics in British Guiana for the Development of Cultural Theory', *American Anthropologist* (Vol. 66, 1964), pp. 1051–77; Despres, *Cultural Pluralism and Nationalist Politics in British Guiana* (Chicago, Rand McNally and Co., 1967). See also B. Benedict, *Mauritius: The Problems of a Plural Society* (London, Pall Mall, 1965); 'Social Stratification in Plural Societies', *American Anthropologist* (Vol. 64, 1962), pp. 1235–46.

[1] Smith, 'Social and Cultural Pluralism', p. 767.
[2] Smith, *The Plural Society in the British West Indies*, p. 14.
[3] Ibid., p. 15.
[4] H. Hoetink, *Two Variants in Caribbean Race Relations: A Contribution to the*

society is not much different from Smith's concept of cultural pluralism. But unlike Smith, Hoetink does not link the plural society with the State and he rightly recognizes the importance of 'race' in the development of cultural pluralism.

Thus this modified concept of 'plural society' which includes both cultural and ethnic variables, is valuable in the study of the political process of a multi-ethnic society. It goes beyond discussing race relations, and it helps us to understand the key cultural institutions of different groups which play the most significant role in the political socialization and recruitment of leadership at all levels of society.

In a plural society, wide variations are always to be found with respect to such basic institutions as family, marriage, kinship, religion, upbringing and socialization process, inheritance of property and ways of life. Each group possesses its own subculture, with distinctive attributes. Hence, for understanding the total cultural patterns and the working of the political process, a comprehension of the ethnic or group subcultures is imperative.

M. M. Gordon, referring to the Negro culture in the United States, observes, 'A sub-culture is a social division of a national culture made up by a combination of ethnic groups (used here as a generic term concerning race, religion, or national origin).'[1] It is within these groups that the socialization process takes place and face-to-face relations are formed. In his opinion ethnic subcultural groups are more significant than rural and urban groups. They provide the basis of 'sub-national' identifications. In multiracial societies it is this group with which an individual feels not only historical identification but also participational identification. He feels not only that his ultimate fate is bound up with his own people but he also feels at home only among them.[2]

Gordon describes four types of cultural pluralism: the tolerance level; the good group relations level; the community integration level; a mixed type—the pluralistic integrational level.[3] The

---

Sociology of Segmented Societies (London, Oxford University Press for the I.R.R., 1967), p. 97. See also J. D. Speckman, 'The Indian Group in the Segmented Society of Surinam', *Caribbean Studies* (Vol. 3, No. 1, April 1963), pp. 3–17.

[1] M. M. Gordon, 'Social Structure and Goals in Group Relations', in M. Berger (ed.), *Freedom and Social Control in Modern Society* (New York, D. Van Nostrand and Co., 1959), p. 143.

[2] Ibid., p. 147.   [3] Ibid., pp. 153–5.

tolerance level is the lowest level of cultural coexistence. The 'good group relations' envisages a society where ethnic groups maintain their social sub-systems, but where the degree of contact across ethnic lines is substantially greater than that existing at the 'tolerance level and where secondary contacts are considerable in number and primary contacts take place in limited frequency'.[1]

The community integrational level, the third level of cultural pluralism, in the structural realm, according to Gordon, 'envisages multiple primary contacts across ethnic lines to the point of complete lack of emphasis on ethnic background as a factor in social relationship'.[2]

The pluralistic-integrational level, the final level of cultural pluralism, allows for the maintenance and the development of subnational or group social heritage within their own respective social structure. It is at this level that the individual can move freely from one group to another.[3]

Accepting M. M. Gordon's four levels of cultural and social pluralism, we can now turn to the description of the pluralistic social structure of Trinidad society, see what level of cultural pluralism Trinidad society has achieved, and examine how this factor influences the political relations between the different ethnic groups.

Characteristics of the Pluralistic Society of Trinidad

Trinidad has been termed one of the most heterogeneous islands of the West Indies in so far as the nature of its population is concerned.[4] As already said Negroes and East Indians form the two major ethnic groups (see Table 1-1).

The history of the Negroes is bound very closely to that of the sugar industry which was founded in Trinidad by the French in 1780. Negroes, who are called 'Creoles',[5] were brought from West Africa to Trinidad and other islands in the Caribbean as slave

---

[1] Ibid., p. 154.

[2] Ibid., p. 155.

[3] Ibid., p. 155.

[4] Vera Rubin, 'Discussion on Smith's Social and Cultural Pluralism', *Annals of the New York Academy of Sciences* (Vol. 83, January 1960), pp. 783–9.

[5] According to M. G. Smith, the Creoles are the 'native West Indians of European, African, or mixed descent. . . . Expressed in terms of color, Creoles form a trinity of black, white and brown.' *Plural Society in the British West Indies*, p. 307.

labour for the newly-developing sugar industry. Slavery was abolished in 1833, and the Negro slaves were emancipated in 1838. The Negro in Trinidad is the descendant of this emancipated slave.

The white population is of diverse national origins. One of the groups is of French extraction. The French were a rich landowning class. Now the Trinidadian French community consists of rich cocoa planters and salaried employees. The French population of Trinidad swelled when many French fled from the French West Indies as a result of outbreaks of violence in those islands and

Table 1-1   *Distribution of Trinidad Population on the Basis of Race*

Ethnic group	Population	% of the total population
Negro	358,588	43
East Indian	301,946	36
White	15,718	2
Chinese	8,361	1
Mixed	134,749	17
Lebanese, Syrian, others	6,714	1

Source Trinidad and Tobago *Annual Statistical Digest*, No. 13, 1963 (Port of Spain, Central Statistical Office, 1963), pp. 14–15.

sought shelter in Trinidad, which was at that time a Spanish possession. The white population also includes the descendants of Scottish, Irish, and Flemish immigrants from Barbados, Grenada, Bahamas, and the Danish and Swedish possessions in the Caribbean.[1] There is also a small percentage of Portuguese population, whose ancestors started arriving in Trinidad around 1846. The Chinese were brought in to serve on the sugar plantations. The first group of Chinese immigrants was brought around 1806 but the major portion arrived between 1852 and 1862.[2] However, the Chinese were found to be unsuited for the hard work on the plantations, and their organized immigration was dropped.

[1] Phil Vieira, 'The Human Mosaic: That is Trinidad. Life and Times of Early Immigrants', *Independence Supplement, Sunday Guardian* (23 August 1962), p. 8.

[2] Ibid.

The lack of adaptability of the Chinese immigrants and the Negro's reluctance to return to sugar plantations brought about in 1845 the introduction to Trinidad of East Indian indentured labour. This immigration continued until 1917. Even after it was abolished, the population of East Indians increased steadily because of their higher rate of natural reproduction. Until 1917, owing to poor medical care, the East Indian population did not show any excess of births over deaths.[1] After 1931 it began to show an increased birth-rate. The 1946 Census noted the increase in East Indian population at the rate of 2·97 per cent per year.[2] Between 1946 and 1960 the East Indian population increased at

Table 1-2   *Religious Distribution of Trinidad Population*

	%
Roman Catholic	38
Hindu	23
Muslim	6
Anglican	21
Various other Protestant denominations	12

Source Trinidad and Tobago *Yearbook*, 1964–1965 (Port of Spain, Yuille's Printerie, 1964), p. 221.

the rate of 4 per cent per year, one of the highest growth rates in the world.

The Arabs came mostly as merchants. The aboriginal Amerindian population called 'Carib' is now almost extinct.

Mixed population has not increased much in Trinidad. In the 1946 Census Report[3] it was 14·12 per cent; in 1960 it was about 17 per cent. Intermarriage between Indian and Negro is strongly disapproved, and the offspring of such marriages is referred to as *Dogala* (bastard) among East Indians.

The Trinidadian society is characterized not only by the multiplicity of ethnic groups but also by religious diversity (see Table 1-2).

[1] George Cumper, *Social Structure of the British Caribbean* (excluding Jamaica), Part III (Mona, University College of the West Indies, Extra-Mural Department, 1949), p. 30.

[2] L. G. Hopkins, *West Indian Census 1946, General Report on the Census Population* (Kingston, Jamaica Government Printing Office, 9 April 1946), pp. 14–15.

[3] Ibid., p. 15.

Trinidad is predominantly a Roman Catholic and Christian country, the Roman Catholic and the Anglican Churches enjoying the highest social prestige.[1] In the lower socio-economic sectors of the Creole substructure of Trinidad society, some African faiths like *Yoruba*, *Shango*, and *Dahomea* (*Rada*) still survive, but the major portion of the African population has embraced Christianity.

Hinduism and Islam are the main religions of the East Indian population of Trinidad. This religious diversity further adds to the heterogeneous character of the Trinidadian society. Daniel J. Crowley notes that almost every religion in Trinidad has been influenced by the others,[2] but followers of Hinduism and Islam hold on to their faiths more tenaciously than ever. The pride which the followers of these religions now take in their faiths was never stronger in Trinidad.

Does religious diversity stand in the way of the development of a homogeneous society, and does it help to strengthen the ethnic loyalties? Do the Hindu-Muslim subgroup loyalties based upon religious differences still play an important role in the life of the East Indian community, or in the face of a common threat from external elements to their existence, have they been presenting a strong united front against Negroes on the basis of common ethnic origin? These are some of the important questions which are considered in this book.

The Numerous Subcultures

When Negro slaves left the plantations and moved into urban areas, they tended to imitate their European masters. Though there was no complete departure from their African cultural heritage,[3] they accepted English as their mother tongue and became

---

[1] Morton Klass, 'East and West Indians: Cultural Complexity in Trinidad', *Annals of the New York Academy of Sciences* (Vol. 83, January 1960), pp. 851–61.

[2] D. J. Crowley, 'Plural and Differential Acculturation in Trinidad', *American Anthropologist* (Vol. 59, No. 5, 1957), pp. 817–24.

[3] Herskovits, who studied the elements of African culture among Trinidad Negroes in 1946, observed that the question of African affiliation was not very strong in Trinidad 'in contrast to Jamaica, Haiti, Dutch Guiana, or Brazil where there is pride in African ancestry and in retention of African custom'. Yet they found retention of numerous African cultural traces and religious beliefs among Trinidad Negroes. M. Herskovits and Frances S. Herskovits, *Trinidad Village* (New York, Alfred A. Knopf, 1947), pp. 22–3 and 331.

westernized in their tastes and cultural values. The cultural ethos of the modern Negro community is provided by the West. 'West Indian uniqueness consists in this, that of all of these hundreds of millions of formerly colonial coloured peoples, West Indians are the only ones who are completely westernized, they have no native language, no native religion, no native way of life.'[1]

The Negro culture is known as the Creole culture and is considered to be a 'variant of European culture'.[2] In the colonial days of the Trinidadian society the local culture was subordinated to the English culture—the culture of the colonial ruling class. However, with the rise of independent African countries there has also been a revival of pride in native African culture and efforts have been made to re-interpret and to rewrite the history so as to assert the cultural maturity of the African (Negro) culture over other cultures.[3] According to Braithwaite, before the rise of independent African states:

The idea of most people was to disassociate themselves as much as possible from anything that sounded 'African'. 'African' was associated with the primitive, the barbarous and the uncivilized, and in fact the idea of Africa and its inhabitants corresponded in no small measure to the stereotype so often found in the United Kingdom.[4]

But, he adds:

Now respectable people started advocating a revival of Africanism. A prominent lawyer, at one time active in the Parent Teachers' Association (now defunct) advocated the teaching of Yoruba and other African languages in the schools. . . . There began a diligent search for folk tunes and attendance at Shango dances became a permissible activity, although actual participation was tabooed. Among certain circles the fact that something was of African origin made it more acceptable than it would otherwise have been.[5]

Organizations like the Negro Welfare and Cultural Association and the Pan African League (West Indies) have been working for

---

[1] C. L. R. James, *Federation: 'We Failed Miserably' How and Why* (published by the author, Tunapuna, Trinidad, 1 Ward Street, 1960), p. 2.

[2] Klass, 'East and West Indians: Cultural Complexity in Trinidad', p. 857.

[3] Eric Williams, *History of the People of Trinidad and Tobago* (New York, Frederick A. Praeger, 1962), pp. 30-9.

[4] Lloyd Braithwaite, 'The Problem of Cultural Integration in Trinidad', *Social and Economic Studies* (Vol. 3, No. 1, June 1954), p. 90.

[5] Ibid., p. 90.

the cause of African culture. But in spite of the revival of interest in the African culture, the Negro in Trinidad is basically western-oriented in his way of life and thought process. However, the African revival provided cultural symbols for the modern Negro nationalism led by the middle-class intellectuals and professionals in Trinidad.

East Indians

Though changes have taken place, and East Indians have accepted a number of socio-economic elements from other communities,[1] nevertheless, they have successfully 'rebuilt in exact and revealing terms the key institutions of their native land, its ancestral but over-reaching social order'.[2] Morris Freilich, who made a comparative study of the cultural diversity of Negro and East Indian peasants in Trinidad, failed to discover significant cultural similarities between the two ethnic groups.[3] Because of their large numbers and their complex institutional and structural relationships, East Indians have been able to reproduce and maintain the basic elements of their native culture.

East Indians, in their value orientation, life goals, beliefs, and institutional structures differ from other ethnic groups. With respect to marriage, family, kinship, way of life, religious ceremonies, festivals, dance, and music they have distinctive traditions and customs. 'Primary group contacts between the Indians and other ethnic groups were limited. This situation arose not only because of mutual prejudices, but also because of certain special aspects of the culture of the East Indian group.'[4] It is held that it was only after the rise of independent India that a cultural revival started among East Indians of Trinidad. However, a look at old Indian magazines and newspapers shows that the people of Indian origin in Trinidad have been taking increasing interest in India since the rise of Indian nationalism under the leadership of Gandhi.[5] The names of Gandhi, Tagore, and Nehru thrilled

---

[1] Crowley, op. cit., p. 820.

[2] Morton Klass, *East Indians in Trinidad: A Study of Cultural Persistence* (New York, Columbia University Press, 1961), p. 18.

[3] Morris Freilich, *Cultural Diversity Among Trinidadian Peasants* (Ann Arbor, University Microfilm Inc., 1961), p. 143.

[4] Braithwaite, 'Social Stratification and Cultural Pluralism', p. 828.

[5] The *East Indian Weekly* and the *Observer*.

many of the East Indians and became objects of national pride. A large number of Hindu and Muslim schools were opened, new and impressive mosques and temples were built, teaching arrangements for Hindi and Urdu were made, strong efforts were made to revive cultural pride among Hindu and Muslim youths through the organization of Youth Clubs and study groups. Many wealthy Indian families maintained links with India either by visiting India or by getting religious and cultural literature from India. Indian 'movies' and Indian music draw large audiences of East Indians in Trinidad. Indian movies are mostly in Hindi and only a small percentage of Indian population can follow the dialogue; still East Indians flock to watch them. They think that Indian movies are closer to their lives and conform to their basic value orientation. Negroes, on the other hand, find Indian movies strange and uninteresting. Recently, Indian cultural troupes have started paying visits to Trinidad. Auditoriums and cinema houses where the Indian artists give their performances are very well patronized by East Indians from every section of the society and a large number of Indian ladies come dressed in saris—the traditional Indian dress. Negroes rarely attend. In Indian majority areas of Debe and Penal, music from Indian films is played over loud-speakers throughout the day—especially at weddings and festivals. Recently local Indian dancing troupes and orchestras have been organized with the encouragement of the Trinidad government.

Well-to-do urban East Indian families are becoming more and more westernized. But westernization, they assert, does not mean in any way the acceptance of the Creole values. They insist that they are not adopting the Negro way of life: though they are becoming westernized, they are different from Negroes. As Morton Klass points out, 'Among rural Hindu East Indians the creolized individual is rare to the point of non-existence, traits and values deriving from India take precedence over those deriving from the non-Indian environment. It is necessary to note, however, that these people are, for the most part, East Indians of the West Indies.'[1] Even westernization, in many ways, encourages ethnocentricity and subgroup nationalism.

Small ethnic groups such as the Chinese and the white also maintain their own subcultural identities. Local whites represent

[1] Klass, 'East and West Indians: Cultural Complexity in Trinidad', p. 858.

the culture of the ruling *élite* of the colonial days. Until recently they looked towards England for cultural inspiration, but now they seem to be increasingly turning to the United States for education, and for the satisfaction of their cultural aspirations.

The Trinidadian society is characterized by an absence of universally acceptable cultural values. However, there are certain ascriptive norms, considered desirable by all, which have been inherited from the colonial past, and are based upon 'social origin and skin colour'.[1] Furthermore, there is a general acceptance by East Indians and Negroes, of the 'social ascendency and high status of the White groups'.[2] With the advent of independence, achievement values and democratic principles are taking root in the society. None the less, both among East Indians and Negroes, light skin is highly prized. In rural Trinidad people still look upon a white man as an embodiment of authority, justice, and fairness.

Within the East Indian community itself, social stratification is based upon caste, colour, and creed. Among the Hindus, the Brahmin—especially in rural areas—occupies a higher status than the low-caste Chamar Hindu. Light-skinned East Indian immigrants from North-West India may look down upon the Madrasis (Indian indentured labour coming from South India), who are very dark. An Indian Christian considers himself more cultured and westernized and looks upon a Hindu as an inferior. Thus individual status is still largely determined by the caste, race, and colour.

Ethnic, Occupational, and Economic Divisions

By and large economic and occupational divisions within Trinidad society have also developed along ethnic and cultural lines. Big industrial units such as Caroni Limited (the island's largest sugar manufacturer) and other large sugar estates like the Trinidad Sugar Estates and the Forres Park, together with such giant oil companies like Texaco and Shell, are British- or American-owned. Most of the banks and large commercial firms such as the Bank of Nova Scotia, Bank of London and Montreal, Barclays Bank, the Chase Manhattan Bank, and the Royal Bank of Canada are run by Canadians, Englishmen, and Americans. Portuguese and French Creoles own medium-sized business houses

[1] Braithwaite, 'Social Stratification and Cultural Pluralism', p. 825.
[2] Ibid.

and occupy executive positions in foreign-owned commercial and industrial firms. Many of the large-scale employers use particularist and ascriptive criteria in the recruitment of their employees as most of the foreign-owned firms prefer to hire light-skinned natives for white-collar jobs.

Chinese and Arab minorities live in urban areas and operate grocery or general stores. Negroes are predominently urban and occupy important positions in civil, judicial, and police services. They also constitute a large section of the professional class. In addition, quite a significant number work as the industrial labour force and supply the bulk of manpower in the oilfields.

An overwhelming majority of East Indians are in agriculture; they work either on their farms or on sugar estates and live in the country (see Table 1-3).

Table 1-3   *Racial Distribution of Rural and Urban Population, 1964*

Race	Urban %	Rural %
Negro	49	51
East Indian	17	83
White	65	35
Chinese	67	33
Mixed	51	49
Lebanese and Syrian	80	20
Others	55	45

Source Rural Development in Trinidad and Tobago (classified confidential) (Port of Spain, UNESCO Regional Office, 1964), p. 8.

As Table 1-3 shows, four-fifths of the Indians live in rural areas and though 51 per cent of the Negro population is technically shown to be rural, a majority of them live in urban areas. Their over-all percentage of rural population increases when it is recognized that they constitute 93 per cent of the population of Tobago which is mainly rural and agricultural.

East Indians have always been under-represented in civil services and professions. After comparing the occupational distribution of East Indians with other ethnic groups, J. D. Tyson, in 1939, observed that there was a very meagre representation of East Indians in services. Conceding that the percentage of illiteracy was quite high among Indians, nevertheless he observed,

'The community has already produced a considerable number of highly educated and successful professionals and businessmen and the figures compiled by the evidence, both for Board and Committees and for the permanent Civil Service, lend considerable

Table 1-4   *Occupational Distribution of East Indians, Late 1930s*

Occupation	Total of East Indians	Other races
Government Service Public officers, messengers, etc. in government offices, police	119	2,019
Professions Legal, medical, ministers of religion, teachers	637	4,494
Commercial Merchants, clerks, shopmen, shopkeepers and hucksters, hotel keepers, spirit dealers	3,574	12,298
Industrial Mechanics, boatmen and fishermen, mariners, laundresses and seamstresses	3,015	40,891
Domestic	1,253	22,796
Agricultural Managers and overseers, peasants, proprietors, *metayers* and farmers, agricultural labourers	40,679	37,927
General Labourers	7,647	Not available
Miscellaneous Proprietors and persons living on private means	3,071	
Unemployed	24,861	
Total	84,856 persons of 15 years and over	

Source Tyson, op. cit., p. 44.

force to the complaint constantly made that there is differentiation against Indians as such.'[1]

He further observed, 'There are only nine Indian Justices of Peace out of about 230 for the whole island and I understand that there is no Indian Justice of Peace in such Indian areas as San Fernando, Chaguanas, Penal, Siparia, Cedros, and La Baria. It is difficult to believe that there are not suitable Indian gentlemen in those areas.'[2]

East Indians in Trinidad were known for ignoring the importance of education for their children. K. J. Grant, the well-known Canadian missionary in Trinidad, wrote: 'There was no appreciation of education on the part of either parents or children. They had no outlook, no prospect in life. With all their latent intellectual capacity, they felt that in Trinidad as well as in India they were doomed to be the children of toil.'[3] There were various reasons for the educational backwardness of East Indians. They came from rural India where the rate of literacy was very low and where the tradition was to keep the children at home to help their parents in field-work. Also, East Indian indentured labour in Trinidad, in the early stages, sought economic stability. A labourer knew that with some savings he could purchase crown land and settle as an independent farmer. Consequently, he brought his children to work on sugar estates instead of sending them to schools. There was also deliberate neglect of East Indian education by sugar planters and the Government, because they were afraid of losing plantation labour.[4] There were also racial prejudices against East Indians as a result of which, as John Morton, the pioneer Canadian missionary, noted, 'There was scarcely an East Indian child to be found in school in the whole island.'[5] It was the Canadian Presbyterian Church which undertook to educate the East Indians.

The Canadian mission did admirable educational work among

---

[1] J. D. Tyson, *Memorandum of Evidence for the Royal Commission to the West Indies* (Port of Spain, Yuille's Printeries Ltd., 1939), p. 41.

[2] Ibid.

[3] K. G. Grant, *My Missionary Memories* (Halifax, N. S., The Imperial Publishing Co., 1923), p. 82.

[4] Murli J. Kirpalani, *et al.*, *Indian Centenary Review* (Port of Spain, Guardian Commercial Printery, 1945), p. 54.

[5] Sarah E. Morton, *John Morton of Trinidad* (Toronto, Westminster Co., 1916), pp. 41–2.

East Indians but the fear of conversion to Christianity kept the Hindu and Muslim parents from sending their children to these educational institutions. In recent years, with comparatively increased economic resources, they are not only building business houses but are also spending larger amounts of money on education. Larger and larger numbers of East Indians are becoming education-conscious and sending their children abroad for higher education.[1] Ahsan, who studied East Indian settlements in rural Trinidad, found that 'of about 80 families investigated more than 60 per cent wanted their sons to go to the University to become a doctor of medicine or a solicitor. About 10 per cent wanted their

Table 1-5   *Number of East Indians in Different Professions*[2]

Profession	East Indians 1945	East Indians 1965	Other races 1965
Barristers	16	61	98
Solicitors	13	14	81
Doctors	19	88	257
Dentists	3	17	76
Druggists	10	31	285

sons to go no farther than elementary school. Thirty per cent wanted high school education for their sons'.[3] There is a general feeling among East Indians in Trinidad that they are now leading in professions because of the rapid strides they have made in the sphere of education. However, as the comparative figures in Table 1-5 will show, with the exception of law, East Indians are still far behind other racial groups in all professions, but their numbers have been steadily rising in the last twenty years.

It is this class which is becoming more and more conscious of the discrimination from which the East Indians suffer. The rise

[1] C. L. R. James, *Party Politics in the West Indies* (San Juan, Trinidad, Vedic Enterprises, 1962), p. 147.
[2] These figures have been compiled on the basis of information provided by Kirpalani, op. cit., pp. 57–8 and the *Trinidad Tobago Year Book 1964–1965* (Port of Spain, Yuille's Printeries Ltd.,) pp. 149, 150, 280, and 286.
[3] Syed Reza Ahsan, 'East Indian Agricultural Settlements in Trinidad: A Study in Cultural Geography' (an unpublished Ph.D. dissertation, Gainesville, University of Florida, 1963), p. 184.

of an educated East Indian middle class also poses a threat to the status of the Negro middle class, which has been dominating civil services and professions up to now.

Even at this stage, East Indians are grossly under-represented in the civil services in comparison with their numerical strength in the total population. In the Supreme Court, the Prime Minister's office, the Governor-General's office, the Parliamentary secretariat, the high-ranking diplomats, and the senior police staff, East Indians have unequal representation. In 1965, out of nine senior officers in the Prime Minister's office, none were East Indian. The situation was the same in the Governor-General's office. Out of eleven judges of the Supreme Court, only one was East Indian. Out of three Parliamentary secretaries, none were East Indian. The civil services, both at home and abroad, are staffed with Negroes.[1] Niehoff, who conducted field research in Trinidad in 1960, noted that there were only two occupations in which East Indians were vastly under-represented, one of which was the civil services (the other was domestic servants). He found that in the whole of St. Patrick County (where 43 per cent of the population is East Indian) there were 150 constables; all were Negroes except three.[2] According to a memorandum submitted to the Government by the Indian Association of Trinidad, out of 2,000 members of the police force, only fifty were Indians (2·5 per cent). In the civil services, the representation of East Indians was between 10 to 15 per cent.[3] Commenting on the position of East Indians in the civil services, Niehoff points out, 'We do not believe that Indians have any particular objection to civil service work in itself. It is probably that the reason comparatively few are found in such occupations is due to the friction between Indians and Negroes.'[4] He found that Negroes in senior positions in the civil services deliberately make the admission of East Indians difficult.

As noted earlier, the Indian community is mainly rural and an overwhelming majority live in South Trinidad. In the words of

[1] Albert Gomes, 'Race and Independence in Trinidad', *New Society* (27 August 1964), p. 16.

[2] Arthur and Juanita Niehoff, *East Indians in the West Indies* (Milwaukee, Milwaukee Public Museum Publications in Anthropology, 1960), p. 52.

[3] *Memorandum submitted by the Indian Association of Trinidad and Tobago on the Draft Trinidad and Tobago Constitution* (St. Clair, Port of Spain, 1962), p. 2.

[4] Niehoffs, op. cit., p. 52.

Albert Gomes, 'it has become the major and indispensable factor in agriculture upon which the whole economy largely rests.'[1] Entry into the civil services being denied to Indians, they seek careers in business and other professions. In some industries such as the cinema, and bus and taxi transportation, Indians have a near monopoly.

Though the fortunes of the Indian community have considerably improved, it is nevertheless an overstatement to say, as Albert Gomes does, that most of the wealth is in the hands of Indians.[2]

The Absence of Interracial Ties

There is little racial admixture to cement the various ethnic groups—African, European, Chinese, Syrian, and Indian—into a Trinidadian whole. Racial lines between the East Indians and Negroes are sharply marked, and there is strong disapproval of interracial marriages. Though C. L. R. James in one of his recent pamphlets has found a trend towards interracial mixing,[3] I asked different groups of East Indians, from urban and rural areas and from various occupational groups, for their opinion and found an overwhelming disapproval of racial intermixing through interracial marriages.

Many of those who approve of interracial marriages approve only in principle. When they are faced with a practical situation where the marriage of their daughter is involved, they concede that they perhaps would not approve of such a marriage. This attitude is also confirmed by an earlier study done by the Niehoffs.[4]

The strongest resistance to interracial marriages among the various groups of East Indians seems to be coming from the Hindus; the Indian Christians seem to be the most liberal. Muslims stand between the two extreme groups.

Religious differences between Hindus and other groups are quite marked. Hindu religion with its caste organization strongly discourages marriage with outside groups. Furthermore, Hindus

---

[1] Gomes, op. cit., p. 15.
[2] Ibid.
[3] C. L. R. James, *West Indians of East Indian Descent* (Port of Spain, IBIS Publication Co., 1965), p. 2.
[4] Niehoffs, op. cit., pp. 60–2.

and Muslims, comparatively speaking, have less direct and primary contact with Negroes than the Indian Christians who, through their church memberships, mix more freely with them.

Among the occupational groups, the strongest objection to marriage with Negroes comes from shopkeepers and small businessmen. The most liberal group is that of the teachers. All other groups show marked resistance and strong disapproval.

The rural-urban variable is not important. In both areas almost the same amount of resistance to integration with Negroes is found. Most of the urban East Indian families maintain close ties with the rural areas. It is difficult for the urban families to save themselves from the censuring eyes of their kinship group. Moreover, Trinidad is small and easy transport facilities make communications between the urban and rural areas almost constant.

The attitude of the East Indian *élite* in politics, business, and the professions, is not much different from the man in the street (see Table 1-6). With the exception of Muslim leaders, all others show a marked resistance to marriage with Negroes. Of all the East Indian religious groups, the Christians are the most educated and westernized; still, the top stratum of the East Indian Christian community shows as much resistance to marriage with Negroes as the Hindus.

Table 1-6 *Attitude of Leaders Towards Marriage with Negroes According to Religion*

Attitude	Religion		
	Hindu	Muslim	Christian
	%	%	%
Approve	5	50	13
Disapprove	93	50	87
Undecided	2	—	—
Total	100	100	100
No. of cases	(39)	(10)	(39)

Even after living in the West Indies for a number of generations there is no significant difference in the attitude of the leadership group.

Leadership groups from all religions show much greater liberalism in their attitude towards marriage with whites.

It is evident that colour and race prejudice with respect to the Negro are very strong. It seems that from all the religious groups,

Table 1-7   *Attitude Towards Marriage with Negroes on the Basis of Generations Lived in Trinidad*

Attitude	Generation Born in Trinidad		
	First	Second	Third
	%	%	%
Approve	9	19	8
Disapprove	91	81	84
Undecided	—	—	8
Total	100	100	100
No. of cases	(33)	(35)	(12)

Hindus are much more reluctant to go outside their own subcultural group for marriage; however, against their wholesale rejection of marriage with Negroes, they are much more liberal

Table 1-8   *Attitude of Leaders Towards Marriage with Whites According to Religion*

Attitude	Religion		
	Hindu	Muslim	Christian
	%	%	%
Approve	41	60	56
Disapprove	54	30	40
Undecided	5	10	4
Total	100	100	100
No. of cases	(39)	(10)	(38)

in their attitude towards marriage with whites. Furthermore, marriage with whites raises social status in the Trinidadian society.

Reasons for the disapproval of racial intermixing through marriage with Negroes range from simple racial prejudices to strong ethnic loyalty, and from strong religious objection to the cultural disparities between East Indians and Negroes.

People motivated by racial prejudices place emphasis on the 'racial inferiority' of Negroes, their colour, and their 'physical appearance'. Their reaction to seeing an East Indian girl with a Negro varies from a feeling of strong revulsion to that of indifference. Many would say that on seeing an East Indian girl with a Negro boy their blood boils or they just cannot see an Indian woman submitting to a Negro. In an Indian majority area like Debe or Penal, open association between an Indian girl and a Negro boy would be very difficult to carry on. In mixed areas there would be greater tolerance.

The *élite* group rationalizes its disapproval of East Indian–Negro racial intermixing on cultural bases. They argue that the East Indian cultural values are directly opposed to the Creole culture, and marriage with Negroes is bound to fail because of the incompatibility of the cultural background. Children of mixed marriages are looked down upon and are not accepted either in the Indian or the Negro society. Some of the *élite* assert that marriage with Negroes will not improve either the race or the culture, whereas marriage with whites will result in improved offspring. Many highly-educated East Indian *élite* point out that the *Dogala*—offspring of East Indian–Negro marriage—is very hard to control, and because he is an outcaste, is prone to develop criminal tendencies. A pure Indian or a pure Negro is easy to handle.

Another basis of rejection of interracial marriage is the fear of loss of Indian identity, shared both by the *élite* and non-*élite*. Though they insist that they do not want to turn Trinidad into a little India, still they do not want to lose their cultural and ethnic identity. Fusion of races would not leave an Indian race, and they do not want to see this happen in Trinidad.

Ethnic endogamy is only one dimension. The other dimension, on the basis of which we can analyse the nature of pluralism existing in Trinidad, is the informal social mixing. One of the bases on which to assess the degree of racial intermixing at the social level is the membership of clubs. I asked East Indian *élites* what type of clubs they go to—whether they go to racially mixed clubs, exclusive clubs, or none. Forty out of eighty-eight do not go to any club at all, and an overwhelming majority of those who go to any club go only to racially exclusive ones (see Table 1-9).

East Indian Christians seem to be racially less exclusive and to be going in the largest numbers to racially mixed clubs. A majority of Hindus and Muslims go only to exclusive clubs.

A large majority of the club-going East Indian *élites* are members either of the West India Club (formerly known as the India Club) or the Himalaya Club—both of which are racially exclusive. Those of the East Indian *élites* who go to mixed clubs go to such clubs as the Rotary Club, which are dominated by the local whites rather than by the Negroes.

Table 1-9   *Club Membership and Religion of Élites*

Clubs	Religion		
	Hindu %	Muslim %	Christian %
Exclusive club	51	50	28
Racially mixed club	10	10	16
No club	39	40	56
Total	100	100	100
No. of cases	(39)	(10)	(39)

Also, the celebration of religious festivals, e.g. the birthday of Lord Krishna or *Holi* (*Phagwa*), and the performance of social ceremonies, weddings, etc., rarely brought the two major ethnic groups together in any significant way. This reinforces the point that social intermixing between different racial groups in Trinidad is very much restricted.

There is also a great deal of cultural pride. East Indians consider the Creole culture as inferior to their own and resent the use of terms like 'the creolization of Indians'. East Indian *élites* insist very strongly that 'creolization' and 'westernization' are two separate processes; westernization does not mean the acceptance of the 'Creole' moral values or ways of living. According to Morton Klass, 'There is a value attached to being "modern"; however, to an East Indian, being modern does not always mean being West Indian.'[1] In the eyes of East Indians, 'Creole' life lacks stability, social virtues, and morality. On the other hand,

[1] Klass, 'East and West Indians: Cultural Complexity in Trinidad', p. 858.

Negroes still look down upon Indians as inferiors and call them 'Coolies', who took up jobs which Negroes refused to carry on after their emancipation. In the words of V. S. Naipaul, 'The Negro has a deep contempt, . . . for all that is not white, his values are the values of white imperialism at its most bigoted.'[1] He adds, 'The Indian despises the Negro for not being an Indian; he has, in addition, taken over all the White prejudices against the Negro with the convert's zeal and regards as Negro every one who has any tincture of Negro blood.'[2] The westernized Negro considers Indian living primitive, their food unhealthy, and every sugar-cane worker a criminal.[3] There is very little effort on the part of the Trinidad Negro to understand the culture, institutional patterns, and life goals of East Indians.

Even after the abolition of the colonial status of Trinidad, the white community still occupies the top stratum of the society. They live in enormous colonial-style houses, as one visitor describes them, with domestic staff, glorious view, and fantastic gardens filled with tropical flowers.[4] The white community sets fashions and patterns of social living which are eagerly copied by Negroes and East Indians. These people still live in a world of their own and they have very few primary contacts with other ethnic groups. Thus different ethnic groups live in close proximity to each other, but do not seem to be moving towards a racially-mixed social system.

Lack of National Identity and the Formation of Political Parties

One of the most crucial factors in the formation of a politically homogeneous culture is national identity. 'National identity,' in the words of Sidney Verba, consists of 'the beliefs of individuals and the extent to which they consider themselves members of their nation state'.[5] Describing the old colonial society of Trinidad, Naipaul says, 'Every one was an individual, fighting for his place

[1] V. S. Naipaul, *The Middle Passage* (London, André Deutsch, 1962), p. 80.
[2] Ibid.
[3] Sheila Solomon Klass, *Everyone in this House Makes Babies* (Garden City, New York, Doubleday, 1964), pp. 128–9. (A very revealing and interesting study.)
[4] *Trinidad Guardian* (10 July 1965).
[5] Sidney Verba, 'Comparative Political Culture', in Lucian W. Pye and Sidney Verba (eds.), *Political Culture and Political Development* (Princeton, Princeton University Press, 1965), p. 529.

in the community. Yet there was no community, we were of various races, religions, sects and cliques; and we had somehow found ourselves on the same small island. Nothing bound us together except this common residence. There was no nationalist feeling, there could be none.'[1] Today Trinidad may not be on the brink of racial war, as Naipaul found,[2] yet Trinidad is far from the development of a common 'national identity'. I asked the East Indian leadership, 'Do you think that the policies of the People's National Movement government endanger the "national solidarity"?' 'There is no national solidarity,' was the flat answer from many of them. There has always been an East Indian nationalism quite distinct from the Negro nationalism. East Indians in Trinidad participated emotionally in India's struggle for independence. With the rise of the nationalist movement in India under the auspices of the Indian National Congress, and subsequently with the rise of charismatic leadership of Gandhi and Nehru, the East Indian young intellectuals always looked towards India for their political inspiration and nationalist pride. As early as the 1930s they started staging island-wide demonstrations in support of India's demand for freedom.[3] The Nationalist Movement in India under Gandhi created a sense of ethnic pride in the East Indians of Trinidad. T. Roodal, an East Indian member of the pre-independence Legislative Council, addressing a public meeting held in support of India's demand for independence, said that East Indians were not inferior to Europeans or any other race. He advised them 'to be proud that they are East Indians and continue to uphold that dignity'.[4] Public meetings held in Indian majority areas opened and closed with the singing of Indian patriotic songs and the Indian national anthem, *Vande Matram*.[5] With the achievement of independence by India many East Indian intellectuals felt a sense of fulfilment. Subsequently, when colonial Trinidad started moving towards independence, they became bewildered by the prospects which East Indians as a minority group would face in independent Trinidad. With Nehru's advice to overseas Indians to forget that they were Indians and to get settled into the countries of their adoption,

[1] Naipaul, *The Middle Passage*, p. 43.   [2] Ibid., p. 80.
[3] *Port of Spain Gazette* (1 January 1930).
[4] Ibid.
[5] *East Indian Weekly* (24 August 1929).

came the climax of their disillusionment and disappointment and they felt badly let down. Before Trinidad became independent, Braithwaite noted, 'In the case of the lower class of Creole Trinidad, the levels of aspirations were "national", the levels of expectations sub-cultural, in the case of the Indian community, both level of aspiration and level of expectation tended, until recent years, to be sub-cultural.'[1]

In spite of these cultural–ethnic cleavages and feelings of racial exclusiveness, I agree with Braithwaite that Trinidad society could be placed at Gordon's tolerance level of cultural pluralism. According to M. M. Gordon:

At the tolerance-level of group relations ethnic groups would maintain such a high degree of social isolation from each other that virtually all primary contacts would be within the ethnic group and most secondary contacts would be either correspondingly confined or if across ethnic lines, completely accommodating, various ethnic groups would be encouraged to have a tolerant attitude toward one another.[2]

Negroes and East Indians have been excluded from each other's social structure—cliques, fraternal societies, religious organizations, and home-visiting patterns. Therefore, 'the good group relation level' is non-existent. At the same time, at least on the surface, the two groups seem to tolerate each other, and are not engaged in open use of violence against each other. East Indians, being a minority, have been on the defensive. Negroes believe that within the next few generations the East Indians will lose their ethnic identity and will become absorbed. East Indians are confident that they would not be lost in the intermixing of numerous West Indian racial groups. Thus it seems that the future does not hold the hope that Trinidad society would rise above the tolerance level of cultural pluralism.

Loyalties or commitments to 'nation-state' are always difficult to achieve in a developing country, but they are much more difficult to achieve in a society like Trinidad where primary loyalties are conceived in terms of ethnic origin. Conflict on political issues is viewed as conflict between different subnational units. In the absence of common historical experience and cultural heritage, any conscious effort on the part of a ruling ethnic group to develop

[1] Braithwaite, 'Social Stratification and Cultural Pluralism', p. 829.

[2] Gordon, op. cit., pp. 153–4.

what David Apter calls 'political religion'[1] is likely to be interpreted by another group as an attack on its subnational identity.

It is obvious that in the absence of a national awareness and
common value patterns, the Trinidad political system lacks con-
sensus. In such a political system the different sections of the society
are held together by force. Earlier this force was exercised by the
colonial power; now it is exercised by the dominant cultural–
ethnic group. In such societies, 'The monopoly of power by one
cultural section is the essential pre-condition for the maintenance
of the total society in its current form.'[2] In the case of Trinidad a
parliamentary type of institutional framework has been superimposed upon a society which is characterized by deep ethnic–
cultural cleavages and which lacks homogeneity.

In such societies formation of stable political parties cutting
across the ethnic-subcultural lines is an ideal highly difficult to
achieve. Therefore, with the advancement of Trinidad towards
independence, both ethnic groups started competing for political
power and ended up with parties relying heavily on ethnic loyalties
and subcultural solidarities. Multiracialism is only for 'window-
dressing' purposes; the P.N.M. (the People's National Movement)
and the D.L.P. (the Democratic Labour Party)—the only parties
at the time of the independence of Trinidad—are basically
representing the Negro and the East Indian elements of Trinidad
society.

[1] David Apter, 'Political Religion in New Nations', in Clifford Geertz (ed.),
Old Societies and New States (Glencoe, Illinois, The Free Press, 1963), pp. 57–104.
[2] Smith, *The Plural Society in the British West Indies*, p. 86.

II

The Main Features of East Indian Subculture

Cultural Diversity and the Process of Political Socialization

TRINIDAD society is characterized by cultural pluralism. In spite of living in close proximity for more than a hundred years, East Indians and Negroes possess distinctive values, institutions, kinship groups, authority patterns, and goals. The East Indian subculture constitutes a distinctive subsystem within the political system of Trinidad. The socialization process of the East Indian community is performed through this subsystem. Political socialization, which consists of 'a set of attitudes—cognitions, value standards and feelings—towards the political system, its various roles, and role incumbents'[1] is a part of the general socialization process. 'The analysis of the political socialization function in a particular society is basic to the whole field of political analysis, since it not only gives us insight into the patterns of political culture and sub-cultures in that society but also locates for us in the socialization process of the society the points where particular qualities and elements of political culture are introduced, and the points in the society where these components are being sustained or modified.'[2] This political socialization process may place emphasis on 'particular' elements or 'universalistic elements', or it may be a combination of both. In Trinidad as in most of the multi-ethnic developing countries, the process of political socialization is ethnic-oriented: the emphasis is on particularistic elements rather than on universalistic elements. It is through the family system and the kinship group, through religious organizations and educational institutions that East Indians have attempted to cling to the basic characteristics of their culture. They are also the main instruments in the process of an individual's socialization, in the development of his personality and beliefs.

[1] Gabriel A. Almond, *et al.* (eds.), *The Politics of the Developing Areas* (Princeton, Princeton University Press, 1961), pp. 27–8.
[2] Almond, op. cit., p. 31.

Role of the East Indian Family System and Kinship Group in the Perpetuation of Ethnic Loyalties

The unit of Hindu society in particular and in the Indian community in general is not the individual but the joint family. According to Mandelbaum, 'The classic form of the family in India is that of the joint family'; it consists 'of a number of married couples and their children who live together in the same household. All the men are related by blood, as a man and his sons or grandsons or a set of brothers and their wives, unmarried daughters and perhaps the widow of a deceased kinsman. At marriage a girl leaves her ancestral family and becomes part of the joint family of her husband.' He adds, 'A very important feature of this social unit is that all property is held in common.'[1]

East Indians have successfully transplanted this institution of Indian social life in its basic form which they brought from their homeland.[2] The East Indian family in Trinidad is still characterized by the inferior or unequal status of women, parental selection of mates, rarity of divorce, sharing of property, and interrelationship with the caste system.[3] In Trinidad, according to Morton Klass, 'an Indian's first allegiance is to his family, his next to his wider circle of kin'.[4] Kinship is one of the most important structural relationships in the community, and it includes numerous real or supposed uncles, aunts, sisters and cousins, grandfather and grandmother—from both the mother's and the father's side. Each person is accorded a status in the kinship group hierarchy and receives his due respect. The Indian child is brought up under a complex structure of kinship relations and family authority patterns. He is taught to obey his elders, pay them respect, and share manifold family responsibilities.

However, the Indian family in Trinidad has undergone a few changes. For a considerable period, marriages performed according to Hindu and Muslim religious rites were not given legal

---

[1] Quoted in T. N. Madan, 'The Joint Family: A Terminological Clarification', *International Journal of Comparative Sociology* (Vol. III, No. 1, September 1962), pp. 10–11.

[2] A. Niehoff, 'The Survival of Hindu Institutions in an Alien Environment', *Eastern Anthropologist* (Vol. XII, No. 3, March–May 1959), p. 185.

[3] Leo Davids, 'The East Indian Family Overseas', *Social and Economic Studies* (Vol. 13, No. 3, September 1964), p. 391.

[4] Klass, *East Indians in Trinidad*, p. 93.

recognition and the offspring of such marriages was considered illegitimate. It is only in recent years (in the case of Muslim marriages, in 1930, and in the case of Hindu, in 1946) that such marriages have been given legal recognition.

The most significant change in the Indian social structure in Trinidad has occurred in the status of women, who enjoy more freedom than their counterparts in India. In the beginning there were less women than men, and rather than wooing the Negro women, Indian men competed among themselves for the hands of Indian women. Being more in demand, women got more freedom. In recent years, with the spread of higher education and increasing westernization among Indian women, they, especially in the urban areas, are seeking greater economic freedom. There is, however, very little participation of Indian women in public and political life. In rural areas, where the joint family exists and where the mother-in-law still rules, women do not move out of their houses for political campaigning or canvassing. Selection of mates by parents or by the older members of the family helps in maintaining caste and religious ties. Parents usually try to arrange matches within their own caste or religious group.

The system of joint property causes a great deal of family bitterness. There is a lack of the tradition of making a will, and most people die without leaving one. Consequently, after the death of the father, many families split apart on the question of the division of the property. Quarrels over the division of the property, and the mutual jealousies nurtured in joint families continue to smoulder throughout the lifetime of a number of joint families. Many times, brothers become each other's bitterest enemies in their public or social life.[1] However, the role of the joint family is declining among East Indian Christians. Table 2-1 shows that about 59 per cent of East Indian Christian *élite* were born into nuclear families, against 33 per cent of Hindus. East Indian Christian *élite*, being more westernized, seem to have moved away from the joint family system more than the two other religious groups. But this does not mean that the role of the nuclear family has declined among East Indian Christians or any other religious groups of East Indians.

The importance of the family is confirmed by the present survey

[1] V. S. Naipaul, *A House for Mr. Biswas* (London, André Deutsch, 1961). (This is an excellent study of the Hindu joint family in Trinidad.)

Table 2-1   *Family Background and Religion of Élites*

Family	Religion		
	Hindu %	Muslim %	Christian %
Nuclear	33	40	59
Joint	64	60	41
No answer	3	—	—
Total	100	100	100
No. of cases	(39)	(10)	(39)

of the East Indian *élites*. Asked what importance they attach to the influence of family in their lives, an overwhelming majority replied 'very much' (see Table 2-2).

Such family- and kinship-centred social life comes very close to what Banfield has called 'amoral familism'. Amoral familism is based on the belief that everybody in the society is pursuing the interest of his own family, and that whoever seeks public office

Table 2-2   *Influence of Family According to Religion*

Influence	Religion		
	Hindu %	Muslim %	Christian %
None	—	—	3
A little	8	10	3
Very much	89	70	91
Self-made	3	20	3
No answer	—	—	—
Total	100	100	100
No. of cases	(38)	(10)	(39)

seeks it for his own good and not for the good of the community. There is always distrust of the outsider. In such societies organization of effective leadership is very difficult to achieve.[1]

[1] Edward C. Banfield, *The Moral Basis of a Backward Society* (Glencoe, The Free Press, 1958), p. 85.

Within their own social circles Indians have a great deal of mutual distrust. 'Indian is the greatest enemy of the Indian,' or 'Do not trust the Indian, every Indian is trying to cut the other's throat,' are some of the most common comments made by East Indians about their fellow East Indians.

However, one cannot minimize the significant contributions made by the stable Indian family system to the rise of the community's business and professional class. Morris Freilich, who studied Indian and Negro peasants, found that whereas the goal of the Negro peasant is the *fête*, e.g. dancing, drinking, and entertainment, that of the Indian peasant is family improvement. 'The magic word for the East Indian around which his whole life is centred is family.'[1] It is through the family that East Indian children learn the values inherited from their culture. The Indian child is much less conscious of social and public life than the Negro child. His life is centred on the family, and he has restricted social relations. Furthermore, the Indian children are rewarded for conformity, accomplishment, and obedience.[2]

This important role of the family in the life of the East Indian introduces numerous traditional elements in an individual's political orientation. It also encourages perpetuation of particularist and ascriptive values, and strong ethnic identifications. Loyalties to family, village, religion, and ethnic group become primary obligations, and strongly promote political participation on ethnic lines.

Religious and Cultural Cleavages Among the East Indians

In the political socialization and recruitment process, religious-cultural diversities play a highly significant role in the life of the East Indian. East Indians are not a solidly united ethnic group, but are divided into various religious groups (see Table 2-3). The Hindu immigrants who came to Trinidad from what was formerly known as the Eastern United Provinces and Bihar States of North India, brought with them three Hindu religious sects, the *Sanatan Dharma*, the *Kabir Panth*, and the *Seunarianies*. The *Sanatan Dharma* is the orthodox sect and claims to represent the traditional body of Hindu beliefs. The main features of the *Sanatan Dharma* are its

[1] Freilich, op. cit., p. 155.
[2] Helen B. Green, 'Values of Negro and East Indian Children in Trinidad', *Social and Economic Studies* (Vol. 14, No. 2, June 1965), pp. 204–16.

emphasis on the *varna-ashrama-dharma*—recognition of the four castes and the four stages of human life, idol worship, and the *Vedas*, the *Puranas*, and the *Smrities* as the main sources of Hinduism.

The four castes into which Hindu social life is divided are the Brahmins (priests and teachers); the *Khshatriyas* (warriors and rulers); the *Vaish* (traders); and the *Sudras* (menials). According to the Sanatanist teachings every man gets his caste on the basis of his birth, which itself is the result of one's actions (*Karmas*) in previous life. Therefore, high and low castes are divinely ordained and a person is incapable of changing his low-caste status through his efforts.

Table 2-3   *Religious Distribution of East Indians*

Religion	%
Hindu	67·9
Muslim	15·0
Christian (various denominations)	16·7
Others	0·4
	100·0

Source Kirpalani, op. cit., p. 61.

The four stages of life are the *Brahamcharya*—starting from birth and lasting until marriage; the *Grihast*—the married householder; *Banprasth*—when a married householder leaves his family and goes into the forest; and the *Sanya*—when man finally renounces the world and seeks salvation through meditation.

The *Sanatan Dharma* places great emphasis on the duties and obligations of a *Grihast*—the householder. Many persons may not reach beyond this stage of life, and therefore a *Grihast* should perform different types of *Pujas*—worship of gods and goddesses. It is the Pundit, the Hindu priest, who performs most of these *Pujas*. Thus the Pundits, who are always from the Brahmin caste, occupy a very important position in the Sanatanist sect. Most of the *Pujas* can be performed at the residence of the householder, and there may not be any need of going to the temples. Though there are numerous temples scattered throughout the island, very few Hindus go to them for worship. A *Pundit Parishad*—a council of Hindu priests—carries on the Sanatanist religious teachings learned from India. The *Sanatan Dharma* has a following among both high- and low-caste Hindus. The organizational leadership of the *Sanatan Dharma* is held by the high-caste Hindus, who have considerably improved their economic status recently.

The *Kabir Panth* originated in North India in the fifteenth century as a revolt against orthodox Hinduism. Mahatama Kabir, the founder of the sect, rejected the caste hierarchy along with the Brahminical rituals and the Islamic orthodoxy. He advocated a compromise between Hinduism and Islam. The followers of the *Kabir Panth* are mostly low-caste and poor Hindus. Therefore the *Kabirpanthies* have not been able to build any significant political influence in Trinidad.

The *Seunarianies* is the smallest Hindu sect to be found in the island. Like the *Kabir Panth* the *Seunarianies* also reject caste hierarchy and Brahminical rituals. They perform most of their ceremonies without a Pundit. The followers of this sect are also low-caste Hindus.

The *Arya Samaj* is another Hindu sect which has a following among the high-caste and rich Hindus. It was founded by Swami Dayanand, a religious and social reformer of nineteenth-century India. The *Arya Samaj* accepted many western ideas and rejected many of the essentials of the Sanatanist sect, such as the caste system, the idol worship, the practice of untouchability, the inferior status of women, and numerous others. The *Arya Samaj* is the only Hindu sect which the Hindu immigrants to Trinidad did not bring with them: *Arya Samaj* missionaries from India who came to British Guiana subsequently paid visits to Trinidad. The highest organization of the *Arya Samaj* is the *Arya Pritinidhi Sabha* which has been running a few schools on the island. Presently the *Arya Pritinidhi Sabha* is bitterly divided into two rival factions which has resulted in a complete stoppage of its work. The influence of the *Arya Samaj* is confined mainly to central Trinidad and the number of its followers is not very large.[1]

Followers of the *Sanatan Dharma* constitute an overwhelming majority of the Hindu population in Trinidad. The religious organizations of the Sanatanist Hindus wield considerable influence in the social and political life of the East Indians. One of the

[1] G. B. Lall, 'A Brief Survey of the Arya Samaj Movement in Trinidad', *The Arya Samaj Brochure* (Vol. I, No. 1, February 1945), pp. 14–17.

Hindu leaders remarked that as long as Sanatanist Hinduism survives in Trinidad Hindus will remain a force to be reckoned with. Until recent years Hinduism has been on the defensive in Trinidad but with the rise of the financial status of Hindu East Indians, it has had a forceful revival. It was reported in 1950 that, 'Hindus of Trinidad are organizing themselves today as they have never done during the last hundred years.'[1] There was a realization that 'Hindus have had no easy time in this country. From the outset they were up against many impediments, the most formidable being the economic question and the proselyting aggressiveness of the Christian missionaries. The Hindus were financially and educationally poor, and were either not organized or ill-organized, whereas the Christian missionaries were better equipped in every way.'[2] In the eyes of Hindus, East Indian subnationalism became identical with Hinduism. 'Hindu Dharma helps us to retain our nationalism. Look at those of our erstwhile Hindu brothers who are today converts to Islam. Many of them do not believe that they are any longer members of the Indian community, look at those who have embraced Christianity. Many of them have sold their birthright for a mess of pottage.'[3]

The *Sanatan Dharma Maha Sabha* and its high-caste leadership played a very significant role in this Hindu revival. Until 1952, there were two organizations of the Sanatanists—the *Sanatan Dharma* Association and the *Sanatan Dharma* Board of Control. In 1952, through the efforts of C. B. Mathura and A. B. Sahay, the Indian Commissioner in Trinidad, the organizations were merged into the *Sanatan Dharma Maha Sabha*. Under the presidency of Bhadase Sagan Maraj, the *Sanatan Dharma Maha Sabha* became one of the most powerful religious and political forces among the Hindus of Trinidad. It has become the strongest base of the political strength of the Hindu community. A candidate seeking election in the Hindu majority areas of Trinidad would be running the risk of losing by openly criticizing the *Sanatan Dharma Maha Sabha*. In the 1956 election, L. F. Seukeran, who was seeking election as an independent candidate, was charged by his opponents with being against the *Maha Sabha*. Seukeran promptly denied the charge and said, 'I am a Brahmin and son of a Brahmin. Seven generations of Brahmin blood flows in my veins. I know more Sanskrit

[1] The *Observer* (Vol. 9, No. 7, July 1950), p. 1.   [2] Ibid., p. 1.
[3] Ibid. (Vol. 8, No. 6, June 1949), p. 6.

D

and Hindi than all the Pandits in Debe. Who told you that I am an enemy of the Hindu religion?' He affirmed amidst applause: 'Seukeran will be the defender of the *Maha Sabha*.'[1] Dr. Eric Williams, the leader of the P.N.M., realizing that he would not be able to win the East Indian vote without breaking the hold of Bhadase Sagan Maraj on the East Indian Hindus, and realizing that Maraj's base of power was the *Sanatan Dharma Maha Sabha*, attacked the organization, linking it with the Hindu *Maha Sabha* of India, which, he charged, was responsible for the assassination of Gandhi. He was corrected by the *Trinidad Guardian* editor who pointed out that since the Trinidad *Maha Sabha* was incorporated in May 1952, while Gandhi was assassinated in January 1948, there could be no possible connexion between the two events. S. N. Capildeo, the then secretary of the S.D.M.S., in a letter to the editor of the *Trinidad Guardian*, made it clear that the *Sanatan Dharma Maha Sabha* was a religious organization and in no way connected with the Hindu *Maha Sabha*, a political body in India.[2] No doubt the linking of the Trinidad *Maha Sabha* with the Hindu *Maha Sabha* was inspired by political motives, but it also signified the political power of the *Maha Sabha*.

The *Maha Sabha* has opened forty schools throughout Trinidad, it employs hundreds of East Indian teachers, and provides education for thousands of East Indian children. Most of these schools are in the Indian majority areas and are staffed completely by East Indian teachers. Non-East Indian students rarely enroll. Religious classes are held daily and children are acquainted with the *Mahabharata* and the *Ramayana* stories. Sunday-school classes are also held with greater emphasis on the teachings of Hindu religion.

Dr. Williams, the present Prime Minister of Trinidad, referred to these schools in 1956 as the political cells of the People's Democratic Party[3] (the predecessor of the D.L.P.). But for the Trinidadian Hindus the establishment of these schools represents the removal of gross injustices against them. By providing employment opportunities for young Hindu teachers, the leaders of the *Maha Sabha* could stop one of the major sources of conversion to Christianity.[4]

[1] *Trinidad Guardian* (30 August 1956).   [2] Ibid. (5 August 1950).
[3] Ibid.
[4] The *Observer* (Vol. 9, No. 7, July 1950), p. 1.

The *Sanatan Dharma Maha Sabha* and its leadership, by the organization of educational activities, the celebration of Hindu festivals and of India's Independence Day in the Indian majority areas,[1] as Niehoff observes, have created a sense of unity among Indians, which has important political implications.[2] It is an important agency of particularist political socialization of East Indians. It is also through the *Maha Sabha* that recruitment of leadership takes place.

Subgroup Rivalries and Emphasis on Particularism Among Different Religious Groups of East Indians

Hindu–Muslim antagonism in India has a long history originating in the conditions of that country. To find out how much these

Table 2-4   *Assessment of Hindu–Muslim Differences According to Religion*

Assessment of Differences	Religion		
	Hindu %	Muslim %	Christian %
Very important	56	20	39
Somewhat important	26	10	33
Not important	18	70	26
No answer	—	—	2
Total	100	100	100
No. of cases	(45)	(10)	(39)

differences still exist among the members of the two religious groups and to what extent they affect their social and political life, East Indian *élite* were asked to what degree Hindu–Muslim differences are important in the social life of Trinidad. A large majority found the differences to be either very or at least somewhat important (see Table 2-4).

Hindus, more than Christians, and Christians more than Muslims, consider the differences between the two groups to be quite significant. Many of the Hindu and Christian *élites* found these differences to be as important as they are in India, and commented that the rise or decline of tensions between India and

[1] *Trinidad Guardian* (14 August 1957).
[2] Niehoffs, *East Indians in the West Indies*, p. 69.

Pakistan will have repercussions in Trinidad too. Whereas Muslims celebrate the birthday of M. A. Jinnah, the founder of Pakistan, the Hindus consider the creation of Pakistan to be a 'calamity', and Jinnah to be a quisling, because he was the author of the division of India.[1] Furthermore, 'when Hindu and Christian members of the India Club celebrated the coming into power of an interim Government in India, Muslims came out with black flags'.[2] Many Muslim-turned-Christian pointed out that the Hindu–Muslim differences were not of much significance in Trinidad until recent times. A large number of Muslim missionaries who emphasize that Muslims are Pakistanis and different from Hindus, have started coming from Pakistan. Another leading member of the Christian *élite* said that Muslims are ready to join any group opposed to Hindus. In 1958, when the Pakistan cricket team visited Trinidad, the *Sunnat-ul-Jamait* arranged a reception in honour of the visitors. A. Khan, the manager of the team, addressed Hindu and Indian Christian guests as 'Indians', and Trinidad Muslims as 'Pakistanis'.[3] The Trinidad Muslims have responded by making efforts to establish closer contacts with Pakistan. Aziza Ahmed, the president of the Trinidad Muslim League, visited Ayub Khan, the President of Pakistan, and urged him to establish a Pakistan Consulate in Trinidad. Said Mohammed, a Minister in the P.N.M. Government, stressing the closer ties between Muslims and people of African origin, pointed out that 50 per cent of the world's Muslim population is of African origin. Thus, as followers of Islam, Muslims are closer to people of African origin than to any other group.[4]

Compared to Hinduism, Islam in Trinidad has shown greater inner strength, and there have been fewer conversions from Islam to Christianity.[5] In his encounter with the Muslim in Trinidad, K. J. Grant noted that, 'The bold truth, "God is the God", gives to this faith of Islam a strength and virility to which Hinduism is a stranger. The followers of Mohammed are not ashamed to declare their faith or offer their prayers wherever they may be.'[6]

[1] The *Observer* (Vol. 8, No. 12, December 1949), p. 7.
[2] Ibid. (Vol. 8, No. 1, January 1949), p. 77.
[3] *Trinidad Guardian* (27 January 1958).
[4] *Nation*, Trinidad (2 January 1962).
[5] Niehoffs, *East Indians in the West Indies*, p. 136.
[6] Grant, *My Missionary Memories*, p. 67.

Numerous sectarian associations like the *Sunnat-ul-Jamait,* *Tackveeyatul* Islamic Association (Society for the Strength of Islam), the Trinidad Muslim League, the Islamic Missionaries Guild, and numerous Muslim Youth Associations have been working to maintain the distinct group identity of Muslim East Indians in Trinidad. It is through these organizations that a particularist process of political socialization and recruitment of leadership continues.

Table 2-5   *Assessment of the Political Affiliation of Muslims by East Indian Élites*

Muslims' Politics	Religion		
	Hindu	Muslim	Christian
	%	%	%
Different party*	77	10	69
Mixed support†	10	50	13
United with East Indians‡	13	40	15
No answer	—	—	3
Total	100	100	100
No. of cases	(39)	(10)	(39)

* % who think Muslims follow a different party.
† % who think Muslims support is mixed.
‡ % who think they stand united with East Indians.

R. J. Smith, who studied the retention of ethnic identity by East Indian Muslims in Trinidad, also referred to the Hindu–Muslim relations and observed that the study of Hindu–Muslim relations in Charlieville reveals the basic clash between the two communities on religious lines. This clash became much more acute during elections, county council elections or legislative elections, reaching a peak in the general election of September 1956.[1] Earlier in the 1950s, in rural Trinidad where there was a considerable Hindu–Muslim population, a type of perpetual war existed between the Hindu and Muslim factions.[2]

[1] Robert Jack Smith, 'Muslim East Indians in Trinidad: Retention of Identity Under Acculturation Conditions'. Unpublished Ph.D. dissertation (Ann Arbor, University Microfilm, Inc., 1963), p. 70.
[2] *Trinidad Guardian* (26 August 1956).

How far does the intergroup particularism of Hindus and Muslims affect the ethnic solidarity of East Indians in the party politics of Trinidad? Both Hindu and Christian *élites* believe that the majority of Muslims do not stand committed to the party supported by other East Indian groups (see Table 2-5).

Most of the Hindu and Indian Christian *élites* believe that Muslims have joined hands with the P.N.M. and have betrayed the cause of the East Indian community. Muslims are seen as using their alliance with the ruling party in the interest of their own community. The feelings of the Muslims have been expressed by Said Mohammed, a Muslim Minister in the P.N.M. Government. He pointed out that until 1956, when the P.N.M. came into power, no Muslim ever became a member of the Legislative Council. He commented that it was only after the rise of the P.N.M. that for the first time in the history of the island, a Muslim not only became a member of the Legislative Council, but a Minister in the Government.[1] Muslims were not satisfied with the treatment which they received from their fellow East Indians. However, it now seems that both the P.N.M. and the D.L.P. are trying to win the support of Muslims.

I was told that in 1956 some sections of urban Muslims voted for the P.N.M. but in 1961 a majority of them supported the D.L.P. In rural areas where Muslims live among other East Indian groups, they show greater ethnic identification than those living in urban areas. With the rise of party politics along racial lines, this ethnic identification was further enhanced.

Another important religious group among the East Indians are the Christians. Ninety-seven per cent of the East Indian Christians belong to the following denominations:[2] Presbyterians (47 per cent), Roman Catholics (33 per cent), and Anglican (17 per cent). Some East Indians belong to the Baptist, the Moravian, and the Wesleyan Churches, but their number is very small. Most of the East Indian Christians are converts from Hinduism or Islam. From the very beginning Christian missionaries of all denominations showed special interest in the immigrants from India. 'But the faith of their fathers was so well engrained in them that it was with the greatest difficulty that conversions could be made.'[3] It

---

[1] *Nation*, Trinidad (12 January 1962).

[2] Ahsan, op. cit., p. 220.

[3] Kirpalani, op. cit., p. 67.

was hard for the poor, indentured labourer to resist the temptations of the economic advantages offered by the Christian Church organizations. K. G. Grant notes that conversion to Christianity was resented by parents a great deal, but 'the gifts of clothing and other supplies from Canada were particularly valuable in those early years in helping to create a favourable opinion and attitude on the part of many toward the mission'.[1]

Among the different Church organizations, the Presbyterian Church of Eastern Canada identified itself most with the educational and social uplift of East Indians in Trinidad. The Presbyterian Church was so closely associated with the East Indians that it almost came to be known as the East Indian Church. A large number of East Indian intellectuals and professionals are the product of the educational institutions run by the Canadian mission.

Massive conversion to Christianity stopped some time in the late 1930s, first because of the rival efforts of Hindu missionaries from India, but mainly because it no longer offered economic advantages. A Canadian mission minister conceded in 1957, 'before that (1937), a man became Christian because it paid him to do so. Now he thinks he can get along without it.'[2]

The intergroup relationship between Christians and Hindus has never shown the type of tension which sometimes appears in the Hindu–Muslim relations. It is mainly because most of the Christians are of Hindu descent, and have close blood relations among Hindus. Also, the nature of intergroup relations between Hindus and Christians depends a great deal on their origins; Christians of Hindu descent are more sympathetic towards Hindus, and those of Muslim descent towards Muslims. However, we did not find it an island-wide attitude. Many Christians of Muslim descent showed strong ethnic identifications and criticized the alignment of the Muslim *élite* with the P.N.M.

Intergroup prejudices between Hindus and Indian Christians are by no means absent. Many East Indian Christians, because of their greater western orientation, look down upon Hindus as inferior. Sometimes they openly criticize the Hindu leaders for not teaching 'good manners' to their Hindu followers. After accepting the embrace of Christianity they look more towards the West than towards India for their cultural orientation. Many Hindus

[1] Grant, op. cit., p. 90.
[2] Niehoffs, *East Indians in the West Indies*, p. 150.

think that most of the Christian converts are former low-caste Hindus. They say that very few high-caste Hindus were converted to Christianity. Further, though it is conceded by Hindus that some East Indians embraced Christianity because of a genuine change of heart, the majority, they hold, were converted to get better economic opportunities. Hindus take pride in the feeling that they did not sacrifice their religion for economic advantage or political expediency. With the revival of Hinduism in Trinidad in recent years, surprisingly, many East Indian Christian professionals and intellectuals praise the Hindus for their continued adherence to their religion.

Religious differences among East Indians tend also to influence their party identification. Hindus make up the largest group who prefer the D.L.P.; in second place, East Indian Christians, and last, Muslims. It seems that though the Indian Christians were not as strongly committed to the D.L.P. in 1961 as were the Hindus, unlike some of the Muslims, they did not vote for the P.N.M. Indian Christians show greater identification with Hindus than Muslims in both social and political life.

The pluralistic social structure of East Indians in Trinidad can be placed at Gordon's community integration level,[1] where primary group relations exist beyond the subcultural lines. Intergroup integration among members of the three religious groups is taking place rapidly. Through fear of absorption by the Negroes and consequent loss of their identity, a larger number of interreligious marriages are taking place among East Indians. Hindu–Muslim marriages which used to be unthinkable, are becoming common in the urban middle classes, though they can still split a family.[2] The strongest resistance to interreligious marriages comes from Hindus (see Table 2-6).

Though 62 per cent of the Hindus disapproved of interreligious marriages, Table 2-6 shows that Hindus, who were quite rigid even in the case of intercaste marriages until recent times, are becoming more flexible towards interreligious marriages. When we compare the attitude of Trinidadian Hindus with that of Indian Hindus for whom interreligious marriage (especially marriage with Muslims) is out of the question, we can understand the significance of this change on the part of Hindus in Trinidad.

[1] Gordon, op. cit., p. 143.
[2] Naipaul, *The Middle Passage*, p. 82.

The reasons given against marriage with Muslims are cultural and religious, but mainly it is due to traditional prejudices carried over from the past.

Marriage with East Indian Christians, especially those of Hindu descent, is not very strongly opposed by the Hindus. East Indian Christians of Hindu descent remain in many ways Hindus, many still read and recite Hindu sacred books like the *Ramayara* and the *Bhagwad Gita*. Hindus oppose marriage with Christians mainly because of the fear of loss of identity of their own subgroup.[1]

Table 2-6   *Attitude of East Indian Élites Towards Interreligious Marriages*

Attitude	Religion		
	Hindu %	Muslim %	Christian %
Approve	36	90	74
Disapprove	62	10	26
No answer	2	—	—
Total	100	100	100
No. of cases	(39)	(10)	(39)

Thus, subgroup loyalties are the strongest among Hindus, but gradually they are moving towards greater ethnic solidarity and a more cohesive Indian social structure due to pressure from external forces. The total East Indian social structure is not as cohesive and homogeneous as that of the Negroes and the whites. Negroes do not possess strong subgroup loyalties built around religion. For an effective and stable organization of an East Indian political party in Trinidad, one would need leadership which could stand above narrow in-group loyalties and have a mass appeal cutting across religious and caste lines.

Hindu society is based on the caste system.[2] Though most of the

---

[1] The *Observer* (Vol. 9, No. 7, July 1950), p. 1.

[2] The four major castes are subdivided into a number of subcastes such as *Maharaj* or *Maraj*, *Dube*, *Gosain*, *Joshi*, and *Misir* within Brahmins; *Chattari* and *Singh* within *Kshatriya; Baniya, Jayaswal, Kayastha*, and *Aheer* within *Vaish*, the middle caste, and *Chamar, Curmi*, and *Dome* within *Sudra*, the lowest caste. Members of Hindu society are assigned status on the basis of their birth in a particular caste.

religious and ceremonial functions such as those related to food, occupational division, and touch and pollution have almost disappeared from the Hindu society of the island,[1] caste as a status symbol, and pride in higher-caste origin, still persist. Out of thirty-nine Hindu *élites* only one stated 'no caste' in the caste column. All others gave their caste origin. Twenty-five out of thirty Christian *élites* of Hindu descent mentioned their caste origin. Only a small percentage of the Christian *élite* of Hindu descent attached significant importance to their caste origin (see Table 2-7).

Table 2-7   *Attitude of Hindu and Christian Élites of Hindu Descent Towards Their Caste Origin*

Importance	Religion	
	Hindu	Christian
	%	%
None	28	63
A little	33	20
Very much	39	17
Total	100	100
No. of cases	(39)	(30)

Among all Hindus as well as among the Christians converted from Hinduism, the words *Dome* and *Chamar* (two low castes) are used in the derogatory sense,[2] and as Niehoff points out, 'Hindus who wish to insult each other will often use the term *Chamar*.'[3]

In the 1956 and 1961 general elections, subtle efforts were made by certain elements of the supporters of the P.N.M. to exploit the caste hostilities existing between the low-caste and high-caste Hindus. Morton Klass in his study of the East Indians of Felicity village in Trinidad noted 'a rough correlation between low caste

[1] Barton M. Schwartz, 'Ritual Aspects of Caste in Trinidad', *Anthropology Quarterly* (Vol. 37, No. 1, January 1964), p. 15.

[2] The *Observer* (Vol. 21, No. 11, November 1962), p. 11.

[3] A. Niehoff, 'The Survival of Hindu Institutions in an Alien Environment', p. 177. For a detailed treatment of caste system in Trinidad, see Barton M. Schwartz, *Caste in Overseas Indian Communities* (San Francisco, Chandler Publishing Co., 1967), pp. 117–200.

and P.N.M. vote, and high caste and D.L.P. vote . . .' in the general election of 1956.[1]

The Hindu *élite* shows greater liberalism on the question of inter-caste marriage: about 80 per cent have no objection to it. Niehoff noted, 'In Trinidad marriage between castes has become quite common, with perhaps as many marriages between castes as marriages within the same caste. Hindu parents prefer to get mates of the same caste for their children, but there are other considerations that they will regard as just as important or more so.'[2] We agree with Niehoff's observation that for Hindus in Trinidad, survival of Hinduism is much more important than the survival of the caste system.

Among the three religious groups, Hindus tend to be the most particularist and exclusive of the East Indians. This fact has an important bearing, as we will see, on the creation of a party competent to articulate and integrate the interests of the Trinidadian community in general and the East Indian community in particular.

This brief survey of the various institutions of the East Indian subculture in Trinidad makes it evident that East Indians have strong subgroup loyalties built around family, kinship group, and religion. Within the framework of this type of social structure, the political socialization process is performed mostly at the subgroup level. Various agencies such as religious associations, youth group organizations, and denominational educational institutions enforce and perpetuate the subgroup loyalties. Whenever the identity of the East Indian community is threatened from outside, ethnic loyalties would prevail over the subgroup loyalties.

This observation is also confirmed by what Niehoff said about the intergroup differences among East Indians. According to him, 'Even though there is a strong objection by many Indian Christians, and some Hindus and Muslims, to the militant Hinduism . . . probably the majority of them still feel that their ethnic identity as an Indian is more important than their religious differences.'[3] The Negro is looked upon by East Indians as an outsider and there exists an antipathy towards him among all groups of East Indians. This attitude plays an important psychological role in the life of the East Indian community, because

---

[1] Klass, *East Indians in Trinidad*, p. 225.
[2] Niehoffs, *East Indians in the West Indies*, p. 98.   [3] Ibid., p. 69.

'antipathy towards the out-group performs a positively integrative function for individual personalities and for the social system in which they participate. It bolsters up the individual's sense of security and self-esteem on the one hand, and promotes in-group solidarity on the other.'[1]

[1] A. H. Richmond, 'Theoretical Orientations in Studies of Ethnic Group Relations in Britain', *Man* (Vol. 57, August 1957), p. 122.

III

Political Perceptions and Attitudes of East Indian Élites

IN this chapter, the focus is on the socio-economic origin, the political perceptions and attitudes of the East Indian *élites*, which include the D.L.P. leadership (studied as a collectivity), East Indian parliamentarians, and the party office-holders. Various background variables of the East Indian *élites* have been studied. They are divided on two important variables: religion and occupation.

Comparison of East Indian Élites on the Basis of Religion

Religion is one of the most important bases of subgroup loyalties among East Indians. We will see how Hindus, Muslims, and Christians differ or have the same socio-economic origin and how they react on different issues.

Although a majority of East Indian *élites* is rural born, Hindus, more than Christian and Muslim *élites*, have rural origin. They continue to be a rural group mainly engaged in agriculture. Because of that, they constitute the group with the strongest element of traditionalism.

The religious differences among East Indian *élites* also find expression in their educational background.

Table 3-1   *An Educational and Religious Background of East Indian Élites*

Level of Education	Religion		
	Hindu %	Muslim %	Christian %
Primary or below	33	30	10
Secondary	36	40	41
University	31	30	49
Total	100	100	100
No. of cases	(39)	(10)	(39)

Table 3-1 shows that almost half of the East Indian Christian *élite* has a university education, which indicates that they are leading in the sphere of education and westernization. We have seen in Chapter II that the Canadian mission did remarkable educational work among the East Indians of Trinidad. Hindu and Muslim parents were most reluctant to send their children to the Christian schools because of the fear that they might be converted to Christianity. The Canadian mission and other Christian organizations gave priority to Indian Christians in appointments to their schools and a large number of East Indian Christians joined the teaching profession. Many of the top professionals and East Indian Civil Servants started as teachers and later acquired university education with their savings.

The Canadian mission founded Naparima College, a secondary school, and later on added a teacher-training college to it. A large majority of Indian intellectuals are the product of this college. However, it is again the East Indian Christian community which made the maximum use of these colleges. The Hindu *élite* constitutes the largest group with primary or below primary education. Many of the Hindu *élite*, with only elementary education, are occupying key positions in the religious or social organizations of Hindus.

Out of the thirty-four university degree-holders, twenty have received their higher education from British universities. East Indian Christians, because of their close cultural contact with Canada, look towards Canadian universities for higher education. In recent years the number of East Indian students going to Indian universities has increased. The Government of India offers scholarships to Trinidad students in numerous fields, including Indian dance and music.

Among the three religious groups to which the East Indian *élites* belong, Muslims seem to be much more organized and conscious of in-group solidarity. Out of ten Muslim *élites*, nine belong to either the *Sunnat-ul-Jamait* or the Muslim League; only one was not a member of any religious organization. In comparison, quite a significant number (31 per cent each) of the Hindu and East Indian Christian *élites* are not members of any religious organization. Most East Indian Christians belong to the Presbyterian Church. (Affiliation of the East Indian Christians with the Presbyterian Church is understandable in view of the pioneering work done by the Canadian mission among East Indians. Many East Indian *élites* refer to the work of the Canadian mission with great admiration.)

Among the Hindu religious organizations, the *Sanatan Dharma Maha Sabha*, the orthodox Hindu sect, seems to be the most powerful organization, as almost half of the Hindu *élite* are members. The *Arya Samaj*, the reformist Hindu sect, has not been able to attract a large number of the Hindu *élite*.

Comparison of Élites on the Basis of Occupation

The *élites* have been divided into six groups: political leaders, which includes most of the present and past parliamentarians; party and trade union officials; leading businessmen; leading professionals; religious leaders; social leaders; and office-holders of such non-political organizations as the West India Club and the Himalaya Club.

Dividing the different types of *élites* on a religious basis, the largest number (50 per cent) of the political leaders come from the Hindus. Six top leaders come from various groups of East Indian Christians. Only two Muslim leaders, Kamaludin Mohammed, a Minister in the P.N.M. Cabinet, and Tajmool Hosein, a former D.L.P. member of the House of Representatives, were mentioned among the outstanding political leaders. K. Mohammed was mentioned mainly because of his efforts to revive Indian music and dance in Trinidad.

If Hindus dominate the group of leading businessmen (67 per cent), a majority (75 per cent) of the top professionals come from the community of East Indian Christians.

The majority of the Indian Christian leaders are converts from Hinduism, and therefore a large number of them (26 out of 39) were able to identify their castes. Thirty-eight out of thirty-nine Hindu leaders could complete the column of 'caste' on the questionnaire; one refused to do so. The Brahmin caste supplies the largest number of leaders in all categories of *élites*. Our survey of 1965 shows that Brahmins dominate the political life of East Indians, as eleven out of fourteen political leaders claimed Brahmin origin; there is no political leader from the second highest caste.[1] In all other groups the two highest castes—*Brahamins* and

[1] In Trinidad, claims to high-caste origins may not be always true. I was told that many Hindus claiming high-caste origin were actually low castes.

Kshataiya—are dominant. Low-caste persons are mainly engaged in trade union activities. Thus, the top stratum of the East Indian community of Trinidad consists of people who claim high-caste origin.

There is a great deal of caste consciousness among some sections of East Indian *élites*. Hindus and Christian converts from Hinduism were asked how much importance they attach to their caste origin. On the basis of their answers we find that the political *élite* is the most caste-conscious group. It is a matter of great importance that a section of political leaders and members of other *élite* groups take pride in their high-caste origin. It is indicative of the *élite*'s belief in ascriptive norms. It is also evident that the caste prejudices, inherited from Indian society, have not altogether disappeared among the *élite* East Indians of Trinidad.

A majority (57 per cent) of the party officials and trade union leaders and half of the political leaders are not members of any religious organization. From more than half of political leaders who belong to religious organizations, the largest percentage are members of the *Sanatan Dharma Maha Sabha*. Many of the political leaders had held important offices in the S.D.M.S. before they entered politics. Bhadase Sagan Maraj, the president general of the *Maha Sabha*, and S. N. Capildeo, the former secretary general, have always been very active in the politics of the island. The *Arya Samaj*, the reformist sect, the *Seunarian Panth* and the *Kabir Panth*, both associated with low-caste Hindus, have no members in the top political leadership of the community. Only one Seunariani holds a leadership position. He is a high trade union official who comes from the low-caste Hindus. The *Maha Sabha* leadership is in the hands of high-caste Hindus, as is the political leadership of the East Indian community.

As the religion of the bulk of the Hindu population is the *Sanatan Dharma*, political leaders of the East Indian community have skilfully used the *Sanatan Dharma Maha Sabha* for consolidation of the Hindu rank and file. Furthermore, the *Maha Sabha* is an important instrument for keeping the traditional elements alive in the Hindu community.

Members of the *Maha Sabha* dominate the business *élite* too,

---

See Judith A. Weller, *The East Indian Indenture in Trinidad* (P. R. Institute of Caribbean Studies, 1968).

38 per cent of them being members of that organization. It is only among the leading professionals that the S.D.M.S. does not seem to have a great following.

Coming back to the political leaders, we find that 14 per cent are members of the Presbyterian Church and 7 per cent belong to the *Sunnat-ul-Jamait*. Thus the leadership of the East Indian community—including the D.L.P.—is dominated by the Sanatanist Hindus and the Presbyterians. Only one of the top former D.L.P. leaders is a Roman Catholic.

The majority of the professionals (50 per cent) is associated with the Presbyterian Church. After the religious leaders, it is the leading professionals who are most active in the field of religious activities; only 25 per cent are not members of any religious organization. Thus, top professionals seem to be more interested in religious and social activities than in political activities. This is perhaps why the political leadership of the community remains in the hands of the traditionalist elements. The other reason may be that most of the professionals are Presbyterians whereas the top political leadership of the community is dominated by Hindus. Hindus, in relation to their population, are under-represented among the professionals.

Like the *Maha Sabha*, Muslim social and religious organizations play an important role in the political socialization and recruitment of Muslim leadership. However, the Presbyterian Church, as an organization, has not intervened directly in politics.

Comparison of Élites on the Basis of Education

When we compare the educational background of the different types of *élites*, we find that the percentage of university-educated is the highest (66 per cent) among the social leaders—the office-holders of social clubs and non-political organizations. The percentage of university education is the lowest (5 per cent) among leading businessmen, who show the lowest level of education in general, 52 per cent having only primary or below primary education.

The religious leaders show the highest percentage (60 per cent) in secondary education, closely followed by the party and trade union officials (57 per cent).

The political *élite* represents a fairly highly educated group. In university education they come after the social leaders and

E

professionals (63 per cent), as 50 per cent hold university degrees. However, 14 per cent have only primary or below primary education, and 7 per cent have no schooling at all.

Out of seven political leaders with university degrees, five got their degrees from British universities, one from the United States, and one has been educated in both English and Canadian universities. Until recent times, political leaders with no university education have been more powerful and influential, because they represented the traditional elements of the society. But recently the balance has shifted and the university-educated group is gradually becoming more powerful. This is perhaps indicative of the new trend in the East Indian community which places greater emphasis on education.

How important a role the Canadian mission played in raising the educational level of the East Indian community is obvious from the fact that almost half of the East Indian *élites* have been educated in the Naparima College of San Fernando. However, its most significant contribution has been in building a class of Indian professionals, as 60 per cent of the East Indian professionals got their education in the Naparima College. Forty-seven per cent of the religious leaders and 43 per cent of the political leaders were also educated in the Naparima College. Until recent years the Naparima College had only East Indian students and faculty. Thus the majority of East Indian *élites* with their East Indian family patterns and exclusive educational institutions have been brought up in a self-segregated society. This process of political socialization has an important bearing on their subsequent political role in the island.

It is also significant to note that only the Christian churches have university-educated religious leaders. Hindu and Muslim religious leaders are mainly the office-holders or the managers of the religious organizations; they use their positions for advancing their political objectives. It is for this reason that one can witness bitter factional fights for control within the *Sanatan Dharma Maha Sabha*, the *Arya Samaj*, and the *Kabir Panth*. Many leading businessmen and professionals hold top positions in these religious organizations. *Pundits* and *Maulvies* (Hindu and Muslim priests), though English-speaking, are without university education. Many of them have been trained in orthodox ways, and they represent a hard core of particularism in their religious groups.

Attitudes of Élites Towards Various Social and Political Issues

An analysis of the attitudes of East Indian *élites* towards educational policies indicates how far they are ready to accept a complete break with their Indian heritage in favour of westernization. I asked the East Indian *élites* whether they would like to place emphasis in education on Indian values by imparting instruction in Indian culture and religion, on westernization, or would they compromise. An overwhelming majority rejected complete westernization outright and accepted making a compromise between traditionalism and westernization. Analysing this resistance to complete westernization on a religious basis, the strongest

Table 3-2   *Attitude of East Indian Élites Towards Education, on the Basis of Religion*

Should Education Emphasize	Religion		
	Hindu %	Muslim %	Christian %
Westernization	10	—	23
Traditional values	8	10	5
Compromise	79	90	62
No answer	3	—	10
Total	100	100	100
No. of cases	(39)	(10)	(39)

opposition comes from the Muslim *élite*. None of the Muslim leaders favoured a complete break with their religious tradition. The largest number of those who favour complete westernization come from the East Indian Christians. But even the majority of East Indian Christians, the most westernized group of East Indians in Trinidad, do not favour a complete break with the traditional culture. A very large number (64 per cent) of the East Indian Christian *élite* feel that their children should also be acquainted with the culture which their ancestors brought with them from India. Hindus stand between Muslims and East Indian Christians; only 10 per cent of them favouring complete westernization (see Table 3-2).

Obviously the interplay of traditional and modern values is

present in almost all the religious groups; no group favours either complete westernization or complete traditionalization. Four Hindu leaders who favour complete westernization through education of their children think that history is against them, and that living in the Western World they would not be able to escape complete westernization. On the other hand, many of the Christians favouring westernization said that they were from the West and therefore westernization was quite natural. Thus for many of the East Indian Christians the process of westernization is quite natural; whereas for Hindus it is the result of historical necessity which they would like to avoid but cannot because of the geographical situation in which they have been placed.

Table 3-3   *Attitude of Élites Towards Marriage with Negroes*

Attitude   Élite

	Political leaders	Party and t.u. officials	Business-men	Professionals	Religious leaders	Social leaders
	%	%	%	%	%	%
Approve	14	14	9	21	13	12
Disapprove	86	86	86	79	87	88
Undecided	—	—	5	—	—	—
Total	100	100	100	100	100	100
No. of cases	(14)	(7)	(21)	(24)	(15)	(8)

We have analysed the attitude of East Indian *élites* towards educational policies on the basis of religion: we will now see how the different types of *élites* react on this issue. When we compared the attitudes of different *élites*, we were surprised to find that even one of the more westernized and highly educated sectors of the East Indian community—the professionals—stands closer to the business leaders, which is one of the most conservative sectors of the community, and overwhelmingly supports the interplay of traditional and modern values in education. Eighty-one per cent of the leading businessmen and 79 per cent of the East Indian professionals advocate an educational policy which makes a compromise of western and traditional Indian values; only a small minority of the business leaders and the professionals advocate complete westernization. Though only a small number of *élites* want to emphasize traditional and Indian culture values in education, the *élites* in all other sectors place emphasis on composite values rather than on complete westernization.

In Chapter I we have referred to the attitude of East Indian *élites* on the basis of their religion towards the controversial question of marriage with Negroes. When we compare the attitude of different groups of East Indian *élites*, we find that liberalism on the question of westernization has no relation to liberalism on the question of marriage with Negroes. Table 3-3 shows that there is practically no difference in the attitude of different groups of East Indian *élites* towards marriage with Negroes, and they reject it almost unanimously.

Though these findings are applicable to a small *élite* population they make evident that even the top leadership of the East Indian community of Trinidad shows a great deal of hostility on the question of racial intermixing of East Indians and Negroes. For a large section of the business community, marriage with Negroes is unthinkable and unbearable; political and social leaders, and top professionals rationalize their objections and say that culturally Negro–Indian marriage would be a failure. They hold that the cultural differences and value orientation of the two groups are so wide apart that at no stage can miscegenation be a success. Cultural factors may be important but it seems that rejection of marriage with Negroes is mainly motivated by colour and race prejudices.

If race and colour prejudices were not important, the *élites* from different groups would have rejected marriage with whites with equal emphasis. But political and social leaders, and top professionals—all the groups which show considerable hostility to marriage with Negroes—show remarkable liberalism on the question of marriage with whites (see Table 3-4).

Whereas marriage with Negroes is approved only by a small minority of the respective *élites*, marriage with whites is approved by more than half of the *élites*. It is here that some of the East Indian *élites* use racial arguments as they assert that there is not much racial difference between whites and East Indians; both are of the same race and therefore, many argue, marriage with whites is not an interracial marriage. There seems to be two groups; one group considers marriage with Chinese also objectionable; the

second one approves marriage with all groups except Negroes.
The second group is motivated mostly by colour prejudice, whereas the first group believes that East Indians are closer to Europeans
in physical appearance and racial stock than to the Mongolians
or Negroes. Besides, marriage with whites raises the social status in
a society where social stratification is based upon ascriptive values
of colour and caste. Whites in Trinidad society, even now, enjoy
a high social status, and East Indians and Negroes consider each to
be inferior to the other. In the eyes of East Indian *élites*, marriage
with Negroes lowers the status of a man or a woman, whereas
marriage with whites raises it.

Table 3-4   *Attitude of Élites Towards Marriage with Whites*

Attitude   *Élite*

	Political leaders	Party and t.u. officials	Business-men	Professionals	Religious leaders	Social leaders
	%	%	%	%	%	%
Approve	64	29	33	65	40	63
Disapprove	29	71	62	35	53	25
No answer	7	—	5	—	7	12
Total	100	100	100	100	100	100
No. of cases	(14)	(7)	(21)	(23)	(15)	(8)

When we divide these *élites* on the basis of their rural–urban
background, there is considerable difference in their attitude
towards interracial marriage. Those born in towns and cities show
considerable liberalism on the question of marriage with both
Negroes and whites. Those born in the countryside or villages
show strong resistance to interracial marriage (see Table 3-5).
They almost unanimously (91 per cent) reject it. Little more than
half (57 per cent) of those born in the city—Port of Spain or San
Fernando—reject marriage with Negroes. Similarly, on the
question of marriage with whites, there is quite a significant
difference in the attitude of these two groups: 46 per cent of those
born in the country and 71 per cent of the city-born approve
marriage with whites. There is a difference of attitude between the
country-born and town-born *élites* on these questions. The sugar

estates and the countryside being more exclusive and segregated, and towns and cities more mixed and desegregated, seem to affect the experience of the *élites* in childhood and thus produce contradictory attitudes between the rural-born and the urban-born.

Table 3-5 *Attitude of Élites Towards Interracial Marriage, on the Basis of Birth-Place*

Attitude	Marriage with Negro Birth-Place			
	Country %	Village %	Town %	City %
Approve	9	9	16	43
Disapprove	91	89	84	57
Undecided	—	2	—	—
Total	100	100	100	100
No. of cases	(11)	(46)	(24)	(7)

	Marriage with Whites Birth-Place			
	Country %	Village %	Town %	City %
Approve	46	48	48	71
Disapprove	45	48	44	29
Undecided	9	4	8	—
Total	100	100	100	100
No. of cases	(11)	(46)	(24)	(7)

It would be important here to see what is the level of informal social intermixing of the different *élites* with other racial groups. Out of 89, only 12 go to racially mixed clubs, 37 said that they were members of racially exclusive clubs, and 40 declared that they were not members of any club at all. Only the professionals and leading businessmen meet more freely at the interracial level in informal social life. All other groups either stay at home and mix with their kinship groups on social occasions, or go only to racially exclusive clubs. Racial exclusiveness on the part of the political and non-political *élites* is highly significant in the context of the pluralistic social structure of Trinidad. Lack of informal intermixing between the political leaders of both sides is bound to create greater ethnic orientation and produce a larger number of racial prejudices.

In the absence of primary relations with other ethnic groups, the *élites* tend to be exclusive in their political organizations, and they cannot build mutual confidence with the members of other ethnic groups. This self-segregation in the social life of the East Indian *élites* of Trinidad tends to make them sectarian in their outlook. We shall see that the East Indian political leadership gradually lost many of non-East Indian supporters due to the presence of mutual suspicion. Lack of informal social relations consolidates the feelings of 'in-group solidarity' against the members of other ethnic groups, who are always treated as outsiders.

East Indians are divided into numerous castes and religious groups. How significant are the prejudices based upon religious and caste differences in the lives of East Indian *élites*? The role of these prejudices was brought out by questions concerning inter-caste and interreligious marriages. Significantly, on the question of ethnic endogamy all groups show greater liberalism. Only the party and trade union officials show strong resistance even to inter-caste marriage (43 per cent). There is very little resistance to inter-caste marriage among other groups. This opposition may not be very strong, but the significant fact is that there are still certain groups in East Indian society which are opposed to intercaste marriages. Obviously caste prejudices or ascriptive values are still alive among the East Indian *élites*.

What is more important is to compare the attitudes of the leaders of the different castes towards intercaste marriage. The strongest opposition comes from the Brahmins. Twenty-five per cent are still unwilling to mix with the middle- or 'low-caste' *élites*. Six per cent of the *Kshatriyas* are also opposed to it. But 100 per cent of the leaders of middle or low castes welcome intercaste marriage. This eagerness of the middle or low castes to marry among the Brahmins or the *Kshatriyas* is understandable in view of the importance they attach to caste origin. Fifty-five per cent of the middle or low caste attach great importance to the caste origin (as compared with 33 per cent of the Brahmins). For the lower-caste Hindu, marriage with a Brahmin is of real significance.

When we move out of the caste structure and ask questions on interreligious marriages among East Indians, we encounter increased resistance, but much less resistance than to marriage with Negroes. An overwhelming majority (88 per cent of the social leaders, 83 per cent of the professionals, and 79 per cent of the political leaders) have no objection to interreligious marriages. However, religious leaders (73 per cent), business leaders (62 per cent), and a significant majority of the party and trade union officials are opposed to marriage outside their own religious groups.

Evidently, only the highly educated and politically-conscious social and political leaders, and professionals are aware of the need for ethnic solidarity and overwhelmingly favour intercaste and interreligious marriages. Subgroup differences, though not significant in the case of caste, are quite meaningful in the case of religion.

The attitude of East Indian *élites* towards these questions shows that, in spite of their internal differences, they would strongly resist any effort by the majority ethnic group to absorb them. Prejudices based upon caste, colour, and creed are prevalent not only among the less educated and less privileged groups of East Indians, but also in the higher stratum of East Indian leadership.

What are the East Indians' attitudes towards the existing Government, its policies, and the political system as a whole? A large majority of the East Indian *élites* does not consider the policies of the P.N.M.'s Government towards East Indians as just. When we divide these groups on a religious basis, Hindus appear to be the most disgruntled with the policies of the Government. East Indian Christians come next, with the Muslims last. East Indian Christians constitute the largest number of those who feel that the Government's policies are conciliatory and that the Government is trying to improve its policies towards East Indians in order to win them over. A majority of those who term the policies of the Government as just towards East Indians are Muslims, compared to a small number of the Hindus and Indian Christians (5 per cent and 3 per cent, respectively) (see Table 3-6). Muslims, on the whole, seem to express greater satisfaction with the policies of the P.N.M.'s Government. This favourable reaction could be understood in view of the fact that in 1965 the two East Indian members of the P.N.M.'s Cabinet were Muslim; Hindus and East Indian Christians had no representation.

There is, however, a strong feeling of alienation towards the political system among all sections of the East Indian population, though these feelings have been most strongly expressed by East Indian Christian and Hindu *élites*. In response to an open-ended question on the nature of the P.N.M. Government, their typical expressions were: 'It is a Negro government;' 'Negro is the ruler in this country and Indian is an underdog;' 'The government's policies are formulated for the betterment of the Negro whereas Indians pay only taxes; no money is spent on East Indian masses;'[1]

Table 3-6   *East Indian Élites' Perception of the P.N.M. Government's Policy Towards East Indians, on the Basis of Religion*

Government's Policy	Religion		
	Hindus	Muslims	Christians
	%	%	%
Harsh	49	30	36
Conciliatory	38	10	46
Sometimes harsh and sometimes conciliatory	8	20	13
Just right	5	30	3
No answer	—	10	2
Total	100	100	100
No. of cases	(39)	(10)	(39)

'The Indians have been discriminated against from the first day they came in this territory until today;' 'Earlier Negroes were the victims of the race prejudices, now those victims of the past have become the aggressors of the present day.'[2] Even Dr. Winston Mahabir who had held office in the P.N.M.'s Government warned against the introduction of 'apartheid in reverse'[3] and against the propagation of a nationalism which excludes a

[1] Many East Indian *élites* cited grants of scholarships to students as one of the examples of discrimination against East Indians. Official figures of scholarships granted to East Indian students are as follows. In 1962, the Prime Minister, Dr. Williams, told the House of Representatives that until 1961 the government offered 303 scholarships out of which 68 were awarded to students of East Indian origin. In 1954 and 1956 no East Indian student was granted any scholarship. *Hansard* (Parliamentary Debates) (Vol. I, Session 1961–2), p. 1203.

[2] *Trinidad Guardian* (13 May 1962).   [3] Ibid. (1 January 1961).

particular ethnic group.[1] The feelings concerning the existing political system are not positive. It is looked upon essentially as representing the interests of the majority ethnic group.

There is a feeling among East Indian *élites* that there are two groups in the P.N.M. One is comparatively liberal on the question of racial policy and is led by Dr. Eric Williams. The other group consists of hard-core racialists headed by Dr. P. V. Solomon (a former Deputy Prime Minister and now head of the Trinidad delegation at the U.N.). Whenever the second group prevails, the policies of the Government become harsh towards East Indians; when the first group dominates, the policies are conciliatory. Another group of East Indian leaders asserts that the P.N.M. is a party controlled by middle-class, educated Negroes, who had never before tasted power. Now that they have it, they will never share it with the rising East Indian middle class.

Under the conditions mentioned above, it is important to see what solutions of racial problems have been suggested by the *élites* of different religions. Leaders from all religious groups assert that the first step towards the solution of the race problem is the recognition of its existence by the leaders of both the Opposition and the ruling party. The tendency of the Government and the government-supported Press and even that of some of the leaders of the Opposition in recent years, the religious leaders assert, has been to deny any racial friction. Political leaders pretend that Trinidad is a happy land of people of different races living together. According to the religious leaders, this is far from the truth and political and social leaders should give up this attitude and frankly recognize the existence of the race problem.

The East Indian *élites* gave numerous suggestions for solving the race problem. The most favoured solution is the provision of equal opportunities and fair treatment of Indians. This has been most advocated by Hindus, next by East Indian Christians, and then by Muslims (see Table 3-7). Another frequently mentioned solution is increased social and cultural intermixing of races. The majority of Muslims support this solution, seconded by East Indian Christians. Only a small percentage of the Hindus favour it. A considerable number of the Muslim *élite* favours the formation of a coalition government between the P.N.M. and the D.L.P. as the best solution. Some East Indian Christian and Hindu *élites* also

[1] Ibid. (16 March 1961).

supported it. The East Indian Christian *élite* seeks the solution of the racial problem through social and educational means, besides fair treatment of Indians and the provision of equal opportunities for them. Only the Christian *élite* considers interracial marriage as one of the major solutions of the problem. Hindu and Muslim *élites* do not even mention it. This attitude of the East Indian Christians is in conformity with their over-all social liberalism. A small minority of East Indian leaders suggests the creation of a separate homeland in the West Indies for East Indians or a partition of Trinidad[1] as one of the solutions of race relations. This has

Table 3-7   *Solutions of Racial Problem Suggested by East Indian Élites*

Solutions	Number of times suggested
Equal opportunities for East Indians	51
Increased social and cultural mixing of races	34
Coalition between the P.N.M. and the D.L.P.	14
Separate homeland for East Indians	4
Indians should take initiative	3
Interracial marriage	3
No solution possible	2

been advocated by a small number of respondents of Hindu and Christian origins. This is perhaps the result of the deep frustration of the Hindu community, born out of non-participation in the decision-making process of the country. It is also the result of a sense of insecurity which comes not only from their being a minority but also from the awareness that the Negro is physically stronger than the East Indian. This feeling is further accentuated because of the increasing accumulation of wealth in the hands of East Indians with the gradual rise of an enterprising business community, as opposed to the rise of the Negro to political power in 1956.

It is obvious that the three major religious groups into which

[1] H. P. Singh, *Hour of Decision* (Published by the author, Port of Spain, Trinidad, 91 Queen Street, 1962), p. 10.

the East Indian community is divided, differ in their assessment of the policies of the P.N.M. Government and in their suggestions for the solution of the racial problem. In fact, religion is an important variable in understanding the political attitude and behaviour of the three communities.

When we divide the East Indian *élites* into different occupational groups, and analyse their reaction to the policies of the P.N.M. Government, we find that the highest degree of dissatisfaction with the policies of the present government has been expressed by the party and trade union officials. However, almost half of the top professionals, political leaders, and a substantial number of leading businessmen, are also dissatisfied.

Only one political leader, three leading businessmen, and two top professionals consider that the policies of the present government are 'just right' towards East Indians. On the other hand, half of the social leaders and the top professionals, and quite a significant number of the religious leaders, leading businessmen, and political leaders, term the policies of the Government as 'conciliatory towards East Indians'. They do not think that the policies are 'just right', but they think that they have changed in recent years and have become conciliatory. They stress that there is still need for great improvement.

One of the most mentioned solutions of the racial problem is the provision of equal opportunities and fair treatment of Indians. It has been most favoured by the party and trade union officials (57 per cent), the business and religious leaders, and the top professionals. East Indians, it was emphasized by the top professionals and social leaders particularly, have been denied their legitimate rights in various ways. Educated Negroes devise various means of keeping East Indians out of civil and police services. The highly educated section of the East Indian community in Trinidad —the professionals and the social leaders—feels that it is being denied its legitimate rights.

A greater social mixing of different races has also been suggested as another solution to the racial problem. This solution comes mainly from the social leaders and top professionals. A small minority of political and business leaders has also advocated it.

Only a small percentage of the political leaders and the religious leaders mentioned interracial marriage as the only permanent and lasting solution of the racial problem; no other group mentioned it. Both groups suggested this as an ultimate solution, but at the same time, it was conceded by many that, personally, interracial marriage was most obnoxious to them. Even when it is realized that the ultimate solution of interracial tension lies in interracial marriages, its practical application is rejected because of strong racial prejudices. Under these conditions, when the people are divided into rigid sections, the Government is bound to be identified with one group.

When a government is considered to represent a particular kinship, caste, or local interests, the citizenry looks upon it as neither just nor representative of the national interest. It makes each section of the society fearful of exploitation and suppression by others, and heightens reluctance to participate in the scheme for which the government needs the assent and will of the ordinary man.[1]

Formation of a coalition government between the P.N.M. and the D.L.P. was another solution offered in order to lessen the racial tension. The suggestion came from the business leaders (33 per cent), with some support from the other groups.

A suggestion for the creation of a separate homeland for the East Indians came from every group except the party and trade union officials and social leaders. One of the top East Indian political leaders when interviewed asserted that the only lasting solution of the problem was the 'creation of a separate homeland for East Indians in the West Indies'. He explained:

The Indian cannot get a sense of being a first-class citizen until he gets his own homeland. There is a basic conflict between the Indian and the Negro. The Indian works hard and saves. It is the Indian community which is building the capital of this country with its hard savings. The Negro does not want to work, especially he does not want to undertake manual labour. The Negro feels that he is of the *élite*, and he wants to leave the dirty work to Indians. The Negro is also afraid of the greater economic abilities of Indians.

He further argued, 'There is also a question of cultural conflict; East Indians cannot leave their culture. If there is an Indian dominion in the West Indies, those Indians who do not want to be treated as second-rate citizens can migrate to this dominion. No other satisfactory solution is possible under present conditions.'

[1] Edward Shils, 'The New States', *Comparative Studies in Society and History* (Vol. II, No. 4, July 1960), p. 270.

He further suggested the partition of British Guiana. He asserted that 'Partition of British Guiana is the only solution. The challenge of Pakistan will come,' but he was confident that the leaders 'will be able to meet the challenge, as Muslims constitute only a small percentage of the population. Jagan will oppose this solution, but he is the only one to oppose, and on this issue he would be swept aside.' Under the present conditions, he maintained, 'The Indian community in the West Indies lives under a constant fear of molestation and even physical destruction. Under such conditions political leadership is unable to press any solution. Had they pressed, like the Negroes in British Guiana, for introduction of proportional representation in Trinidad or asked for some type of parity in the formation of governments or in the civil services, before independence of the country, Negroes would have resorted to the use of violence against East Indians in Trinidad, as they did in British Guiana. It was only in order to save the East Indian community from being subjected to violence and humiliation, that the demand for proportional representation was given up.' However, the people who supported this suggestion are in a small minority. We found that a majority of the East Indian *élite* seeks the solution of the racial problem under the existing structure and through political and economic means. Very few recognize that the problem is also social.

British Guiana is not far from the thoughts of East Indians in Trinidad. In order to discover the depth of ethnocentricity of East Indian *élites*, I asked them a few questions about the conflict between Negroes and East Indians in the political situation in British Guiana. An overwhelming majority of the East Indian *élites* reacted emotionally. Some of the typical expressions were: 'Indians have been betrayed.' 'Indians are doomed in British Guiana.' 'Negro rule has been imposed on the Indian in British Guiana.' The Hindu *élite* betrays the strongest ethnic orientation and expresses the greatest concern about the fate of the East Indians in British Guiana, whereas the Muslim and Christian *élites* exercise the greater restraint. But the number of objective and non-ethnic oriented persons is very small in all of the East Indian groups. The situation in British Guiana is viewed mainly as a struggle between an East Indian majority and a Negro minority for political power. Their sympathies are unmistakably with the East Indians, and they think that the East Indians as a majority

ethnic group should run the country. Higher ethnic orientation of the Hindu *élites* is the result of their own distinctive
social and religious institutions. As we have seen, Hindus
are more exclusive in their social relations than the Muslims and
Christians. Higher ethnic orientation of the Hindu *élites* is
further confirmed by their greater expression of sympathy towards Cheddi Jagan, the outstanding political leader of British
Guiana, than that of the *élites* of the two other religious groups. The
data show that an overwhelming majority of East Indian *élites*
(68 per cent) are sympathetic towards Jagan. They praise him for
his non-racial attitude, while a majority term Burnham a 'racist'.
They regard Jagan as an honest politician, and many of them
believe that he cannot be called a communist, as Shastri, the late
Indian Prime Minister, could not have been termed a communist.
Hindus constitute the largest group of sympathizers with Jagan.
The smallest group is that of East Indian Christians who show
either a greater indifference or an attitude of hostility towards
Jagan than any other group of East Indians. Many of those who
express hostility towards Jagan argue that Jagan foolishly betrayed East Indian interests in British Guiana by placing too much
emphasis on ideology. This ethnic bias is further evidenced in the
rejection by a large majority of East Indians of Jagan and his
P.P.P. as a model on the basis of which the D.L.P. can be
organized. Christians and Muslims overwhelmingly reject Jagan's
People's Progressive Party as a model for the D.L.P., but a significant number of the Hindu *élite* advocate its acceptance. This is
understandable since it is the Hindu *élite* which shows the highest
percentage of ethnic orientation and expresses the strongest
sympathy for Jagan.

The reason most frequently mentioned for the rejection of
Jagan's P.P.P. is the impression that he is a communist. Here,
East Indian *élites* contradicted themselves. When they were asked
questions on the situation in British Guiana, they expressed
sympathies with Jagan and overwhelmingly denied that he was
a communist. But, subsequently, they rejected the P.P.P. as a
model for the D.L.P., saying they think that Jagan is a communist. The Muslim *élite* forms the largest, and the Hindu *élite* the
smallest, group to do so. East Indian Christians stand between
Hindus and Muslims, but closer to the Hindus than the Muslims.
Another reason given for the rejection of Jagan's P.P.P. is that he

and his party have failed to achieve their objectives. His failure is twofold; he failed to achieve his cherished ideal of a genuine multiracial party, and he failed to put the East Indians in a position of power.

Another group consisting of *élites* from all religions, reject Jagan and his P.P.P. because they think that Trinidad is much less racial than British Guiana. In Trinidad, they assert, there is a need for mixed political parties rather than a party based upon ethnicity. This argument is advanced mainly by East Indian Christians, but has also been supported by a small number of Hindus.

A majority of those who support the P.P.P. as a model for the D.L.P. believe that Jagan is one of the most honest politicians in the West Indies. They also admire his dedication to the cause of his people, his devotion to his country, and, above all, his determination to stay with his people through thick and thin. These are the qualities, they say, which the D.L.P. leadership in Trinidad needs most. In other words, this appreciation of Jagan is an implicit criticism of the D.L.P. leadership.

When we analyse the reaction towards the situation in British Guiana on the basis of occupations, the political and business *élites* and party and trade union officials betray the highest degree of ethnocentricity. Their expressions are extremely emotional and they exercise little restraint in condemning Burnham or Britain and the United States for their roles in British Guiana. One is impressed with the complete absence of ideological orientation in the expressions used by the *élites*. The reaction of the political leaders, for example, found expression in sentences like: 'The situation is most unfortunate.' 'It is a rape of the people.' 'It is the violation of all democratic principles.' 'It is the result of the dishonesty of educated Negroes which enabled them to capture political power.' 'The situation is lamentable; it is most distressing.'

Although the *élites* from all occupational groups have a sympathetic attitude towards Jagan, the highest degree of sympathy is expressed by the political leaders (86 per cent). Even when they say that the entire situation is the result of the folly of Jagan, they would add: 'He is one of the most sincere men in the western hemisphere, though he is simple and naive.' 'He [Jagan] is totally lacking in political subtleties. He should have, first, won freedom and

F

then he could have talked about communism.' Many of them criticize him for placing too much emphasis on ideology. One of the political leaders remarked: 'He may be an honest man but he is not a shrewd politician; he failed to understand that honesty and idealism are not the only desirable factors. He behaved most foolishly and lost an opportunity of establishing a safe place for Indians in the West Indies.'

Thus the East Indian political *élites* of Trinidad look upon the entire question of Jagan and the position of the East Indians in British Guiana from an ethnic viewpoint. They are afraid of the rising political power of Negroes and feel a sense of insecurity in the loss of British Guiana to Negroes.

Sympathy towards Jagan and East Indians in British Guiana has also been expressed by *élites* from other sectors. However, almost half of the top professionals assume an attitude of indifference or hostility towards Jagan.

While expressing their sympathy with Jagan, a majority of the East Indian leaders either do not speak about his communist affiliation or, if at all, refer to communist beliefs only to express the view that they do not know whether he is a communist.

Élites from all sectors, though especially the political *élite* and the social and religious leaders, throw the entire blame on Great Britain and to a lesser extent on the United States for imposing the minority rule over the majority and thus depriving East Indians of their legitimate right of running the Government of the country. Strong feelings of the political and social *élites* find expressions in statements such as: 'The situation in British Guiana is a disgrace for the British and Americans.' 'British Guiana is one of the blackest spots on British colonialism.' 'British Government must be held responsible for this situation.' 'British Guiana Indians have become victims of British and American dishonesty.' 'The situation in British Guiana is the result of the Negro militancy actively encouraged by the British and American Governments.' Many people among the East Indian *élites* hold that this policy of western discrimination against East Indians in the West Indies is the result of a deep-rooted hostility. Both British and Americans distrust Indians. They know that the Negro can be manipulated whereas it is difficult to manipulate Indians; therefore, they did not want to see the rise of an Indian dominion in the Caribbean. They argue that the Negro has no business sense; he does not know how to manage an economy and therefore he would never be a challenge to British and American business interests in the West Indies. The Indian, on the other hand, with his business skill and organizational abilities, is already posing a threat to the local whites, who until now had been exercising an undisputed monopoly in certain trades. Therefore, some of the members of the East Indian *élites* assert that Jagan has not been displaced because of his communist beliefs but because he is an Indian. Those who do not blame the British or American Governments, or blame them moderately, do not argue on ethnic lines. They concede that Jagan posed a communist threat in the Caribbean, and the British and Americans were justified in removing him. They assert that Jagan failed to recognize that he was living in the western hemisphere.

A few of the political leaders and a small minority of the professionals criticize the Government of India for its indifferent attitude concerning the people of Indian origin in the West Indies. The view is that had the Government of India taken some interest in their fate, perhaps it could have saved them from falling under the subjugation of a racist like Burnham.

The East Indian leadership in Trinidad has been distinctly pro-West. Time and again it has supported the presence of the United States naval base in Trinidad. The anti-West expressions are basically the result of the strong ethnic-oriented response to the situation existing in British Guiana. Thus East Indian *élites* conceive national loyalty on the basis of ethnicity. In spite of their sympathies with Jagan and East Indians in British Guiana, an overwhelming majority of East Indian *élites* from all sectors reject the P.P.P. as a model for the D.L.P. Even the political leaders, who expressed great appreciation for Jagan, reject the P.P.P. as a model for the D.L.P. The political *élites* reject the P.P.P. mainly on two grounds, first because the P.P.P. failed in achieving its objectives. An important party office-holder of the D.L.P. said that Jagan 'should follow our philosophy. He was too idealistic to accept the racial problem; he brought many Negroes in power.' 'This he did,' a former East Indian M.P. said, 'in order to enlist the Negro support, but he failed.' Thus this section of East Indian leadership does not believe that any political partnership with Negroes can be a success. Another section rejects the P.P.P. model for the D.L.P. because of its leftist orientation. An

East Indian M.P. of Trinidad commented that Trinidad has a large middle class, the standard of living of the people is sufficiently high, and the conservative tendencies are very strong in a large proportion of the population: a radically leftist party would not be popular. One of the professionals remarked: 'The sooner we forget our affiliations with Jagan, the better it is for us; mainly because of his communism, he led his people into trouble.' On the other hand, a leading businessman argued that: 'Jagan forgets many times that he is an Indian. Jagan was backing Mao in the case of the Sino-Indian border war. In Trinidad, the Indian leaders still carry on Indian traditions. The only thing which we have in common is the support of the Indian peasantry.'

Also, the top professionals and leading businessmen of the East Indian community expressed the view that the situation in British Guiana is different from that of Trinidad. In Guiana, there is too much racialism, Trinidad has not yet reached that stage. Jagan and the P.P.P. have shown us that we should not make enemies with the people with whom we live. A few top professionals who accepted him and his party believe that 'his honest position can be a model for the D.L.P. although not his leftist policies'.

Obviously East Indian *élites* in Trinidad do not think in terms of a 'class struggle'. They are conservative and sectarian in their outlook and seek limited objectives. The whole of their socio-economic background and their value orientation tend to make them defensive. As a rising property-owning class, they seek peace rather than political instability; they seek maintenance of the *status quo* rather than any radical change in the economic and political structure of the country. Under these conditions the political organization of East Indians, as we will see, has become narrow and sectarian in its character, and conservative in its political outlook.

IV

The Rise of Party Politics in Trinidad and the Birth of the D.L.P.

The Birth of Representative Institutions

THE development of representative institutions in Trinidad has not been different from most of the other British colonies, where colonial people, inspired by the British parliamentary model and the system of Cabinet government, demanded and gradually attained self-government and afterwards attempted to frame their political institutions on the British pattern.

As in many other British colonies, the institutional structure in colonial Trinidad consisted of a Governor, an Executive Council, and a legislative body. The legislative body in Trinidad was first established in 1831, and it was known as the Council of Government. In 1863, the name was changed to the Legislative Council.[1] It was mainly an advisory body and its members were 'nominated' (appointed) by the Governor. In 1831, the Council consisted of a Governor, who presided over its meetings, and twelve members, six of whom were officials and six non-officials. Thus it was purely an appointive body.[2]

By 1898, the number of members of the Council had grown to twenty-one, ten official and eleven non-official members.[3] A demand for the introduction of the elective process in the selection of the Council was made by the English settlers, but it was opposed by the French settlers who did not look favourably upon representative institutions.[4] At any rate, the demand was rejected by the British Government, and unlike Jamaica, Trinidad planters failed to get an elective legislative body. The major reason for this refusal was the presence of a large number of non-white free people in the

---

[1] Hewan Craig, *The Legislative Council of Trinidad and Tobago* (London, Faber and Faber, 1951), p. 13.
[2] Ibid., p. 18; the term 'nominated' means appointed in the formal usage in British colonies—'nominated' will be used in this study to indicate that positions are appointive.
[3] Ibid., p. 28.
[4] H. O. B. Wooding, 'The Constitutional History of Trinidad and Tobago', *Caribbean Quarterly* (Vol. VI, Nos. 3 and 4, May 1960), p. 149.

colony. Introduction of elections would have meant extending to them the right to vote which the Colonial Office was reluctant to do but denying it would have created widespread discontent. Another reason was the general backwardness of the colony. Both East Indians and Negroes were considered unqualified for participation in any representative political system.[1]

At the beginning of the twentieth century, an educated coloured middle class gradually arose and started making demands for representative institutions. However, the Government of the colony was of the opinion that the demand for direct representation lacked popular support, as it held the view that 'The great bulk of the people were peasants or agricultural labourers who neither understood nor agreed about the meaning of the change proposed by the gentlemen. . . .'[2] The Government pointed out that the demand was 'supported by the Creole Negroes and coloured people, many of whom have no settled occupation. They are represented by the educated men of their race and it is the latter who have organized the agitation for a change in the form of government; some of them being actuated simply by racial feelings.'[3] The Government also asserted that the demand for representative government was opposed by the important merchants and planters, especially by the old and established French families.[4] The British Government sent E. F. L. Wood, a Member of Parliament and a Parliamentary Under-Secretary of State for the Colonies, as a one-man commission to the West Indies and British Guiana in order to examine the whole issue of representative government in the light of changed conditions in this part of the empire.

Wood, who travelled throughout the British West Indies and British Guiana towards the end of 1921, found that the demand for representative government arose because of the stimulation of democratic sentiment as a result of World War I, the spread of education and the consequent rise of a native intelligentsia, and the return of army personnel from abroad at the end of the war.[5]

[1] Craig, op. cit., p. 28.

[2] 'Governor's Dispatch to the Secretary of State for Colonies, dated November 21, 1921', Trinidad Archives.

[3] Ibid.   [4] Ibid.

[5] Great Britain, *Report by the Hon. E. F. L. Wood on his Visit to the West Indies and British Guiana 1921–1922*, Cmd. 1679 (London, H.M.S.O., 1922), p. 6. (Hereafter known as the Wood Commission Report.)

Wood was of the opinion that with the acceptance of the British way of life by Negroes in the West Indies, the rise of a demand for representative government would be natural. 'The whole history of the African population of the West Indies inevitably draws them towards representative institutions fashioned after the British model.'[1] According to Sir H. O. B. Wooding, the demand for representative institutions was also stimulated by the Bolshevik Revolution, which gave impetus to workers to unite and also led to widespread labour disturbances in the colony in 1921, which forced the British Government to reconsider its policies.[2] However, Major Wood rejected the demand for the introduction of fully representative government on account of the political under-development of the area, the existence of racial and cultural cleavages, and the non-existence of a leisured class which could take an active part in political life. Introduction of representative government, he thought, was much more difficult and complex in Trinidad than in any other part of the West Indies.[3] He found that Trinidad lacked a 'homogeneous public opinion' and that socially it was 'divided into all kinds of groups which have very few relations with one another'.[4] He specially referred to the heterogeneous mass of East Indians in Trinidad, whom he re-garded as illiterates and political underdogs, incapable of partici-pation in representative government.

The demand for reforms was mainly being pushed by what was known as the Legislative Reform Committee, led by Captain A. A. Cipriani (a French Creole who called himself a socialist and devoted himself to the organization of labour in Trinidad).[5] The Legislative Reform Committee felt that the people of the colony were well advanced in the fields of education and political consciousness. They claimed that they had achieved success in the operation of town governments, and that the people were mature enough to be given a direct share in the representative bodies.[6] This demand was supported by an East Indian leader, Rev.

---

[1] Ibid., p. 6.
[2] Wooding, op. cit., p. 151.
[3] *The Wood Commission Report*, p. 22.
[4] Ibid., p. 23.
[5] C. L. R. James, 'A. A. Cipriani: The Greatest of All British West Indian Leaders', Independence Supplement, *Sunday Guardian* (26 August 1962), p. 17.
[6] *Trinidad Guardian* (29 January 1922).

C. D. Lalla.[1] On the other hand, a powerful and influential section of the East Indian community led by A. R. Sinanan, James Mungal, and L. D. Boodoosingh (East Indian leaders from South Trinidad) strongly opposed the introduction of representative government and demanded the continuation of Trinidad's crown colony status. They asserted, 'We believe that the East Indians will be hopelessly outvoted if the election system is granted and even the only seat now held by the Indians will be lost.'[2]

The East Indian National Congress, an organization claiming to represent an overwhelming majority of East Indians, in its memorandum submitted to Mr. Wood did not reject outright the demand for representative government. It advocated the introduction of partial measures of representative government, but demanded safeguards to protect the rights of East Indians as a minority group. It held that 'in the opinion of the East Indian Community, the Communal or Proportional Form of Representative Government provides the most adequate safeguards against'[3] the danger of East Indians being absorbed by the West Indians. It pointed out that already the West Indians dominated the civil and police services, and they were reaping the rewards of the prosperity built by East Indian labour. They claimed that there were no religious differences among East Indians and demanded representation for East Indians on the basis of race.[4] The demand for communal representation or proportional representation was opposed by the Legislative Reform Committee, which argued that introduction of communal representation would cause frictions in the life of the community.[5] The Wood Commission, however, rejected the demand of the East Indian National Congress for communal or proportional representation. Wood held that the demand was opposed, first of all, by the advocates of the constitutional changes and secondly, he asserted that it would increase and perpetuate the differences between the diverse elements of

[1] *Port of Spain Gazette* (13 August 1921).

[2] Ibid.

[3] Quoted from 'The Memorial of the East Indian National Congress of Trinidad', submitted to Mr. E. F. L. Wood and signed by Rev. H. H. Imamshah, secretary (Trinidad Archives, 3 February 1922) pp. 3–4.

[4] Ibid., p. 3.

[5] *The Wood Commission Report*, p. 23.

the population and stand in the way of development of a homogeneous community in the island.[1]

On the other hand, Wood found that the demand for increased representation was irresistible. Consequently, in his recommendations, he suggested introducing elected members in the Legislative Council by reducing the number of the nominated majority. Further, in place of the official majority, he recommended the creation of a majority of nominated non-officials and elected members. He held also that the Governor should continue to exercise his power of nominating the members of the Legislative Council. He recommended that when all the elected members were opposed to a legislative measure, the case should be referred to the Secretary of State for the Colonies.[2] He recommended an increase in non-official members from seven to thirteen. Out of these thirteen non-official members, six were to be nominated and seven were to be elected on the basis of one member for each 60,000 persons for a term of five years.[3] The formation of electoral constituencies was left to the local governments.

Wood's recommendations were put into effect in 1924. The colony was divided into seven constituencies: The City of Port of Spain; The County of Caroni; The County of St. George; The Eastern Counties (including the counties of St. Andrews, St. David, Nariva, and Mayaro); The County of Victoria; The County of St. Patrick, and The Ward of Tobago.[4]

The right to vote was granted according to property or income qualifications. High financial qualifications were fixed for the candidates seeking election to the Council to insure that only men of considerable means could become members of the legislative body.[5]

Thus for the first time in the history of the colony, the elective element was introduced in the legislature. In the first election, out of seven elected members, two were East Indians. Subsequently the number of elected East Indian members was raised to three.[6] In spite of the new system, the official bloc was still in a position to outvote the non-official bloc. Furthermore, the elective element in the legislature could get almost no effective control over the Executive Council.

[1] Ibid., p. 27.   [2] Ibid., p. 9.   [3] Ibid., pp. 25–6.
[4] Kirpalani, op. cit., p. 72.   [5] Craig, op. cit., p. 39.
[6] Kirpalani, op. cit., p. 72.

The next important stage in the development of representative institutions came with the appointment of the West Indian Royal Commission, in the wake of the labour disturbance of the late 1930s. Under the chairmanship of Lord Moyne, the Commission started its work in August 1938. During 1938–9, the Commission spent about six months in the West Indies. The Commission not only probed into the socio-economic problems faced by the areas but also investigated the issue of political reform. The Commission found the basic cause of the labour disturbance to be socio-economic conditions. It pointed out that 'The crux of the West Indian problem . . . is the demand for better living conditions.'[1] It recognized that, 'rightly or wrongly a substantial body of public opinion in the West Indies is convinced that far reaching measures of social reconstruction depend . . . upon greater participation of the people in the business of government'.[2] Although it rejected the demand for independence, the Commission conceded that 'participation by the people in the work of government is a great necessity for lasting social advancement'.[3] The Commission also recognized that the exclusion of non-official elements from the administration encouraged them to adopt an attitude of hostility towards its officials. At that stage, the Commission expressed its concern mainly for increasing the representative character of the legislative bodies in the area and to insure that the ultimate object of such a policy 'should be the introduction of universal adult suffrage'.[4] In the case of Trinidad the Commission recommended an increase in the number of elected members and the reduction of nominated officials to three. It provided for the appointment of a local committee to examine the ways and means of introducing the adult franchise in the colony. The Commission also pointed out the need for giving adequate representation in the Executive Council to all important sections of the society.[5]

In 1940, on the basis of the recommendations of the Royal Commission, the practice of nominated official members was terminated. The next year the number of elected members was

---

[1] *The West Indian Royal Commission Report*, Cmd. 6607 (London, H.M.S.O., 1945), p. 423.
[2] Ibid., p. 375.
[3] Ibid., p. 449.
[4] Ibid., p. 450.   [5] Ibid.

raised from seven to nine.[1] The Legislative Council now consisted of eighteen members, out of which nine were elected, six were nominated non-officials, and three were *ex officio* members. By 1941 the elected members constituted the largest single bloc in the Legislative Council.

The second important step in the introduction of representative institutions in Trinidad came with the appointment of a Franchise Committee, which consisted of 34 members, six of whom were East Indians. The Franchise Committee recommended granting the right to vote to every adult on the basis of no more than proof of knowledge of spoken English. The two East Indian members of the Committee, Adrian Cola Rienzi and C. E. Abidh, in a minority report, opposed the provision for a language test. The Trinidad Legislative Council, on the pleas of Captain A. A. Cipriani and Albert Gomes, accepted the majority report and refused to remove the provision for the language test. Evidently, the language test was intended to deprive a large majority of East Indians of their right to vote, since they constituted the largest bloc of non-English-speaking people. East Indians launched an island-wide protest campaign for the removal of the language test. They ultimately triumphed when the Secretary of State for the Colonies approved the Franchise Committee's recommendation on adult suffrage but at the same time dropped the provision for a language test.[2]

The first election with universal suffrage was held in 1946. The percentage of registered voters increased from 6·6 per cent (in 1938) to 46 per cent. Numerous independents and quite a large number of political groups contested in the election. These political groups, which were called political parties, were organized around prominent personalities. They lacked common programme and policies. Election was held on the basis of single-member constituencies without any special safeguards for East Indians. This enabled different groups to form electoral alliances. Albert Gomes, a Trinidadian of Portuguese descent, organized a United Front and put up the largest number of candidates.

East Indians obtained four out of the nine elected seats and thus, although they formed only 35 per cent of the island's population, they captured 44 per cent of the elected seats.[3] The

---

[1] Craig, op. cit., p. 144. [2] Kirpalani, op. cit., pp. 109–10.
[3] Craig, op. cit., pp. 153–5.

East Indian leadership formed alliances with other sections, although the main basis of their strength was the solid mass of East Indians who stood behind them.

The politically enlightened section of Trinidad was not satisfied with the constitutional reforms introduced in 1946. Only half of the members of the Legislative Council were elected; the rest of them were nominated by the Governor who also possessed a casting vote. Albert Gomes pointed out, 'It is impossible to produce truly representative legislation within a body which is not truly democratic.'[1] The Executive Council was still dominated by the Governor and the elected members did not have any real power. The Executive Council was also not responsible to the Legislative Council. An unanimously-passed resolution of the legislature appointed a committee in 1947 to make further recommendations on constitutional reforms. No official member of the Legislative Council was on the committee; it consisted entirely of non-officials and included several elected members. The Committee reported to the House in February 1948. There were two reports—the Majority Report and the Minority Report. The Majority Report recommended a Legislative Council consisting of twenty-seven members, out of which eighteen should be popularly elected, six nominated, and three *ex officio* members.

It also recommended that a Speaker, who should have only a casting vote, should be appointed by the Governor from outside the House.[2] The Executive Council should consist of three *ex officio* members, nine non-officials, all of whom should be elected by the Legislative Council. Among the nine non-official members, three should be nominated and six, elected. The Governor would preside over the meetings of the Council, but should have only a casting vote. The Majority Report also recommended the appointment of a 'leader' of the Executive Council from among the non-official members of the Council. The Governor should make the allocation of portfolios in consultation with the Leader of the Executive Council.[3]

The Minority Report recommended the introduction of the Cabinet system on the British model along with an entirely

[1] Quoted in Ann Spackman, 'Constitutional Development in Trinidad and Tobago', *Social and Economic Studies* (Vol. 14, No. 4, December 1965), p. 285.
[2] Craig, op. cit., p. 158.
[3] Spackman, op. cit., p. 285.

elected legislative body. It recommended the complete abolition of the system of nominated members, asserting that it was not in conformity with democratic principles.[1]

A constitutional structure, based mainly upon the Majority Report, was introduced in 1950. The new system reduced the number of nominated members of the Legislative Council from six to five. Against the recommendations of the Committee, the Speaker, a nominated official, was given no vote. The Executive Council was to consist of three *ex officio* members, one nominated member, and five elected members. The five elected members were made responsible to the Legislature. For the removal of the elected members of the Executive Council, a two-thirds majority

Table 4-1   *Racial Distribution of Members of the Legislative Council, 1950*

White	Negro	East Indians	Chinese	Syrian	Mixed	Total
2	5	7	1	1	2	18

was needed. The Governor, with his casting vote, was to preside over the meetings.

The new Executive Council was termed as one of the 'most advanced in the crown colonies. Unlike the former purely advisory Executive Council, it is executive in fact as well as in name, and it lies in the power of the five elected members, provided they vote together and subject to the use of the Governor's reserve powers, to control the policy of the administration.'[2] The 1950 Constitution was another major step towards further extension of representative institutions in the island.[3]

The colony was divided into eighteen single-member constituencies with almost equal population. The election was held in September 1950. Fifty-one candidates were put up by five different political groups, and ninety sought election as independent

---

[1] Ibid., p. 286.

[2] Craig, op. cit., p. 160.

[3] Ronald V. Sires, 'Government in the British West Indies: An Historical Outline', in H. D. Huggins (ed.), *Federation of the West Indies*, (Jamaica, University of West Indies, B.W.I., Institute of Social and Economic Research, 1958), p. 128.

candidates. Five Independents were elected and thirteen were returned on party tickets.[1]

Among the seven East Indian members of the Legislative Council, four were Hindus and three Christians: two Presbyterians, and one Roman Catholic. No Muslim East Indian was returned. Five were Brahmins and two were Kshyatrias. Obviously the leadership of East Indians was in the hands of high-caste Hindus, and as we have seen in Chapter III, it has not changed hands; the high-caste Hindus, especially the Brahmins, have been successful in maintaining their hold on the East Indian masses.

In 1950, East Indians held 38·9 per cent of the total elected seats against 44·4 per cent in 1945.[2] East Indians, thus, still presented the largest and most solid voting bloc.

The 1956 Constitutional Reforms and the Introduction of Self-Government

A Constitutional Reform Committee under the chairmanship of A. S. Sinanan, an East Indian member of the Trinidad Legislative Council, was appointed in January 1955, to examine extending the representative principle further in the composition of both the Legislative Council and the Executive Council. In its majority report, the Sinanan Committee recommended the creation of a unicameral legislature in place of the bicameral one. It recommended the retention of the nominated element in the legislature but at the same time suggested an increase in the number of elected members. The Legislative Council was also to elect a Chief Minister, who was to be the leader of both the Executive Council and the legislative body. Nominated members of the Executive should be reduced to two: only the Colonial Secretary and the Attorney-General should be *ex officio* members. The Executive Council should consist of ten members, including the Chief Minister. The principle of ministerial responsibility was recognized and the Sinanan Committee recommended the creation of the British type of Cabinet government under the popularity elected Chief Minister. The Governor was to allocate the portfolios but only in consultation with the Chief Minister.[3]

The Minority Report was submitted by U. Butler, a Negro

---

[1] Craig, op. cit., p. 167.

[2] The *Observer* (October 1950), p. 2.

[3] *Trinidad Guardian* (12 February 1956).

labour leader. Butler opposed the retention of nominated members, and urged the removal of the Governor as chairman of the Executive Council.[1]

The recommendations made in the Majority Report, with some minor modifications, were implemented by the Trinidad and Tobago (Constitution) Order in Council of 1956. The final composition of the Legislative Council is given in Table 4-2.

Table 4-2 *Composition of the Legislative Council (Constitutional Set-up of 1956)*

Ex officio members	2
Nominated members	5
Elected members	24
Total	31

The Executive Council was to consist of eight elected members (including the Chief Minister), two *ex officio* members, and the Governor.

The introduction of these reforms was widely hailed in the island. L. F. Seukeran, an East Indian leader, said that the creation of the office of the Chief Minister was the greatest advance yet made. Mitra G. Sinanan, an East Indian Member of the Legislative Council, asserted that 'it was the biggest move which we can make at present' and expressed the hope that it would give Trinidad the highest degree of autonomy.[2] On the other hand, R. N. Donaldson, the Leader of the Caribbean People's Democratic Party, criticized the constitution as 'ultra modern'.[3] Gerald Montano, a local white, expressed the hope for the development of the party system as a result of the introduction of the Cabinet system of government.[4] It was realized that with the development of organized parties the new constitution could be turned into fully responsible government.[5]

The 1956 General Election and the Birth of Party Politics

The institutional framework provided by the Constitution of 1956 gave impetus to the rise of party politics in Trinidad, as the new

---

[1] Ibid.   [2] Ibid. (14 February 1956).   [3] Ibid.   [4] Ibid.
[5] Spackman, op. cit., p. 289.

constitutional structure promised full internal self-government. The competition for capturing power necessitated organization, constant campaigning, and shrewd electioneering. The election was to be held under the new constitution.

The parties and different political groups which existed until 1956 were organized around personalities, and they lacked nation-wide organization. As a large, well-established, and influential middle class did not exist, most of the political parties directed their appeals to lower income groups by identifying themselves with labour and by paying lip-service to its welfare.[1] An appeal to ethnicity, in order to win election, was not uncommon and one or two political groups were organized on ethnic basis, but ethnicity was not yet a dominant feature of the politics.

In the 1956 election there were as many as eight parties and political groups which put up 89 candidates for 24 seats.[2] Among these, the Trinidad Labour Party and T. U. Butler's Party were the two oldest parties of the country. The Trinidad Labour Party was founded by Captain A. A. Cipriani, one of the earliest local whites to lead the labour movement. He had earlier founded the Working Men's Association which in the opinion of F. W. Dally, should have been registered as a trade union under a 1933 ordinance.[3] Although the Trinidad Labour Party appealed to the imagination of the common man, still 'the new party was . . . largely a one-man affair, despite its island-wide character and its numerous branches, and although its founder and leader had great admiration for the British Labour Party, he seems to have lacked a political philosophy or even a considered programme adapted to the needs of the situation. Not unnaturally the Party advocated self-government, the adult franchise, and equal opportunities for natives also, interestingly enough, in view of the present day development of the Federation of the British West Indies.'[4] The East Indian leadership at this stage was divided into two groups. One consisted of East Indian leaders like Sarran

---

[1] Morley Ayearst, 'A Note on Some Characteristics of West Indian Political Parties', *Social and Economic Studies* (Vol. III, No. 3, September 1954), pp. 186–96.

[2] *Trinidad and Tobago Report on the Legislative Council General Elections 1956* (Port of Spain, Government Printing Office, 1958), p. 73.

[3] F. W. Dally, *Trade Union Organization and Industrial Relations in Trinidad* (London, H.M.S.O., 1949), p. 5.

[4] Ibid.

Teeluck Singh and T. Roodal, both rich cinema and land proprietors, and A. C. Rienzi, a barrister, all associated with Captain
Cipriani's Trinidad Labour Party. Timothy Roodal was the
second president general of the Trinidad Labour Party.[1] Teeluck
Singh and Roodal were also associated with Cipriani's Working
Men's Association. Rienzi helped Cipriani to organize the southern
branch of the Working Men's Association. But with the decline
of Cipriani's popularity among the working classes, Rienzi joined
hands with Butler, another labour leader.

Another section of East Indians was organized into the East
Indian National Congress and the East Indian National Association and on many issues followed independent lines. Neither
organization put up any candidates for election.

In subsequent years the Trinidad Labour Party came to be
dominated by well-to-do people, and it moved away from
Cipriani's pro-labour policies. In 1956, A. P. T. James was the
leader of the parliamentary wing of the Trinidad Labour Party.
James, a wealthy Negro from Tobago, was associated with a
number of different parties at various times in his political
career. He was the secretary of the Working Men's Association
and then one of its presidents, then joined Butler's Party, the
rival of Captain Cipriani's organization. Later on he left it,
and in 1946 joined Dr. P. V. Solomon's party, the Caribbean
Socialist Party. He advocated nationalization of oil and sugar
industries but said that the time was not yet ripe. In 1950 when
somebody called him 'middle class', he replied, 'I am a working
class, middle class and capitalist together.'[2] He called himself a
socialist, 'but the only thing clear about him is his Tobagoism'.[3]
He was always advocating increased government spending for
Tobago.

T. U. 'Buzz' Butler, the founder of the British Empire Workers
and Citizens' Home Rule Party—popularly known as Butler's
Party—called himself the 'Chief Servant'. And it is said, 'The
"Chief Servant" is a Revivalist gone wrong, a shouter who was
diverted from the lanes to the Legislature, a missionary, who missed
his way.'[4] In 1956, at the age of 59, Butler was termed as the
'oldest practicing demagogue in the island'.[5] The Bible was his

---

[1] Kirpalani, op. cit., p. 161.
[2] *Trinidad Guardian* (29 August 1956).
[3] Ibid.   [4] Ibid. (2 September 1956).   [5] Ibid.

handbook and the minor prophet was his model. Butler was born in Grenada, a small island in the Caribbean, and came over to Trinidad where he was employed in the oilfields. He soon became engaged in organizing oilfield workers. Butler, like most of the labour leaders of the West Indies in the early 1930s was considered to be a simple man, 'without a great deal of training, education or reading. The manner in which he expressed himself was . . . that of religion.'[1] He came into prominence in 1935 when he organized and led a hunger march to Port of Spain. In 1936, he was expelled from Cipriani's Trinidad Labour Party due to his extremist tendencies, and it was at this stage that he formed the British Empire Workers and Citizens' Home Rule Party. Butler, it was reported, 'flourished in and on a situation born of passionate emotional upheaval, strikes, riots, demonstrations and tableaux'.[2] In many ways he could be compared to Sir Alexander Bustamante, Leader of the Jamaican Labour Party, but unlike Bustamante, Butler failed to attract professionals. If some of them joined his camp, they left him as soon as they found him to be useless for their purposes. The Forster Report described him as 'a fanatical Negro'.[3] 'Women, as always, gave him full support, surrounding him with pure worship or mother love in their eyes.' It was observed that 'the most loyal Butlerites were women'.[4] Butler's management of the party and the union funds also came under fire. Charges of financial irregularities against him were carried in the *Trinidad Guardian*,[5] which seem to have been based upon rumours and hearsay rather than facts.

In 1950, an alliance was formed between Butler and East Indian leaders and Butler's Party succeeded in capturing the largest number of seats in the Legislative Council. It seems that East Indian leaders aligned with Butler only in order to attract extra Negro votes, because when Butler's Party was completely ignored by the Governor in the formation of the Executive Council, Mitra G. Sinanan and his brother, Ashford S. Sinanan, left Butler and became independent or joined other parties.

[1] 'Arthur Calder Marshal's Memorandum on Trinidad (1938) to the West Indian Royal Commission' (Trinidad Archives, 1938-9), p. 20.

[2] *Trinidad Guardian* (2 September 1956).

[3] Dally, op. cit., p. 14.

[4] *Trinidad Guardian* (2 September 1956).

[5] Ibid.

In 1956, at the time of the general election, Butler returned to Trinidad from England and told his audience, 'The Lord told him to go back to Trinidad, win elections with a large majority and then He would get him self-rule.'[1] He considered his party to be his personal affair. The nature of the relationship between Butler and his subordinates could be judged from the following incident between him and his deputy, S. C. Maharaj. The incident, as reported in the *Trinidad Guardian*, occurred in August 1956, when the general election was due in September of the same year. Stephen C. Maharaj nominated K. Dougdeen as a candidate for the Nariva-Mayaro constituency. The nomination was first approved by Butler but subsequently he cancelled it. Maharaj threatened to resign. Butler told him, 'I am the supreme commander of my party. I am the only person to decide on the candidates the party will put up. If you want to resign, you can do so, but I will not accept your resignation until after the elections have taken place.'[2] None the less, Butler's efforts have resulted in furthering constitutional and economic reforms in Trinidad. Although lacking in polish and sophistication, Butler is still respected as some sort of West Indian national hero.

Another party which was in the field for the 1956 election was the People's Democratic Party (P.D.P.). The founder of this party was Bhadase Sagan Maraj, one of the two top leaders mentioned by the East Indians in this survey. B. S. Maraj has become a legendary figure in Trinidad politics of the mid-fifties. He has been described as a tough and durable character by inheritance. At one stage he was an undisputed leader of thousands of his fellow East Indians. In 1956 it was said of him that 'he wields an influence in the business of government which, though probably overstated, is certainly more effective and far reaching than his modest political office should warrant, and he has at least one finger in every Trinidad pie of any importance'.[3] The methods which he uses for the exercise of his power include traditional Hindu ways of giving liberal donations for the poor and needy, spending huge funds on temple and school buildings, organizing big Hindu festivals and other celebrations, and on the receptions of Hindu holy men on visits to Trinidad from India. He also skilfully relates his business activities to the employment of his

[1] Ibid. (4 September 1956).   [2] Ibid. (28 August 1956).
[3] Ibid. (26 August 1956).

loyal supporters. It is in this way that Bhadase builds what Klass calls *praja* relationships. The *praja* relationship is born when a 'superior'—a 'big man'—obliges an 'inferior'. Bhadase with his wealth and wide influence has been able to oblige numerous persons of the community who feel duty-bound to follow him.[1]

Fairly tall and sturdy, Bhadase has been thought to carry a gun in his pocket and to be surrounded by two or three East Indian bodyguards. He is known for helping people in distress and granting them loans, but he is also known for using rough methods to keep his followers under his control and to silence his opponents. There is nothing idealistic about Bhadase; he is a tough and practical-minded individual. Many people, even though afraid of his methods, admire him, believing that he is the type of leader whom Hindus in Trinidad need most. Klass noted that in villages, 'He is admired for his wealth, respected as a Brahmin, and hailed as the East Indian "Chief" who has advanced the status of the entire ethnic group.'[2] Some, on the other hand, dislike his manners and turn their faces away on the mere mention of his name.

Bhadase Sagan Maraj was born in February 1919 in Caroni, an East Indian majority area where factions were organized on the basis of religion and where fights between Hindus and Muslims were a traditional way of life. His father, Mathew Sagan Maraj, was the leader of the Hindu faction for thirty years in the Charlie village area where his word was law. He was a self-appointed judge who settled all disputes, and approved major settlements. There was no appeal against his decisions. It was under the shadow of this Indian tradition of village headmanship (as embodied in his father's leadership) that Bhadase spent his childhood. When he was 13, his father was shot dead on the porch of his own house by a rival faction. After some time, his brother-in-law was strangled to death. Bhadase was next on the list and therefore he had to be constantly vigilant. Under the close protection of his mother— whom Bhadase still remembers with a great deal of gratitude—he started to work in the sugar-cane fields at the rate of four dollars (Trinidad dollars) per week. At the age of 19, Bhadase was able to purchase a boat with his savings, and set himself up as a small-scale contractor selling construction material to Americans, who were building military bases in Trinidad during the Second World

[1] Klass, *East Indians in Trinidad*, p. 199.
[2] Ibid., p. 223.

War. 'At the end of World War II hostilities, Bhadase was able to buy the United States Army installations at Docksite, lock, stock, and barrel, from the United States Government for a reported $182,000. . . . The profits were enormous but not more enormous than from his next deal—purchase of equipment from Walher Field—the biggest U.S. base in Trinidad and possibly in the West Indies.'[1] Since then his fortunes have risen steadily. It is said that Bhadase was a 'refugee at 13, a father at 20, independent at 25, a millionaire at 30, a grandfather at 35, and a fanatically energetic promoter of the Hindu, and his own, interest from birth. . . . His reputation is that he is a generous friend, an implacable enemy, a great lover and merciless payer of debts. His cause is Hinduism. His wide smile is the end product of his million dollars —which itself is the end product of the most fantastic story even in West Indian history.'[2]

He was first elected as an independent member of the Legislative Council in 1950 after defeating a candidate 'with a good social position' put up by the India Club.[3] Since then his influence in the politics of the island has increased steadily. The main bastion of his political strength became the *Sanatan Dharma Maha Sabha*, which was formed in 1952. From its very inception, Bhadase Maraj has been its president general. In 1953, Bhadase founded the People's Democratic Party and in the same year became president general of the Federation of the Union of Sugar Workers and Canefarmers—an overwhelming majority of whom are East Indians. Evidently Bhadase was now the most powerful and influential leader of the East Indian community because of his undisputed control of the East Indian religious and secular organizations.

Under his leadership the All-Trinidad Sugar Estates and Factories' Workers Trade Union went on a general strike in 1954 to get recognition. The strike lasted three weeks. Bhadase told us in an interview that the workers were ready to go back to work; they could not have held on without wages. They would have starved. In order to maintain their morale, he loaned money to the workers at the rate of three dollars per person per week. He said that he lost around 50,000 dollars during the strike. Ultimately, through his tactics, the union won its cause. In 1955, Bhadase resigned

[1] *Trinidad Guardian* (26 August 1956).   [2] Ibid.
[3] The *Observer* (Vol. 9, No. 10, October 1950), p. 10.

from the presidency of the union. In the following year, the union lost its identity when the sugar manufacturers withdrew their recognition and refused to bargain with it.[1] In 1957, Bhadase went back to the trade union and became its president general, a position which he still held in 1970. Whenever any opposition was organized against him among the East Indian sugar workers, he resorted to various tactics in order to maintain his position. Many of his opponents alleged that he had never been democratically elected to some of the offices which he has held. In the absence of a democratic process of election in many of these organizations, Bhadase's leadership in the *Maha Sabha* and others has come to be challenged in recent years. People generally agree that he has not entertained ministerial ambitions either in the Government of Trinidad or in the former Federation of the West Indies.

When Bhadase's political power and influence rose in the East Indian community, he was joined by the Sinanan brothers— Mitra G. and Ashford—the two ablest parliamentarians which the East Indians have so far produced. By 1956, both brothers had tasted power. First they were elected, one after another, as Deputy Speakers of the Legislative Council, and subsequently, they both held ministerial positions in the Governor's Executive Council. The Sinanan family has produced outstanding professionals and Mitra is recognized as one of the top lawyers of Trinidad. Their Brahmin father, A. R. Sinanan, was a highly successful businessman and was also interested in the politics of the East Indians of the island. Like most of the colonial *élite*, Mitra Sinanan received his university education in the United Kingdom and qualified as barrister-at-law from the Middle Temple. While in England, he was closely associated with the movement of Indian students and was elected vice-president of the Indian Students' Association after defeating V. K. Krishna Menon, a fellow law student. Like many Indian nationalists, Mitra Sinanan studied at the London School of Economics and Politics for some time.[2] When he returned from England, many East Indians looked to him for leadership with the hope that he might form a political party based upon secular principles.[3] However, he became busy in establishing his legal practice and only occasionally dabbled in politics.

---

[1] *Trinidad Guardian* (26 August 1956).   [2] Ibid. (15 August 1956).
[3] The *Observer* (Vol. 10, No. 6, June 1951), p. 3.

He made his name and earned island-wide popularity when, along with Sir Stafford Cripps, he defended Butler and obtained his freedom after the 1937 riots.[1] In the 1947–8 strike, he was the lawyer for the Butlerites and did not charge a fee. This won him Butler's esteem, and brought him and his brother Ashford, a solicitor, into Butler's Party. In the 1950 election, they were candidates of Butler's Party, Mitra Sinanan for the Caroni South and Ashford Sinanan for the Victoria South, both East Indian majority areas. They were elected but could not co-operate with Butler for long. Butler, having little formal education and being associated with the working class, lacked the sophistication of the Sinanan brothers, who came from a rich East Indian family. When the Butler bloc, even though constituting the largest single bloc of elected members in the legislature, was completely ignored by the Governor in the formation of the Executive Council, both brothers found the alliance with Butler to be fruitless. Mitra Sinanan left the party in April 1951,[2] and while Ashford Sinanan asserted that he never severed his relation with Butler's Party, he did walk out informally.

Like many of the Trinidad politicians, both brothers are looked upon as political opportunists. Sinanan is a name disliked by many politicians in Trinidad. After leaving Butler's Party, Mitra Sinanan joined the Trinidad Labour Party, but was subsequently expelled on account of his vote on the federation issue against the party directives. He afterwards became Bhadase's adviser and helped him to build the sugar workers and canefarmers organizations.

In 1956, both brothers rode on Bhadase's bandwagon and became members of Bhadase's People's Democratic Party. With the Hindu revival of the 1950s and the rise of the *Maha Sabha* as a powerful organization, the political leadership of East Indians in Trinidad passed into the hands of the Sanatanist Hindus. Since Hindus constitute 64 per cent of the East Indian population, it became difficult for non-Hindu East Indians to assume political leadership. Therefore, like the Sinanan brothers, both of whom are Presbyterians, other politically ambitious East Indians started rallying around Bhadase.

Another political group took part in the election in 1956. Albert Gomes, a Trinidadian of Portuguese descent and a

---

[1] Ibid.   [2] Ibid.

Minister of the Trinidad Government, was its head. This Party of Political Progress Group was organized in 1947 to protect the interests of a section of the well-to-do community of Trinidad. It was openly termed as a party of the Chamber of Commerce. Its main basis of support were in urban areas. It was also a stronghold of orthodox Roman Catholics—mostly local whites. It was not a party of national influence and did not put up candidates for all seats. The candidates did not have island-wide reputations, except Albert Gomes. There were rumours that the P.O.P.P.G. candidates were ordinary people of humble origin (such as teachers), who were given money by big business to fight in the election.[1] The party had too close an identification with the old colonial system, it failed to win over a significant number of supporters from lower income groups.

The local whites in Trinidad did not build a third party as Peter D'Aguiar built the United Force in British Guiana, which had a heterogeneous composition made up of Portuguese and Chinese businessmen, rich East Indians, and light-skinned Negro professionals. The Trinidad whites finally split their support and backed one of the two parties organized on an ethnic basis. Other minor political groups which made an effort to put up candidates were the Caribbean National Party, the West Indian Independence Party, and the Caribbean People's Democratic Party. The number of candidates put up by these groups was very small, and therefore they were insignificant in the election of 1956.

Until 1956, political parties in Trinidad were organized round personalities or they represented particular interests, rather than having a mass base. They lacked grass-root organization and were unable to conduct skilful and well-organized election campaigns. Most of these parties did not differ from each other in their programmes and policies. They did not have any ideological orientation.

The Founding of the People's National Movement and the Democratic Labour Party

The most important event in the development of party politics in Trinidad was the rise of the P.N.M. in 1956. The People's National Movement's inaugural conference was held on 1 January 1956, and the party was formally launched nine days later. The birth

[1] *Trinidad Guardian* (1 August 1956).

of the Democratic Labour Party is linked with the rise of the People's National Movement. 1956 was termed the year of the P.N.M. and the subsequent period in which the P.N.M. held power has been described as the P.N.M. decade. The P.N.M. has been in power in Trinidad since 1956.

Whereas the old-style electioneering was based upon rum and *roti* (East Indian bread),[1] the P.N.M. emphasized policy, programme, organization, and discipline. It was with the rise of the P.N.M. that the 'lone wolf' in politics disappeared and party politics became a reality. Until the rise of the P.N.M. a gap existed between the sophisticated western-oriented Negro middle class and the illiterate or semi-literate and poor Negro mass. The Negro middle class was, in the words of C. L. R. James, 'excluded from the centers of economic life, they have no active political experience, they have no political education'.[2] He further said, 'they as a class of people have no knowledge or experience of the productive forces of the country'.[3] They formed mainly the class of professionals and Civil Servants, and aimed at capturing the jobs and the opportunities which the colonial government offered them.

The Negro mass, on the other hand, was led by such demagogues as Butler, and a large majority of the Negro middle class avoided associating with a man like Butler. Until 1955, the Trinidad Negro middle class failed to produce a responsible, educated, and polished Negro leadership as Norman Manley and G. Adams could provide in Jamaica and Barbados. It was at this stage that Dr. Eric Williams, a brilliant intellectual, Trinidad scholarship-holder, and D. Phil. from Oxford, appeared on the political scene in Trinidad. He had a cause to serve. This cause was to rehabilitate the Negro's self-respect in the West Indies. Like many left-wing colonial intellectuals, Williams' writings were radical with an overtone of anti-colonialism and anti-imperialism.[4] In *The Negro in the Caribbean*, he 'praised the rise of working-class leaders in the West Indies and exorted the traditionally aloof coloured middle class to join the struggle'.[5] In his famous work *Capitalism*

---

[1] V. S. Naipaul, *The Suffrage of Elvira* (London, André Deutsch, 1958), gives a very good account of old-style electioneering.

[2] James, *Party Politics in the West Indies*, p. 133.

[3] Ibid., p. 132.

[4] Ivar Oxaal, *West Indian Intellectuals in Power* (Davis, Ph.D. dissertation submitted to the University of California, 1963), p. 137.   [5] Ibid.

and Slavery, Williams seemed to be guided by the Marxist interpretation of history, as he saw economic self-interest as the motive
for freeing the slaves in the West Indies rather than the humani-
tarianism of the English abolitionists.[1] Elsewhere he said, 'The
State existed in Caribbean society to maintain the property
relations. The state became the organ of the plutocracy and the
enemy of the people. . . .'[2] Thus, Williams, in the tradition of
colonial *élites*, gave a radical overtone to his expressions in order to
attract mass support.

After spending a couple of years as an associate professor at
Howard University, a Negro university in Washington, D.C., he
became associated in 1948 with the Anglo-American Caribbean
Commission. It was while working with the Commission that
Williams developed a greater interest in the area of his origin.
After his departure from the Commission in 1953, he began to
take an active interest in Trinidad–Tobago politics. He toured
the island, addressed meetings in Woodford Square—which
he called 'the university'—and educated the people in politics,
sometimes appealing to their emotions and sometimes to their
reason. He bridged the gap between an educated, westernized,
and polished Negro middle class and the disinherited Negro mass.
In Williams the Negroes found the 'hero' element which was
missing until this time. Soon he came to dominate the life of the
Trinidad Negro as a charismatic leader. Oxaal notes that, 'For
many lower class Negroes, particularly Creole women, Williams
was nothing less than a messiah who came to lead the black children into the Promised Land.'[3] He further points out that 'the
image of Williams as a racial messiah was not limited to the black
lower class, although it was strongest there, but could be found in
the Creole middle class as well. Among members of the latter,
however, the belief in personal and collective salvation through
Dr. Williams often shaded over into a more secular varient of the
True Believer in which the *rationality* and *honesty* of the Doctor
were so fervently espoused as to occasion the willing surrender of

[1] Ivar Oxaal, 'C. L. R. James and Eric Williams: The Formative Years',
Trinidad and Tobago Index (Vol. I, No. 2, Fall 1965), p. 21.

[2] Eric Williams, 'Race Relations in the Caribbean Society', in Vera Rubin
(ed.), *Caribbean Studies: A Symposium* (Seattle, University of Washington Press,
1960), p. 55.

[3] Ivar Oxaal, *Black Intellectuals Come to Power* (Cambridge, Schenkman
Publishing Co., 1968), p. 100.

independent judgement and will, associated with an intense hostility to any form of criticism, direct or implied, of the political leader.'[1] According to Oxaal, Williams alone became the central point of the aspirations and ambitions of the Negro masses. It was Williams, again, who, in the eyes of the people, provided the essential bond without whom the P.N.M. would split into rival factions.[2] Even though a middle-class intellectual, his approach was that of direct communication with the masses—especially with the people of the lower stratum. He denounced political expediency and advocated honesty and integrity in politics. However, it was pointed out that Williams, like Butler, was most often surrounded by singing, chanting, and shouting Negro masses.[3] But, unlike Butler, Williams was successful in attracting a number of brilliant Negroes to his camp.

With his excellent background in Caribbean history and his strong feelings about the servitude of Negroes in the western hemisphere, time and again Williams impressed upon his followers the greatness of the African heritage[4] and successfully created a sense of racial dignity among his own people. With his interpretation of slavery and the slave economy, with his onslaught on colonialism and the 'Massa'—by which he meant 'absentee European planters exploiting West Indian resources, both human and economic',[5] but a term which in the popular mind is associated with the local white—Dr. Williams could capture the imagination of the people. In his writings and speeches the racial element was not entirely absent. Even Oxaal concedes, 'On the one hand,' Williams 'would always denounce racial prejudices and affirm the multi-racial convictions of the P.N.M. but on at least a few occasions at the University he insinuated a racial undertone into his oratory.'[6]

Williams, with his charismatic hold on the Negro masses, his organizational abilities, and his dedication to the restoration of Negro self-respect, became a serious challenge to those who, until then, held positions of power. With the organization of the P.N.M.

[1] Oxaal, op. cit., p. 101.
[2] Ibid., p. 96.
[3] *Trinidad Guardian* (5 August 1956).
[4] Williams, *History of the People of Trinidad and Tobago*, p. 31.
[5] Williams, *Massa Day Done* (Port of Spain, P.N.M. Publishing Co., 1961), p. 2.
[6] Oxaal, *West Indian Intellectuals in Power*, p. 184.

in 1956 under his leadership, a new and highly significant element was introduced in the politics of the island. At the beginning of the election campaign of 1956, Dr. Williams declared:

Our policy in this matter has been simple, straight forward and honest. We cannot agree to inheriting the prejudices and antagonism of others, we will not be compromised by them, we decline, for the sake of winning an election, to participate in deals, arrangements or alliances with parties or individuals which we have every reason to believe, from the past history of Trinidad and Tobago, are as dangerous as shifting sands.[1]

The P.N.M. entered the election campaign with a clear-cut programme. It declared that the people of Trinidad and Tobago had had 'six years of corruption, mismanagement, maladministration and party acrobatics, in public affairs',[2] and it called for ending all this by voting the P.N.M. to power. The P.N.M. promised to promote the general welfare, to achieve constitutional, economic, and political reforms, and to reduce the costs of administration.[3] The P.N.M. tried to present a multiracial slate of candidates and based its appeal on West Indian nationalism—which to many East Indians was another name for Negro nationalism.

As a result of the P.N.M. declaration of policy and programme, the number of independent candidates declined and dependence on political parties increased. Among the other political parties and groups opposed to the P.N.M., the People's Democratic Party, with its stronghold in the East Indian majority areas, emerged as the second strongest party in the island. Under pressure from the P.N.M., the leadership of the P.D.P. tried to modify its purely East Indian character and started speaking in terms of multi-racialism and secularism from its platforms. It also sponsored some non-East Indian candidates.[4] The P.D.P. brought a Baptist minister and two Catholic nuns to speak in its favour and to testify to its secular and multiracial character.

In contrast to the P.N.M.'s declared policy of making no elec-

---

[1] *Trinidad Guardian* (2 January 1966), p. 3.

[2] *People's National Movement Election Manifesto 1956* (Port of Spain, printed for the P.N.M. by the College Press, 1956), p. 1.

[3] Ibid., pp. 2–3.

[4] *Trinidad and Tobago Report on the Legislative Council General Elections 1956*, Appendix No. 1.

tion alliances, the P.D.P. lent its support to Albert Gomes, the then Minister of Labour, Industry, and Commerce and head of the Party of Political Progress Group; Roy Joseph, Minister of Education and Social Services, and a close friend of Bhadase Maraj; T. U. 'Buzz' Butler; and A. P. T. James, leader of the parliamentary wing of the Trinidad Labour Party.[1] The P.D.P. was even supporting some of the independent candidates. The P.N.M. became the target of attacks—both from the opposition parties and the independents. Butler called the P.N.M. 'a Godless group'.[2] Ashford Sinanan, a P.D.P. candidate, expressed great admiration for Butler, and denounced Williams 'for preaching racialism'.[3] Mr. Seukeran, an independent candidate seeking election to the Legislative Council, described Williams as public enemy number one, expressed admiration for Butler and Bhadase, and promised to support them in the Legislative Council, if elected.[4] Albert Gomes accused Williams of creating an immoral rift in the community by spreading racialism in order to satisfy his personal political ambitions.[5]

Recognizing the P.D.P. as his main opponent, Williams attacked its Hindu leadership by delving into his favourite arsenal, history. He equated the *Sanathan Dharma Maha Sabha* of Trinidad with the Hindu *Maha Sabha* of India and quoted Nehru against the *Maha Sabha*.[6] The P.D.P. leaders stormed back by calling Williams a West Indian Malan[7] and the arch reactionary of the country.[8] S. N. Capildeo, a P.D.P. leader and secretary general of the S.D.M.S., wrote, 'Let Dr. Williams know, although the public is not highly educated as he is, they understood his anti-White lectures in the Public Library, they understood his anti-Indian speeches today; for whatever racial disturbance comes in the colony, which is inevitable if Dr. Williams continues his evil work, he must bear full responsibility.'[9] Evidently the contest between the P.N.M. and the P.D.P. engendered bitterness among the two ethnic groups. However, because of the close identification of Bhadase with the *Sanathan Dharma Maha Sabha*, his efforts in the cause of Hinduism, and the close association of the Sinanan brothers with the old régime, the P.D.P. alienated some sections of

---

[1] *Trinidad Guardian* (9 August 1956).   [2] Ibid.   [3] Ibid.
[4] Ibid. (16 August 1956).   [5] Ibid.
[6] Ibid. (12 August 1956).   [7] Ibid.
[8] Ibid. (5 August 1956).   [9] Ibid.

the East Indian population—especially East Indian Christians and Muslims. But the associations of Dr. Winston Mahabir or Dr. Ibbit Mosahib could not prevent the P.N.M. hecklers from making it impossible for the P.D.P. leaders to address public meetings. Both Bhadase and Gomes accused the predominantly Negro police of being pro-P.N.M. and of failing to provide protection for those opposed to the P.N.M.[1]

Eight parties or political groups put up candidates for the election. Six parties put up more than eight candidates each, two political groups presented one candidate each. There were forty independent candidates. The election was held by secret balloting on 24 September. Only four parties could return their candidates. The P.N.M. won the largest number of seats (13) with 39 per cent of the votes (see Table 4-3). The P.D.P. was the second largest party with five seats and 20 per cent of the votes polled in its favour. P.O.P.P.G. with its nine candidates was unable to capture a single seat. Albert Gomes and Roy Joseph, both former Ministers, were beaten by the P.N.M. candidates.

The P.N.M. won mainly in the urban areas where the Negro population formed the majority. In the East Indian majority areas, especially in the sugar belts, the P.D.P. swept the polls. In areas where the racial population was evenly divided, the P.N.M. won by a narrow margin.

Table 4-3   *Election Results of 1956*[2]

Political Party	Seats contested	Won	Total votes polled
P.N.M.	24	13	105,153
P.D.P.	14	5	55,148
Butler's Party	18	2	31,071
Trinidad Labour Party	11	3	13,692
P.O.P.P.G.	9	—	14,019
Independents	40	1	40,523

In Tunapuna constituency, where Learie Constantine, chairman of the P.N.M. fought against Surajpat Mathura, a P.D.P. candidate, the former won by only a narrow margin.[3]

[1] *Trinidad Guardian* (21, 22 September 1956).
[2] *Trinidad and Tobago Report on the Legislative Council General Elections 1956*, p. 72.
[3] Ibid., p. 45.

The P.N.M. put up candidates for the twenty-four seats; the P.D.P. put up only fourteen candidates. It did not fight the election in any of the Negro majority areas like San Fernando, Port of Spain, and Laventille; the P.N.M. set up East Indian candidates from East Indian majority areas—none of whom were returned.

Butler's Party, which returned the largest number of legislators in 1950, now could capture only two seats, one of which went to Butler and the other to Stephen Maharaj, an East Indian, who was returned from an East Indian majority area.

Unmistakably the trend was towards the division of votes on racial lines. It became clear that there was no future for independent candidates. It also became obvious that unless all those who were opposed to the P.N.M. united, they would not survive. The P.N.M. victory was the result of better organization and superior electoral technique. It was also the result of the assertion of Negro self-respect and self-confidence through its nationalism, led by the Negro middle class.

Although the P.N.M. had secured thirteen out of twenty-four elected seats and formed the largest party in a House of thirty-one members, it could still be outvoted and be excluded from office, just as Butler's bloc was in 1950. The P.N.M. could form the Government either by forming a coalition with elected members or by requesting the Governor to nominate its supporters as members of the Council, thus providing a comfortable majority. The P.N.M. adopted the second course.

On the suggestion of the Secretary of State for Colonies, the Governor allowed the P.N.M. to nominate two of its supporters to the Legislative Council, so that with the support of the *ex officio* members, the P.N.M. could have a comfortable majority to run the Government. Thus with the help of the Governor and with the blessings of the Secretary of State, the P.N.M. was able to form the Government.[1] Party government came to be introduced under the Constitution of 1956, and the rise of an Opposition Party now became inevitable.

The P.N.M.'s rise to power with the support of the Governor and its unwillingness to share power with the minority group, led to further division and consolidation of forces on racial lines. Formation of the Government by the P.N.M. raised the morale

[1] Spackman, op. cit., p. 290.

of ordinary Negroes sky high. As a result, racial tension rose. Recalling the days after the 1956 election, Stephen Maharaj, still a member of Butler's Party, wrote:

After the elections I think that Trinidad witnessed its worst period of racial tension. If I can recall those days, it was never safe for any member to come to the Legislative Council; when you alighted from your car you virtually met what I may call a cordon of supporters of the PNM all along the path you walked. And I can recall in those days the seating accommodation for the public was usually crowded, even one hour before the session started. The crowd stood on every little spot they could find and when Williams would alight from his car there was always a crowd to greet him and clap him. When he delivered a speech and left, the crowd was there to clap him. We were always the pack of victims. We had to face these angry crowds. And if you dared criticize the Government in those days you were always in danger of being mobbed and even beaten by that angry crowd. There was hardly any protection from the police for the members of Parliament. To my mind it appeared that if at any time an M.P. were stabbed on his way to the House, it did not matter to anyone whether he was alive or dead.[1]

Members of the Legislative Council belonging to the Opposition were insulted even inside the House by persons sitting in the public gallery. The *Trinidad Guardian* said, 'We cannot conceive of any enlightened West Indian Government in the mid-twentieth century deliberately encouraging such behaviour, far less bringing into the public gallery of the Legislative Council a group of rowdies schooled in insulting tactics intended to embarrass the opposition.'[2]

Under these conditions, the need for the formation of unified opposition consisting of all political groups was widely felt. However, the initiative did not come from the politicians of Trinidad but from outside. When in 1958 the Federation of the British West Indies was formed, and Trinidad and Tobago joined it, election for the Federal Parliament was announced for April of the same year. Norman Manley, Leader of the People's National Party of Jamaica, started negotiations with the leaders of the political parties of the different islands for the formation of a

[1] Stephen C. Maharaj, 'Politics in Trinidad and Tobago 1950-1965', *We The People* (Vol. I, No. 15, October 1965), p. 7.
[2] *Trinidad Guardian* (1 March 1958).

federal party. He successfully persuaded the P.N.M. to join his federal party.

In order to counteract the efforts of Manley, Sir Alexander Bustamante, a cousin of Manley and his political rival, began trying to form another federal party, named the Democratic Labour Party. He came to Trinidad on 17 May 1957, and had talks with members and executives of the P.D.P., headed by Bhadase Maraj, Victor Bryan of the Trinidad Labour Party, Albert Gomes and Carlton Achong of the Party of Political Progress Group, and Stephen C. Maharaj of Butler's Party, to found the Trinidad unit of the federal Democratic Labour Party. During his private and public appearances Bustamante made it clear that his party, though pro-labour, would be opposed to socialism. He declared that it was only in the absence of any kind of socialism that the West Indies could get outside capital.[1]

The Trinidad unit of the Democratic Labour Party was launched on 23 May 1957. The political parties which declared their affiliation were the People's Democratic Party, the Trinidad Labour Party, and the Party of Political Progress Group. The office holders also came from three different groups; its provisional chairman, Ashford Sinanan, came from the P.D.P., its first vice-president, A. P. T. James, came from the T.L.P., and its provisional treasurer, Carlton Achong, came from the P.O.P.P.G.[2]

Williams denounced the new party in very strong terms. He declared that, 'The D.L.P. denounces socialism and advocates free enterprise all the more vehemently because it understands neither.'[3] He also expressed the fear that it would be the P.D.P. which would dominate the newly-formed party.[4]

The rise of the Trinidad unit of the federal D.L.P. proved to be the first step towards the formation of a united opposition at the local level. The East Indian political *élite*, as represented in the P.D.P., was simply ignored by the P.N.M. in the formation of the Government. At some stage it was reported in certain circles that there was a possibility of the formation of a coalition between the P.N.M. and the P.D.P. but the P.N.M. ruled out this possibility. By excluding the P.D.P. from any share of power, the rift between East Indians and Negroes was bound to increase. All those who were toppled by the P.N.M. from positions of power naturally

---

[1] Ibid. (22 May 1957).   [2] Ibid. (24 May 1957).
[3] Ibid. (28 May 1957).   [4] Ibid.

H

rallied round the P.D.P. which, with East Indian mass support, could provide the basis for the formation of an effective opposition. Soon after the departure of Bustamante from Trinidad, therefore, efforts increased for the formation of a united front, at the local level, of all the parties affiliated with the D.L.P. at the federal level. The initiative in this direction was taken by W. W. Sutton, a trade union leader and secretary of the Trinidad Labour Party, and its president, Victor Bryan (both non-East Indians).[1] There was the realization in other groups, too, that it would be a waste of time and energy if they continued to oppose each other in local politics and unite in federal politics.[2]

On 18 July 1957, a meeting of the special committee of the representatives of the three parties—the P.D.P., the T.L.P., and the P.O.P.P.G.—was held, and the decision made to dissolve their parties and form the Democratic Labour Party of Trinidad and Tobago.[3] A six-man special committee, with Ashford Sinanan of the P.D.P. as its chairman, was formed to draw up the rules and regulations of the D.L.P. of Trinidad and Tobago. Its inaugural conference was opened by Sinanan on 1 September 1957. Victor Bryan, the former president of the Trinidad Labour Party and a non-East Indian, was elected provisional chairman of the party. Louis Rostant (another non-East Indian) and Surajpat Mathura (an East Indian of the P.D.P. group) were elected vice-chairmen.

No special policy pronouncements were made at the party conference. In his inaugural address, Ashford Sinanan simply asserted that 'the D.L.P. was going to play a much more constructive role and its sole purpose was not just to oppose'.[4] In one of his subsequent speeches, Sinanan spelled out a little more clearly the differences in the approaches of the D.L.P. and the P.N.M. when he said, 'The P.N.M. stood for the dictatorship of one man and the tyranny of a clique while the Democrats stood for democratic government by the people's elected representatives.' He further said, 'The P.N.M. stood for state socialism or the regimentation of the life activities of the citizens while the Democrats stood for freedom of enterprise and respect for the right of individual.'[5] He opposed any control of denominational education institutions and told his audience, 'We should first seek the

---

[1] *Trinidad Guardian* (9 June 1957).   [2] Ibid. (16 July 1957).
[3] Ibid. (19 July 1957).   [4] Ibid. (2 September 1957).
[5] Ibid. (10 April 1958).

Kingdom of God and all peace, prosperity and happiness will be added upon us.'[1]

A clearer pronouncement of the party's policies came in an article which appeared in the *Guardian* on behalf of the D.L.P. The D.L.P. was determined to

> stand for the democratic rights of the people and it has with equal determination stated its rigid and inflexible stand against any type of socialism. The DLP is not fighting a party or a personality, it is fighting the disrupting evils which socialism brings into the lives of people everywhere. . . . Within the framework of democracy national welfare is promoted, agriculture and natural resources of the country, under the private enterprise system, are encouraged and developed.[2]

Anti-socialistic pronouncements of the D.L.P. were quite natural in view of the fact that an overwhelming majority of its leaders—especially the East Indians—belonged to the business community or came from well-to-do middle-class families. They hoped to get the support of the local white, Chinese, Arab, and other miscellaneous groups, who were afraid of the P.N.M.'s socialism. These pronouncements also appealed to the East Indian masses, who are known for their passion for land ownership.

By the beginning of 1958, the P.D.P. faction of the D.L.P.—the East Indian leadership—established itself in full command of the D.L.P. On 8 January 1958, B. S. Maraj, the former head of the P.D.P. and president general of the *Maha Sabha*, was unanimously elected leader of the parliamentary wing of the D.L.P.—which by this time had come to be recognized as the official Opposition in the Legislative Council of Trinidad and Tobago.[3] Subsequently Sir Alexander Bustamante announced that Sinanan would become the Prime Minister of the Federation of the British West Indies should the D.L.P. win the election at the federal level.[4] Evidently, the non-Indian element in the D.L.P. had to take a subordinate position and accept the dominance of the East Indian leadership if it wanted to get East Indian mass support.

The two-party system seemed to have arrived on the political scene. The P.N.M. with its Negro support and the D.L.P. with its

[1] Ibid.
[2] Pearl Cameron, 'New Democratic Party Upholds People's Rights', *Trinidad Guardian* (5 June 1957), p. 8.
[3] Ibid. (9 January 1958).
[4] Ibid. (16 January 1958).

East Indian base became the main contestants in the political struggles of the island. Polarization was taking place on racial lines. Stephen C. Maharaj, an East Indian and deputy leader of Butler's Party, had joined hands with the D.L.P., but Butler, a Negro, though still not a member of the P.N.M., became its outspoken supporter and a critic of the D.L.P.[1]

The 1958 Federal Election

Under the leadership of Bhadase Sagan Maraj, the D.L.P. became a much more effective organization. This became apparent in the electoral mobilization and organization of its followers in the federal election of 1958. The election was fought on local, not federal, issues. The P.N.M. and the D.L.P. were the major contestants in the fight for ten seats in the Federal Parliament. The issue was not merely the federal election. The P.N.M. was determined to vindicate its victory of 1956.[2] The D.L.P. put up a racially-mixed slate of East Indians and non-Indians. Many of the old guard, such as Albert Gomes and Roy Joseph, the former Ministers badly beaten by the P.N.M. in 1956 and both prominent non-East Indians of the island, were launched as candidates by the D.L.P.

The campaign was rough. In the Negro majority areas it was difficult for the D.L.P. to get public hearing, and in the East Indian majority areas the P.N.M. leaders were shouted down. When Denis Mahabir and his brother Winston, along with Mathew Ramcharan—all East Indian supporters of the P.N.M.—went to address a public gathering in the sugar belts, the East Indian masses refused to listen, shouting that they were the stooges of the P.N.M.[3] In Tobago, where Negroes constituted 95 per cent of the population, the D.L.P. leaders were greeted with bottles and rotten eggs.[4]

The D.L.P. fought the election on a mediocre platform in which it reasserted its faith in free enterprise, opposed socialism, denounced heavy taxation, welcomed foreign capital with open arms, and asserted a square deal for labour. In its election manifesto, it declared, 'The general approach to economic development must be through private capital and private enterprise. It would be a tragedy if the Government of this Federation should fall in the

---

[1] *Trinidad Guardian* (14 December 1957).   [2] Ibid. (5 March 1958).
[3] Ibid. (12, 13 March 1958).   [4] Ibid. (19 March 1958).

hands of socialists whose fundamental policy is government ownership, unnecessary and frustrating controls and bureaucracy.'[1] At the same time it declared that, 'The economic and social welfare of all is best achieved under a government which never forgets that the State is the servant and proctor of the people.'[2] It further said, 'We believe in promoting cooperation and unity among all sections of the people regardless of colour, race, or creed, and in the upliftment of the working people of all categories.'[3]

The D.L.P. convincingly defeated the P.N.M. winning six out of ten seats; the rest went to the P.N.M. Men like Albert Gomes and Roy Joseph, beaten by the P.N.M. in 1956, now defeated the P.N.M.'s candidate on the D.L.P. ticket. Mohamed Shah, an East Indian Muslim candidate of the D.L.P., defeated Butler in his home constituency of St. Patrick. The P.N.M. defeated A. P. T. James, a D.L.P. candidate from Tobago, a heavily Negro-populated area. The P.N.M.'s victories were confined to Port of Spain and suburban areas. The P.N.M.'s defeat in the San Fernando–Naparima constituency was a particularly bitter pill for the ruling party because, since the general election of 1956, the P.N.M. had always swept the polls in San Fernando. The election returns examined on the basis of census statistics supplied by the Central Statistical Office, Port of Spain, explain the victories of the D.L.P. East Indians were in an absolute majority (above 60 per cent) in the electoral districts of Caroni and Victoria, and the D.L.P. candidates polled above 60 per cent of the votes in these constituencies. In St. Patrick, the East Indian population was 42 per cent, but the Negro vote was divided between Butler, 34 per cent of the votes, and the P.N.M. candidate, 23 per cent of the votes. Mohamed Shah (D.L.P.), won with 43 per cent of the votes. The P.N.M. Government combined the city of San Fernando (26 per cent of East Indians) with the thickly-populated Naparima, where the East Indian population was 63 per cent. There was a higher turn-out of East Indian voters in all constituencies.[4] The D.L.P. made inroads into Negro majority areas only in two

---

[1] *Federal Election Manifesto of the Democratic Labour Party* (of the West Indies) (Tunapuna, Trinidad, Gem Printery, 1958), p. 4.

[2] Ibid.

[3] Ibid.

[4] *Trinidad Guardian* (28 March 1958).

electoral districts. In the Eastern counties, Victor Bryan (D.L.P.), a non-East Indian, defeated the P.N.M. candidate and got 41 per cent of the votes. Among the four eastern counties, only two are heavily populated; St. Andrews and Nariva which have 39 per cent and 58 per cent respectively, of East Indian population. The counties of St. David and Mayaro have a combined population of only 12,000 and the percentage of East Indian population is 5 per cent and 17 per cent respectively. Thus Bryan got appreciable support from non-East Indian elements, though East Indians formed the main basis of his support.

In St. George East, where Albert Gomes defeated the P.N.M. candidate with 53 per cent of the votes against P.N.M.'s 47 per cent, the East Indian population percentage for the whole county is 24 per cent. However, the electoral district of St. George East contained some wards where East Indian population was above 40 per cent. Evidently Albert Gomes also got support from the non-East Indian element.

The demarcation of electoral boundaries, the higher turn-out of East Indian voters,[1] the division of Negro votes, and the defection of some non-East Indian elements to the D.L.P. led to its victory.

Albert Gomes attributed it to the able leadership of Bhadase Maraj.[2] M. E. Farquhar, the *Trinidad Guardian* columnist, termed the election result as a censure of the P.N.M.'s demeaning tactics. 'The P.N.M. literally overreached themselves in their frenzied campaign and fanatical vendetta of personal abuse and political smearing.'[3] The P.N.M. after its victory in 1956 and after securing a dominant position in subsequent municipal election, came to be considered impregnable.[4] The results of the federal election made it clear that the P.N.M. was not invincible and that during the two years it had lost considerable mass support.[5]

After remaining silent for a number of days, Williams came out

[1] Morton Klass, who witnessed the 1958 election, refers to a rumour current in the top stratum of the non-East Indian society of Port of Spain. According to it, before the start of elections, 'agents of the Maha Sabha go from house to house in the rural districts with a *lota* (ceremonial brass vase) fitted with Ganges water, ordering the illiterates—and presumably the otherwise politically unconcerned East Indians—to swear on the *lota* that they will turn out to vote and will vote for the East Indian candidate'. *East Indians in Trinidad*, p. 222.

[2] *Trinidad Guardian* (26 March 1958).

[3] Ibid. (30 March 1958).   [4] Ibid. (27 March 1958).   [5] Ibid.

with a strong denunciation of the D.L.P. and the East Indians. Speaking before an overwhelmingly Negro audience, he accused the D.L.P. of using race for getting votes. He said that the election was fought on one issue, 'Our Indian nation'. He asserted that the campaign conducted by the D.L.P. was an appeal for Indian votes for the D.L.P. to insure an Indian Governor and an Indian Prime Minister.[1] He further revealed that, 'Religion figured prominantly in the D.L.P. campaign. By hook or crook they brought out the Indian vote, the young and the old, the literate and illiterate, and lame, the halt and blind.'[2] He called them a 'recalcitrant and hostile minority', who were 'prostituting the name of India for their own selfish and reactionary political ends'.[3] Dr. Williams' speech gave only an indication of the working of the mind of the Negro middle class which was always plagued with the nightmare of the rise of the East Indian middle class to a position of political power. They feared that the D.L.P., back by an East Indian bloc vote and with its successful manipulation of other disgruntled elements—including disgruntled Negroes —would gain control of the colony. The election results made it evident that had even a small percentage of the Negro vote gone over to the D.L.P., it could have toppled the P.N.M. from its position of power. Williams' accusations of the use of race by the D.L.P. for getting votes did not make any sense, as both parties were fundamentally based upon the support of one or the other of the ethnic groups. The D.L.P. got a majority of votes in the East Indian majority areas; in the Negro majority areas, Negroes overwhelmingly voted for the P.N.M. The P.N.M. was disappointed this time, because some of the Negro voters switched their votes to the D.L.P. and thus enabled the D.L.P. to win. Williams actually sought an escape route for his party by shifting the blame of the P.N.M.'s defeat on to the shoulders of East Indians. Commenting on Dr. Williams' speech, the *Trinidad Guardian* pointed out:

The PNM came into power in 1956 on a manifesto which started out by maligning the party's predecessors . . . it went on to claim that the PNM was the only party that was national in scope and dedicated to the promotion of the general welfare. Yet if the Chief Minister's Woodford Square address on Tuesday conveyed anything, it showed that this 'national' party had failed to gain the confidence

[1] Ibid. (2 April 1958).   [2] Ibid.
[3] Ibid.

and win the respect of a very important minority group which forms a third or more of Trinidad's population.[1]

Moreover, if East Indians were capable of defeating Williams' party, why did they not defeat it in 1956? And if they supported him and his party in 1956, Williams should have asked himself why he lost their confidence in 1958. It was openly asserted that no Indian voted for the P.N.M. And Indians who said 'they voted for the P.N.M. were often abused, maligned and discredited'.[2] Some persons of non-East Indian origin charged that Williams' accusations helped to cultivate the myth of 'Indian domination' prevailing in a section of the community.[3] Another non-East Indian pointed out that after the victory of the P.N.M., Negroes started thinking in terms of their right to dominate the country 'even to the extent of subscribing to the belief that other elements were mere trespassers. It was during this phase that the so-called racialism, for which Dr. Williams sought to blame the D.L.P., was born.'[4] Albert Gomes wrote that 'decent citizens were the victims of the most vulgar abuse on the streets for no other reason than that they did not look like the sort of people who would be P.N.M. supporters'.[5] He predicted that henceforth racialism would be the main weapon of the P.N.M.[6]

It was charged by the P.N.M. that the D.L.P. mainly put up rejected candidates—like Albert Gomes and Roy Joseph—previously defeated by the P.N.M. But this had no meaning in the context of Trinidad politics, as the P.N.M. itself put up Dr. Patrick V. Solomon and Chunilal Saith as candidates, though they had previously suffered defeats at the polls.

Thus the 1958 federal election further accentuated the feelings of racialism and the polarization of the parties on racial lines. It also put the Negro middle class on guard. They realized that East Indian leadership could topple them from their position of power, if they were not vigilant, and if they let the East Indian leadership exploit the discontented Negro elements. With this realization, the appeal to racism became the main strategy of party politics.

[1] *Trinidad Guardian* (3 April 1958).   [2] Ibid.   [3] Ibid. (13 April 1958).
[4] Ibid. (13 April 1958).   [5] Ibid.   [6] Ibid.

V

The Democratic Labour Party: Its Development and the Changes in its Leadership

THE birth of the D.L.P. took place with the coming together of the leaders of the various political groups in their common opposition to the P.N.M. No common programme or ideology bound the D.L.P. together. It lacked a grass-roots organization, and it depended heavily on Bhadase Maraj for getting the support of the East Indian masses.

After 1958, according to Stephen C. Maharaj, the D.L.P. was actually being run by F. E. Brassington, Albert Gomes, and Romal Gomes, all non-East Indians who represented the local whites and opposed the P.N.M. They hardly had any party branches, except a few men and they met only off and on. The rank and file were willing to keep the branches going but there was no cohesive force at the party headquarters.[1] The D.L.P. victories in the 1958 election were not the result of organized and concerted efforts. They were mainly the result of the efforts of one man, Bhadase Sagan Maraj, who was successful in maintaining the solidarity of East Indians and at the same time was shrewd enough to manipulate the non-East Indian discontented elements of Trinidad and Tobago.

Bhadase might have been popular among the East Indian masses, but the younger generation of East Indian professionals, Civil Servants, and other educated and enlightened groups found him embarrassing as their leader. Bhadase lacked education. In their eyes he had no polish, his manners were crude, and they were suspicious of his methods. He could not match Dr. Williams who not only had the education, but a charismatic hold on the Negro masses. To match the intellectual glamour of Williams, a section of the D.L.P. looked for leadership elsewhere.

In 1959, Bhadase Sagan Maraj became sick and bedridden and gradually started losing his central position in the party machinery of the D.L.P. He was no longer very active in politics. Due to his prolonged absence from the sessions of the Legislative Council, the

[1] Stephen C. Maharaj, 'Trinidad and Tobago Politics 1950–1965' (II) *We The People* (Vol. I, No. 19, 29 October 1965), p. 6.

D.L.P. as an Opposition Party, became ineffective. It had some able individual parliamentarians, but none of them were capable of leading the party and maintaining the discipline within its ranks. Under these conditions, the D.L.P. became a travesty or a mockery of genuine parliamentary opposition. Williams either ignored it or denied its existence. In the absence of B. S. Maraj, A. P. T. James, former Leader of the Trinidad Labour Party and a wealthy Negro from Tobago, acted as the Leader of the Opposition in the Legislature. He was a nominee of B. S. Maraj and seemingly was never actually elected as the acting Leader of the Opposition by the D.L.P. Members in the House.

In the absence of a democratic process for the election of the party leader, the D.L.P. leadership became an object of internal party intrigues and backdoor manipulation. It could be transferred from one person to another without being referred to the party for election. This was how Mr. S. N. Capildeo, a staunch Sanatanist Hindu, became the acting leader of the D.L.P. in place of James. Both the rank and file and the East Indian professionals were extremely frustrated over the squabbles and manœuvring. Furthermore, Bhadase and Capildeo were so much identified with the *Maha Sabha* and with the Hindu cause that many East Indian Christian and Muslim intellectuals, in their disappointment with the East Indian leadership, joined the P.N.M. in 1956. (We have seen that Dr. Winston Mahabir, an East Indian Christian, and Dr. I. Mosaheb, an East Indian Muslim, and their factions were actively associated with the P.N.M. in 1956.) In the late 1950s many of these East Indians had become disenchanted with the P.N.M. and its policies, but at the same time the D.L.P., in their eyes, lacked intellectual respectability and secular orientation. It was in order to win over this group of people and to match the intellectual glamour of the P.N.M. that the name of Dr. R. N. Capildeo was mentioned for the leadership of the D.L.P.

Dr. Capildeo[1] was the younger brother of S. N. Capildeo. Like Dr. Williams, he was an island scholarship-holder of 1938, and he earned his Ph.D. from London University in physics, where he read physics and mathematics. In 1958–9, he was Principal of Trinidad Polytechnic and thus available locally. It was believed that if Dr. Capildeo headed the D.L.P. he would be able not only to bag the votes of the uncommitted fence-sitters—Indian

[1] Dr. Capildeo died in London in 1970.

intellectuals and professionals—but would also provide the 'hero' element for the rural East Indian masses. Dr. Capildeo would also provide the non-East Indians alienated from the P.N.M. with the intellectual calibre they wanted.

One of the greatest failures of the East Indian community had been its inability to produce intellectually mature and secular political leadership. None of the East Indian leaders of the D.L.P. at that stage, was capable of providing intellectually enlightened and dedicated leadership. All of them had become discredited in the eyes of the masses as 'spoils-seeking' individualist politicians. R. N. Capildeo possessed the academic qualifications to match those of Dr. Williams. He had an unspoiled reputation and had never been in politics. Although a high-caste Hindu by birth, in no way could he be identified either with the *Maha Sabha* or with the Hindu cause. He could be equally popular among all sections of the East Indian community.

But in the absence of issue orientation and clear-cut objectives, the change of leadership could easily lead to personal fights among the East Indian leadership of the D.L.P. The extreme individualism of East Indian leaders not only created a lack of discipline but also bred mutual jealousies and distrust. It was only after bitter factional fights that Dr. Capildeo could become the leader of the party. At the end of the succession from Bhadase to Capildeo, the East Indian political leadership, for a while, stood deeply divided. The fear of a P.N.M. victory in the forthcoming elections, and consequently another five years of Negro rule, forced them to close their ranks behind the new leader.

Though firmly entrenched as Leader of the D.L.P. Dr. Capildeo was no politician. Unlike Dr. Williams, he had not created a party of his own; rather, he was placed at the head of a party by a group of experienced politicians who wanted to use him and his academic achievements for getting votes. Capildeo seemed to have been lured by the hope of becoming Prime Minister of Trinidad.

From the very beginning, he was ill at ease in politics. He soon made it evident by his inconsistent utterances, contradictory statements, and rash behaviour that he was a trained scientist but lacked statesmanship.

The first policy statement which Dr. Capildeo made gave the clear indication that he could speak the artless truth, which might not be politically adroit and advantageous. In the first meeting of the D.L.P. parliamentarians which he called, he gave instructions on the stand they were to take on a motion introduced by the P.N.M. Government in support of Jagan's demand for internal self-government in British Guiana. A statement was prepared by Capildeo, and Dr. E. A. Lee, a D.L.P. member of the Legislative Council, while speaking on the motion before the House, read this statement on behalf of the D.L.P. leadership. The D.L.P. leadership lent its support to the demand for self-government in British Guiana only under certain conditions:

British Guiana is like Trinidad from the point of view of population. In British Guiana there are two large racial groups—Indians and Africans—with the Indians in a majority. In Trinidad we have two racial groups, again Indians and Africans, with the Africans in a majority.

The main process of democratic rule is the government of the country by a majority. When parties are grouped together on racial lines then it is clear that in British Guiana, you will have the majority rule of the Indians over Negroes, while in Trinidad you will have the majority rule of the Negro over the Indian.

We on this side of the House have again and again accused the Government party of preaching and practicing racialism. We see no reason to modify that charge, let alone withdraw it.[1]

The statement further asserted that it was open knowledge to all concerned that since the advent of the P.N.M. party and its Government, racialism had become a major consideration in Trinidad politics. It added, 'British Guiana is polarized on racial lines. Unfortunately, the same has been held to be true in Trinidad and Tobago. The P.N.M. has claimed that the D.L.P. is an Indian party and the D.L.P. has claimed that the P.N.M. is a Negro party. We cannot agree with free conscience to a situation in which the Indian majority in British Guiana would be given full latitude to tyrannise over the Negro minority.'[2]

This was an important policy statement which pointed out how Capildeo looked upon the question of independence for Trinidad. There was bluntness in this statement, but it was essentially true. However, in a multi-ethnic society, where the D.L.P. leadership was hoping to get support from the non-East Indian element, this type of statement was highly inadvisable. Capildeo, instead of exercising sobriety and restraint as the election of 1961 drew near,

[1] *Trinidad Guardian* (9 April 1960).   [2] Ibid.

became more and more aggressive. When the P.N.M. Government decided to introduce voting machines in place of ballot boxes and provided for a permanent registration of voters under the new election law, Dr. Capildeo told a huge audience in San Fernando, 'I appeal to 1000 of you to come forward on election day and smash up 1000 voting machines.'[1] He asked for mass-burning of the identity cards and hinted that if his demands were not met, he might start a civil disobedience movement. He also declared that he would not mind going to jail in order to get this election law repealed.[2] In another violent speech he told his predominantly East Indian audience, 'Today I have come, but I have not come to bring peace, but to bring a sword. We have brought peace long enough and they cannot understand. . . .'[3] Finally, in the thick of the election campaign, when Negro supporters of the P.N.M. tried to disrupt a mass meeting of East Indian supporters of the D.L.P., Capildeo lost his temper and gave a call to arms. He called upon the East Indian masses to retaliate against the P.N.M. by disrupting its meetings. He asked them to get ready to march on the White Hall and the Government House and to be prepared to take over the country. He said that all these measures were being taken in self-defence, but he made it clear that 'if self-defence comes to violence, we are not going to stop at it'.[4] This statement was widely regretted by the East Indian *élites*, though many said that it was an outburst provoked by the P.N.M. hecklers who had been regularly disrupting the D.L.P. meetings. They conceded that it was perhaps the worst mistake of the D.L.P. electioneering, and an unfortunate utterance which cost the D.L.P. a large proportion of the votes of the minority groups. This incident also made it evident that Capildeo lacked the temperament to lead a mass party in a multi-ethnic society.

The D.L.P. Campaign Strategy in the 1961 Election

In the 1961 election, the D.L.P. bitterly criticized and opposed the following aspects of the election procedure:

The voter's registration rules as provided under the Representation of the People Bill.

The Government's demarcation of electoral boundaries.

The introduction of voting machines in place of ballot boxes.

---

[1] *Trinidad Guardian* (11 September 1961). [2] Ibid. (28 August 1961).
[3] Ibid. (12 September 1961). [4] Ibid. (17 October 1961).

The voter's registration rules, as provided in the Representation of the People Bill 1961,[1] have been praised in some circles as the world's most modern,[2] but they were termed by the *Trinidad Guardian* as quite complex and 'intended to confuse the vast majority of country voters, who as every one knows, are the backbone of the opposition camp'.[3] Under the voter's registration rules the prospective voter was asked questions not only concerning his age, sex, and colour, but also on his height, the colour of his eyes, his marital status—whether he was lawfully married or living in concubinage and the like. There were twenty questions relating to various personal matters. The voters were to be photographed and supplied with permanent identification cards for voting purposes.[4]

The D.L.P. leadership, while speaking on the Representation of the People Bill before the House, charged that the registration rules were prepared by the 'racialist backroom boys of the P.N.M.'[5] in order to disfranchise the East Indian masses on the same pattern as the American Negroes had been disfranchised in the southern states of the United States.[6]

L. F. Seukeran introduced a motion in the House for setting up an independent body consisting of the members of the Federal Parliament to examine these rules before they were passed by the Trinidad Legislative Council.[7]

Dr. P. V. Solomon charged that the Opposition was only following delaying tactics because it was afraid of facing the electorate. The Government agreed to some amendments, but the main provisions regarding identification cards and photographs remained. Seukeran's motion was defeated by 7 to 13.[8] Ashford S. Sinanan, the organizational leader of the D.L.P., expressed his dissatisfaction over the amended legislation: the entire measure should have been abandoned.[9] The D.L.P. leadership commented that under the Representation of the People Bill of 1961 too many powers were granted to the registration officers who were mostly

---

[1] *Trinidad and Tobago, Representation of the People Bill, 1961* (Port of Spain, Government Printing Office, 1961).

[2] Gordon K. Lewis, 'The Trinidad and Tobago General Elections of 1961', *Caribbean Studies* (Vol. II, No. 2, July 1962), p. 3.

[3] *Trinidad Guardian* (5 January 1961).

[4] *Trinidad and Tobago Representation of the People Bill, 1961*, pp. 152–6.

[5] *Trinidad Guardian* (21 January 1961).

[6] Ibid.

[7] Ibid.   [8] Ibid. (22 January 1961).   [9] Ibid. (15 January 1961).

Negroes and therefore pro-P.N.M. They declared that they did not expect free and impartial registration of voters under the conditions existing at that time.

Most of the D.L.P. leaders and non-political *élites* interviewed strongly denounced the way in which the electoral districts were demarcated. Under the Trinidad and Tobago (Electoral Provisions) Order in Council of 1960, a Boundaries Commission was created, consisting of four members: A. C. Thomosos, Speaker of the Lower House, chairman; Dr. P. V. Solomon, Home Minister, Justice Clement E. Phillips, and Stephen C. Maharaj. S. C. Maharaj was the only East Indian and nominee of the D.L.P. All others were Negroes. Stephen Maharaj expressed his violent disagreement with the other members of the Commission.[1] He declared that the Commission's proposals were intended to create majorities in most of the seats according to returns of previous elections. To North Port of Spain, where the Government was defeated in two successive elections, a part of Belmont, where the Government had won in the last election, was added in order to destroy any attempt by another party to get a seat.[2] Maharaj charged that the Commission was packed with government supporters and even Justice Clement Phillips, who should have been impartial, was very much partial to the views of the Government nominees and supported them in every case. The D.L.P. leadership declared that the findings of the Commission were biased and the whole document irregular and immoral.[3]

L. F. Seukeran, another East Indian and D.L.P. member of the Legislative Council, said that he wondered how the P.N.M. could justify calling itself 'national' when it had divided the country according to ethnic groupings. He charged that although the 'P.N.M. did not talk race, they practiced it with all the viciousness at their command'.[4] The interviews showed that the Trinidad Government had not been able to remove the impression from the minds of East Indians that the elections were rigged and that the Opposition Party was not given a fair chance.

The D.L.P. leadership was also opposed to the introduction of

---

[1] *Report of the Electoral District Boundaries Commission to the Legislative Council with a Minority Report by Hon. S. C. Maharaj* (Port of Spain, Government Printing Office, 1961), p. 21.

[2] Ibid.

[3] *Trinidad Guardian* (12 March 1961). [4] Ibid. (12 March 1961).

voting machines. It wanted to know why voting machines were being introduced when ballots were in use everywhere else. Stephen C. Maharaj openly declared that, 'Every sentence, every clause in the Ordinance' (referring to the Representation of the People Bill and the introduction of voting machines), 'contains one aim and purpose and that is to make sure that the present Government keeps itself in power. Make no mistake about it.'[1] Addressing the Government directly, he said, 'You are beating your chest because you feel you control the police. You control communications, you are having things [sic] under your feet.'[2]

Since the defeat of the P.N.M. in the 1958 federal election, the D.L.P. leaders asserted, the middle-class leadership of the P.N.M. had made up its mind to use every means to keep the power in its hands. The D.L.P. requested that the Home Minister hold a referendum as to whether the people wanted to vote by ballot or by the voting machines. The D.L.P. sought permission to buy a Shoup voting machine so that it could demonstrate it to D.L.P. supporters. It also demanded radio time in order to explain its position on such important questions as the introduction of voting machines and permanent personal registration as proposed under the Representation of the People Bill. These demands were rejected by the Government.[3] Many of the D.L.P. fears concerning the voting machines might have been baseless, but at the same time the Government failed to remove the distrust in voting machines from the minds of those who were opposed to their introduction.

The D.L.P. proposed as many as 118 amendments to the Representation of the People Bill, seeking to remove the provisions relating to permanent personal registration, identity cards, and the introduction of the voting machines,[4] but it failed to achieve any of its objectives. The Government held that the introduction of the voting machines was economical and that registration rules and identity cards were essential for ensuring clean voting, but it gave the assurance that people would be educated to use the voting machines.

Programme and policy were the secondary questions in the election of 1961: it was primarily a struggle between the two ethnic

---

[1] House proceedings reported in *Trinidad Guardian* (15 September 1961).
[2] Ibid.   [3] Ibid. (17 September 1961).
[4] *The Statesman* (16 September 1961), p. 6.

groups for political power. It remains worthwhile, however, to have a look at the election platform of the D.L.P. In its 'Guide to the D.L.P. Policy',[1] the leadership made a statement of its policies and programme. The party promised full support for federation and assured that it would make every effort to develop and sustain the alliance. On the issue of the American bases in Chaguaramas, it expressed dissatisfaction with the existing agreement, arguing that too much land was tied up in the bases, and suggesting that the surplus land should be released for the people of the island. More important, it demanded a joint management of the base and increased employment of local labour. The D.L.P. expressed its full support for the denominational educational system and promised to encourage it in the future. It promised to further the cause of secondary education and pledged to establish a full university college in Trinidad. To promote exportation of skilled migrants to other countries, it promised to introduce technical education.

The D.L.P. also expressed its intention to improve local industrial conditions in order to attract foreign capital. It said, 'We must encourage investors by offering attractive tax concessions, land grants and stable conditions of labour.'[2] With respect to labour, it promised to provide for old-age pensions, insurance policies, increased health facilities, and better housing. It pledged to reduce the general cost of living but at the same time pleaded for the separation of trade unionism from party politics.

It advocated the introduction of a system of social security and promised to create a Social Assistance Service. The D.L.P. declared that it would restore agriculture to its former position as the first industry of the country, with stress on food production. It promised to increase refrigeration facilities for food products and to introduce a system of farm subsidies in order to keep the prices down.

Surprisingly, the D.L.P. policy declaration stated that consideration would also be given to the establishment of a nuclear power plant.

The D.L.P. also said that it would restore and expand the powers of the local self-governments. It placed special emphasis on the maintenance of the system of rule of law and declared, 'The

[1] Ibid. (30 September 1961), pp. 9–10.
[2] Ibid.

I

Democratic Labour Party pledges to maintain . . . the complete independence of judiciary at all levels.'[1]

In its last policy declaration, made before polling began, the D.L.P. listed eight problems facing the country: water shortage; a rise in the cost of living; a rise in rents and totally inadequate housing for persons in the lower income group; a rise in school population, and the near impossibility of obtaining places for children in secondary schools; totally inadequate health facilities; high cost of drugs; inadequate old-age pensions; the absence of pensions and social security for most workers in the territory.[2]

The D.L.P. declared that in order to solve these problems there was no need for a tax increase; on the contrary, it assured that the taxes would be reduced as soon as possible. The tax reduction, it said, would enhance the purchasing capacity of the lowest income group. The D.L.P. promised a welfare state, but it did not spell out how it was going to meet the expense involved in the introduction of welfare services.

Compared to the election platform of the D.L.P. the P.N.M.'s election manifesto was an impressive document, which spoke about its achievements and its clear objectives for the country's future political and economic development. The P.N.M.'s programme outlined its political achievements in obtaining a greater degree of internal self-government for Trinidad and Tobago, and it promised to carry on the economic development of the country through five-year plans.[3]

However, as stated before, the programme and the policies were not of much consequence in the election. Very few people exhibited any interest in the platform of the parties. As the election campaign stood, the Negroes were opposed to the elevation of a 'Coolie' to the position of Prime Minister, and the East Indians were afraid of a Negro government.

The 1961 Election Campaign

The 1961 election campaign was perhaps the roughest in the history of the island. Fully-awakened Negro nationalism under

[1] *The Statesman* (30 September 1961), p. 10.
[2] *For the Sake of Trinidad and Tobago Vote D.L.P.* (San Fernando, Rahman's Printery for the D.L.P., 1961), p. 2.
[3] *People's National Movement Election Manifesto General Election, 1961* (Port of Spain, P.N.M. Publishing Co., 1961), pp. 3–5.

Williams was quite assertive of its rights, and one of the most important claim was the right to rule Trinidad as the majority ethnic group of the colony. The Political Leader of the P.N.M. had nothing but contempt for the D.L.P. He described the members of the D.L.P. as the 'shoe shine boys of planters and merchants of Port of Spain'.[1] He maintained that the D.L.P. was opposed to self-government; it was thoroughly a reactionary party. Speaking in Marxist terminology, he asserted that the vested interests were trying to stage a counter-revolution through the D.L.P. In the 1961 election, 'The struggle was between the social revolution wrought by the P.N.M. and the counter-revolution being mounted by the D.L.P.'[2] In spite of the differences in their election manifestoes, this distinction between the P.N.M. as a revolutionary party and the D.L.P. as a reactionary party was just a fiction created by Williams. Albert Gomes remarked: 'In the ideological sense this is a battle between Tweedledum and Tweedledee, both of whom are driving hard on the right.'[3]

The P.N.M. and the D.L.P. both presented multiracial slates for election. The P.N.M. adopted eight East Indian candidates, contesting election in East Indian majority areas. Twenty-one non-East Indians fought the election in Negro majority or predominantly mixed areas. Out of the eight East Indian candidates, three were Muslims.

The D.L.P. put up twenty non-East Indians and nine East Indian candidates. Two Negro D.L.P. candidates were given safe seats in East Indian majority areas. Out of its nine East Indian nominees, two were Muslims.[4]

In all the constituencies where East Indian population was not more than 20 per cent, such as the electoral districts of Diego Martin, Maraval, St. Joseph, and Barataria the D.L.P. put up only non-East Indian candidates. But it was mainly concentrating on such marginal seats as Tunapuna, Ortoire-Mayaro, and Arima where the East Indian population in some wards was considerable and non-East Indian candidates were expected to attract Negro votes.

---

[1] *Trinidad Guardian* (9 November 1961).
[2] Ibid. (10 November 1961).
[3] Ibid. (19 November 1961).
[4] *Trinidad Guardian* (3 December 1961). There were thirty seats; the election for the remaining seat was postponed due to the death of one of the candidates.

The D.L.P. strategy was to make inroads into the P.N.M. areas by putting up Negro candidates. The D.L.P. was also expecting support from minority ethnic groups, such as the white, Arab, and Chinese. Accordingly, the D.L.P. like the P.N.M. made particular efforts to recruit non-East Indian elements. Some of the key positions in the D.L.P., such as the chairmanship of the party, were held by non-East Indians.

In spite of the multiracial line-up of the candidates of the two parties and their avowed objective of racial integration, both parties used ethnicity as their major support. Dr. Williams, who is considered by many East Indian *élites* to be a moderate racialist, had declared in 1958, 'The P.N.M. bulldozers are digging deep into the hillside, and God help any minority group that gets in the way.'[1] And now, exhorting a Negro audience, he declared again, 'Indians as a group may not be with us and be against us. So what? We beat them in 1956 and we will beat them again. Laugh at them, ask them for their programme, tell them to follow their leader if they can find him, analyze the contributions of their choice in 1956 and 1958.'[2] The Press reported that Isabella Teshea, vice-president of the P.N.M. and a Government Minister, remarked, as she looked over the crowd at a public meeting, 'that few, if any D.L.P. faces could be seen and she saw that as a good sign for the people of the area'.[3] Apparently she identified East Indian faces with the D.L.P., few of whom were present at the meeting.

'He is a coolie, he is D.L.P.' 'All coolies are D.L.P.' 'We do not want a coolie Prime Minister.' These remarks flowed effortlessly from the tongues of Negroes. On the other hand, in East Indian majority areas, every Negro was P.N.M.

The political struggle at this stage was not motivated by desire to capture power in order to serve some ideological goals. It had become a desperate struggle between the two ethnic groups to secure victory in order to assert their wounded racial pride. The Negro desire for assertion of his self-respect found significant expression in this calypso,

> Soon, in the West Indies,
> It will be please, Mr. Nigger, please.

[1] *Trinidad Guardian* (8 January 1961).   [2] *Nation* (2 February 1962).
[3] *Trinidad Guardian* (3 October 1961).

One of the major means of campaigning and electioneering was the organization of public meetings. Most were open-air meetings held at street corners, public parks, or in parking lots. On the P.N.M. side, Williams was the main speaker, whereas the D.L.P. battery of speakers was led by Dr. R. N. Capildeo. One of the main complaints of the D.L.P. was that it was not given a fair chance to conduct its election campaign through public meetings. The D.L.P. public meetings were broken up by P.N.M. supporters. Many times, due to organized heckling of P.N.M. supporters, the D.L.P. speakers were unable to address the public gatherings.[1]

The election was to be held in December 1961, but as early as January and February, the D.L.P. was finding it difficult to hold meetings in non-Indian or mixed areas. The D.L.P. was chased out of Woodford Square, which is in the heart of Port of Spain. Even when it held meetings in other parts of Port of Spain, the D.L.P. was not spared by the hecklers. Stephen Maharaj went to address a meeting in the St. Ann's area, and he faced there a hostile crowd of 400-strong 'booing, jeering and laughing'.[2] The D.L.P., Maharaj said, 'was fighting for freedom of speech, but freedom of speech was given to only one man in Trinidad—Dr. Eric Williams; he had hooligans and the Police Forces behind him'.[3] The D.L.P. leadership charged that they were not getting protection from the Negro-dominated police.[4] Although the P.N.M. Executive advised its followers to behave themselves and to keep the law of the land,[5] Williams may have indirectly encouraged his followers to treat the D.L.P. differently when he advised them to give Butler a fair hearing but added, 'don't treat him like you treat the D.L.P. candidates'.[6] Organized heckling and hooliganism were witnessed mainly at the D.L.P. meetings.[7]

In November, hostile demonstrations by Negro workers in support of the P.N.M. led to an outbreak of violence in the San Juan area. The Negro dock workers raided a gasoline station, looted shops, and threw stones at the D.L.P. office and candidates' houses. As a result of this mob violence, the D.L.P. was forced to suspend its public meetings. It declared that until the general election was over it would not hold any public meetings. For three

[1] Ibid. (7 February 1961).   [2] Ibid. (18 June 1961).   [3] Ibid.
[4] Ibid. (12 November 1961).   [5] Ibid. (11 November 1961).
[6] Ibid. (29 November 1961).   [7] *The Statesman* (3 August 1961), p. 2.

weeks before the election, the D.L.P. conducted only house-to-house canvassing. The D.L.P. requested the Government to provide paid radio time in order to explain its position to the people, but the Government refused.[1] Unlike British Guiana, where the four major parties of the country were allowed a series of election broadcasts,[2] in Trinidad, the radio remained a P.N.M. Government monopoly. Both parties also conducted mass rallies, torchlight processions, and motorcades.

Organized labour played a significant role in the election campaign. Whereas an overwhelming majority of sugar workers are East Indians, oilfield and industrial workers are mostly Negroes. With the rise of political parties on an ethnic basis, the workers also became divided on ethnic lines. All the major trade unions excepting that of sugar workers are dominated by Negroes. The National Trade Union Congress, the most powerful labour organization of the island, is led by Negro trade unionists. The Sugar Workers Union, on the other hand, is headed by Bhadase Sagan Maraj.

At the opening of the election campaign, the D.L.P. organ, *The Statesman*, laying down the labour policy of the D.L.P., cautioned the country about the disturbed state of industrial peace and advocated some positive action on the part of the Government to check the tide of labour unrest.[3] Subsequently Dr. Capildeo, the D.L.P. Political Leader, also came out against labour strikes, pointing out that disturbed industrial peace would discourage the investment of foreign capital. He accused the P.N.M. of using the trade unions for its own ends. He advocated separation of trade unionism from politics and opposed any alignment of trade unions with the political parties.[4]

Carl Tull, then secretary general of the National Trade Union Congress (and now a P.N.M.-nominated senator) declared that Dr. Capildeo's statement was a threat to the trade union movement.[5] The Negro-dominated National Trade Union Congress, looking for an excuse to make such charges, condemned Dr. Capildeo for his anti-strike stand and pledged its support to the

[1] *Trinidad Guardian* (22 November 1961).
[2] C. Paul Bradley, 'Party Politics in British Guiana', *Western Political Quarterly* (Vol. XVI, No. 2, June 1963), p. 367.
[3] *The Statesman* (15 April 1961), p. 2.
[4] *Trinidad Guardian* (8 November 1961).   [5] Ibid. (12 November 1961).

P.N.M.[1] J. F. Rojas, the Negro boss of the N.T.U.C., charged that the D.L.P. carried a labour name but was a conservative party supported by big business.[2] The D.L.P. leadership claimed that both the Marxist Rojas and big business firms were supporting the P.N.M.

The N.T.U.C., meanwhile, decided to hold a series of mass demonstrations in favour of the P.N.M. The East Indian members of the N.T.U.C. and the Oilfield Workers Union disassociated themselves from these activities and strongly condemned the decision of the N.T.U.C. to pledge its support to the P.N.M.[3]

Negro workers, under the banners of different unions, and the N.T.U.C., staged demonstrations against the D.L.P. Some of the placards carried the slogans, 'Vote peace not murder,' 'Down with the D.L.P. and Adams, stooges of the colonial Regime,' 'I'd rather live in a P.N.M. Grave than be a D.L.P. Slave,' 'Vote D.L.P. and suffer a Hell.'[4] Williams declared that it was significant that the party which proclaimed itself a labour party should find the whole mass of the labour movement marching against it.[5] But as noted, all the labour unions in favour of the P.N.M. were Negro-dominated. The All-Trinidad Sugar Estate and Factories Workers Union, the East Indian-dominated labour union, refused to participate in any demonstration staged to support the P.N.M. When the Cane Farmers Association, a predominantly East Indian organization, came out against the P.N.M. two days before the elections, Williams declared, 'Such lickspittlers will get the order of the boot—and I used to play a lot of football.'[6] Williams welcomed Negro labour support for his party but became infuriated when any labour organization pledged its support to his opponents. An important result of labour demonstrations and parades in support of the P.N.M. was the outbreak of violence in the areas adjacent to Port of Spain. As noted, the D.L.P. office and the houses of D.L.P. supporters and candidates in St. Augustine, San Juan, and Barataria were stoned. A state of emergency was declared in the East Indian majority area, and later extended to the electoral districts of Caroni East and Chaguanas,

---

[1] *The Statesman* (25 November 1961), p. 10.
[2] *Trinidad Guardian* (8 November 1961).
[3] *The Statesman* (25 November 1961), p. 10.
[4] *Trinidad Guardian* (14 November 1961).
[5] Ibid. (2 December 1961).   [6] Ibid. (8 December 1961).

populated heavily by East Indians and D.L.P. supporters. The police, equipped with guns and rifles, moved into these areas and conducted a house-to-house search for arms and ammunition. The Government suspected hoarding of illicit arms in these areas, but the police failed to discover anything illegal. East Indian leaders strongly denounced these actions of the Government which, they held, were undertaken to terrorize the D.L.P. supporters.

Thus the 1961 election campaign was marked with an overtone of racialism and with an aggressive determination on the part of the majority ethnic group to defeat its opponent by any means in order to keep the power in its own hands.

Ethnicity: The Primary Determinant of Voting Behaviour

The election took place on 4 December 1961. The main contestants were the P.N.M. and the D.L.P., though Butler's Party and the African National Congress also put up some candidates. When the final results were in, including the delayed returns from Siparia, the P.N.M. had won twenty seats out of thirty and the rest of the ten seats were captured by the D.L.P. The P.N.M. polled 57 per cent of the popular votes, the D.L.P., 42 per cent.[1]

Although both parties made limited inroads into each other's areas, the primary determinant variable in the voting behaviour appears to be ethnicity. For instance, the P.N.M. secured heavy majorities in four Port of Spain constituencies and two San Fernando constituencies, where East Indian population was only 9 per cent and 26 per cent respectively.[2] On the other hand, in such heavily East Indian majority areas as Point-a-Pierre, Couva, Chaguanas, Caroni East, Naparima, Nariva, Princes Town, Siparia, and St. Augustine, the D.L.P. won with heavy majorities, although in all these constituencies except St. Augustine, the P.N.M. put up only East Indian candidates. Similarly, in the electoral districts of Diego Martin, Laventille, San Juan, and La Brea where East Indian population was in many cases less than 20 per cent, the P.N.M. won with heavy majorities. A close contest between V. Jamadar (D.L.P.) and Mariel O. Donawa (P.N.M.) and the narrow victory of the former, gave a true

---

[1] *Trinidad and Tobago Report on the General Election of 1961* (Prepared by the Supervisor of Elections, Port of Spain, 1965), p. 74.

[2] Trinidad and Tobago, *Census of 1960, Bulletin No. 1* (Port of Spain, Central Statistical Office, Population Census Division).

representation of the almost equally divided ethnic composition of the population of the electoral district.

The importance of race as a major determinant of voting behaviour is confirmed by another study. K. Bahadoorsingh, a native of Trinidad, conducted a sample study of the voting behaviour of East Indians and Negroes of three constituencies—Naprima, Laventille, and Fyzabad—and concluded that 'race is the main determinant of voting behaviour in Trinidad'.[1]

The D.L.P. put up two Negro candidates in two heavily Indian-populated areas—Point-a-Pierre and Nariva—who were opposed by two East Indian P.N.M. candidates. However, the P.N.M. failed in its strategy to draw East Indian votes away from the D.L.P. by putting up East Indian candidates. The people voted

Table 5-1   *Voter Participation in Elections of the Trinidad Legislative Council*[2]

Votes	1946	1950	1956	1958	1961
	%	%	%	%	%
Cast	52·9	70	80	73·6	88·11
Accepted	93·9	95·7	97·4	98·2	99·96
Rejected	6·1	4·3	2·6	1·8	0·04

for the party rather than the candidate, regardless of his ethnic origin, which shows the strong identification of the parties with the two distinct racial groups of the island in the minds of the masses.

There was a higher turn-out of voters in the East Indian majority areas, the highest (95·17 per cent) being in St. Augustine where Dr. Capildeo was a candidate. St. Augustine was closely followed by Couva where Dr. Capildeo's brother, S. N. Capildeo, was a candidate, the turn-out being around 94 per cent. There were only two East Indian majority constituencies where the voters' turn-out was below 90 per cent. Compared with other election years, the general turn-out of voters in 1961 shows an over-all larger participation of the voters (see Table 5-1). There

[1] Krishna Bahadoorsingh, *Trinidad Electoral Politics: The Persistence of the Race Factor* (Institute of Race Relations, Special Series, 1968).
[2] *Report on the General Election of 1961*, Appendix VIII.

was a greater awareness of the major political issue involved: vindication of the racial pride of the respective ethnic groups.

The D.L.P. candidates were returned from rural areas, mainly the sugar belts. Out of ten D.L.P. members of the Legislative Council, eight were East Indians, two were Negroes or mixed. The eight East Indians consisted of three Hindus, one Muslim, and four Christians—three Presbyterians and one Roman Catholic. One of the Negroes was Anglican and the other Roman Catholic.

Out of ten members, four were re-elected to the Legislative Council. They were S. N. Capildeo, A. S. Sinanan, L. F. Seukeran, and Stephen C. Maharaj. The six new members were Dr. Capildeo (Political Leader of the D.L.P.), Tajmool Hosein, V. Jamadar, B. Ramdeen, M. Forrester, and Peter Farquhar.

Out of these ten members, five were university graduates and five had a secondary school education. One was a university teacher, two were solicitors, two were barristers, one a medical practitioner, one a druggist-chemist, and one a company director.

We have seen that the five most frequently mentioned East Indian leaders had not originated from the impoverished masses; they came from comfortable middle-class families. Therefore, in their political outlook, they have tended to lack imagination and to be closer to the conservative and conformist forces of the society.

Both parties are fundamentally middle class. This becomes evident when we compare the socio-economic backgrounds of the candidates. For instance, if there were two company directors on the D.L.P. slate, the P.N.M. also launched two company directors and one industrialist. If the P.N.M. put up one trade union official, the D.L.P. too had one trade unionist on its list. Both parties had university teachers, professionals, druggists, land proprietors, peasants, farmers, solicitors, school teachers, and journalists among their candidates.[1] If the P.N.M. was supported by the Negro-dominated trade unions, the D.L.P. was supported by the sugar workers.

But whereas the middle-class leadership of the P.N.M. has been more broad-minded, clear, and determined about its objectives and has also been successful in winning over some minority groups, the middle-class East Indian leadership of the D.L.P., on

[1] *Report on the General Election of 1961*, Appendix I.

the other hand, has been much more sectarian and narrow-minded, and has failed to attract disgruntled Negroes and other miscellaneous elements.

The D.L.P. Defeat in the 1961 Election as Seen by the East Indian Élites

An examination of census figures published by the Central Statistical Office demonstrates that Negro candidates of the D.L.P. were very rarely able to poll a higher percentage of votes than the East Indian ratio of population warranted. As the ethnic composition of the population stood, the D.L.P. would not have been able to win the election. For instance, in the electoral district of Maraval, where the East Indian ratio of population was around 20 per cent, the D.L.P. Negro candidate could get only 33·45 per cent of the votes. Similarly, in Toco-Manzanilla, where the median of East Indian population was 16 per cent, the D.L.P. Negro candidate secured 33 per cent of the votes against 67 per cent for the P.N.M. candidate. In heavily Negro-populated areas like Diego Martin, La Brea, and Laventille, D.L.P. Negro candidates were given crushing defeats.

I asked a number of East Indian social and political *élites* how they explained the poor showing of the D.L.P. in the election of 1961. Some replied that under the conditions then existing the D.L.P. could have won but they were robbed. An overwhelming majority of party and trade union office-holders (71 per cent), political leaders (64 per cent), more than half of the religious leaders (53 per cent), a large percentage of top professionals (38 per cent) and leading businessmen (33 per cent) thought that one of the major reasons for the defeat of the D.L.P. was the use of voting machines. It is difficult to say how much this in fact influenced the final result but it is commonly held among the East Indian *élites* and the masses that the election was not fair and the voting machines were rigged. Even Dennis Mahabir, a prominent East Indian supporter of the P.N.M. and a former P.N.M. Mayor of Port of Spain, said: 'The D.L.P. lost the elections at several points. First with the delimitation committee, second at the Queen's Park Savannah, and third with the voting machines.'[1] Top D.L.P. leaders, including Dr. Capildeo and his former

---

[1] 'The Hammer and the Anvil: The Indian Case for Proportionate Representation in Trinidad and Tobago' (mimeographed pamphlet, Port of Spain, Indian Association of Trinidad and Tobago, 1962), p. 16.

colleagues, Peter Farquhar and Dr. Forrester (leaders of the Liberal Party at the time of writing), and the East Indians were convinced that the D.L.P. was cheated by the introduction of voting machines. To quote various *élites*: 'P.N.M. was not the only one to be fought, we fought against the voting machines, they cheated us.' 'All agencies of the Government were loaded against the D.L.P.' 'They were robbed by the voting machines.' 'There were no fair elections.' Peter Farquhar, a Negro, who was elected on the D.L.P. ticket told me that: 'There were no fair elections, there was widespread intimidation of the voters and the voting machines were rigged.' Dr. Forrester, another Negro, a former chairman of the D.L.P., said: 'There was organized break-up of the D.L.P. meetings at many places and we were unable to address public gatherings. The voting machines were deliberately intro- duced in order to defeat the D.L.P. through underhanded means.' They also referred to the unfair demarcation of electoral districts. They held that the effort of the P.N.M. Government was to see to it that the East Indian should not be in a majority in more than ten constituencies.

Subsequently, the D.L.P. filed an election petition and based its case mainly on the inaccurate working of the voting machines, but lost by a 2 to 1 decision. Mr. Justice Corbin gave a dissenting judgement and conceded that 30 per cent of the voting machines in the constituency showed discrepancies in the recording of votes and that there were no satisfactory arrangements for inspection of the machines. He found that the machines were not constructed according to the rules laid down by the legislature.[1] The Super- visor of Elections in his report found various discrepancies in the working of the voting machines, but said that it was difficult to establish the reason for these inaccuracies as the election law did not allow re-examination of the voting machines.[2]

The second most frequently mentioned reason for the defect of the D.L.P. by the social, political, and religious *élites* was lack of organization. The D.L.P. did not have even the semblance of an organization. The P.N.M. possessed a model grass-roots organiza- tion, strict party discipline, and a united leadership. The D.L.P. did not have any efficient party machinery and it was difficult to enforce discipline among the leaders. While in the thick of

[1] *The Statesman* (30 March 1962), pp. 1–2.
[2] *Report on the General Elections of 1961*, p. 64.

battle, they were more often fighting each other than the P.N.M.

The third most frequent explanation was the unfair conduct of the election. This was advanced mostly by the political *élites* (71 per cent), party and trade union officials, and quite a few of the top professionals and leading businessmen. A senior East Indian parliamentarian charged that the Home Minister, Dr. Solomon, who was in charge of the election, made a very careful selection of the officials, and all key positions were held by Negroes. Out of seventy-two election officials, only ten were East Indians.

Table 5-2 *Racial Distribution of Election Officials Appointed by the P.N.M. Government in 1961*[1]

Officials	East Indian	Non-East Indian	Total
Returning officials	4	26	30
Clerks	4	26	30
Registration officials	2	10	12
Total	10	62	72

A significant number of East Indian *élite* groups believed that Capildeo's intemperate outbursts were also responsible for the D.L.P.'s defeat. They held that many minority groups were frightened by his aggressiveness and switched their support to the P.N.M. We have seen above that during the 1961 election period some people felt that he had not behaved in the manner of a responsible leader.

Very few said that the D.L.P. was defeated because of its lack of ideology or programme. Even D.L.P. candidates conceded that race was the major issue in the election and that they got elected from the areas where East Indians were in an overwhelming majority. They thought that 90 per cent of the East Indians voted for them, whereas 90 per cent of the Negroes voted against them.

The demarcation of electoral districts or unfair election practices

[1] The racial distribution of election officials presented in Table 5-2 is based upon East Indian and non-East Indian names of the officials given in the *Report on the General Elections of 1961*, Appendices II and III.

could not be denied as one of the reasons for the defeat of the D.L.P. But primarily the D.L.P. seemed to have failed to win only because of the narrow and sectarian base of its top leadership, its lack of internal cohesion, and the absence of an efficient party organization.

When asked how successful they thought the D.L.P. was in mobilizing East Indian support, an overwhelming majority of the social and political *élite* groups thought that the D.L.P. in spite of itself, was highly successful in winning over the mass support of East Indians in 1961 (see Table 5-3).

Table 5-3   *Assessment by the Élites of the Success of the D.L.P. with East Indian Voters*

	Political leaders	Party and trade union officials	Business leaders	Professionals	Religious leaders	Social leaders
	%	%	%	%	%	%
It was successful	100	100	86	96	80	88
It was not	—	—	14	—	20	—
No answer	—	—	—	4	—	12
Total	100	100	100	100	100	100
No. of cases	(14)	(7)	(19)	(24)	(15)	(8)

The mass identification of East Indians with the D.L.P. is actually based upon their antipathy towards the out-group. East Indian men in the street stated their party preference as follows:

'I like the D.L.P. because I like the Indian side.' 'I am Hindu, my party is Hindu, I love my Hindu Dharma.' 'I still prefer D.L.P. because I am Indian, we should stick to our own.' 'We will always support our own party whether it wins or loses, we can not run away from our Dharma.' 'D.L.P. is we people.' 'In Trinidad elections are run on race, I vote for the people of my own race.' 'I want to follow my own religion, the P.N.M. is trying to wipe out Hindus from the island.' 'I am Indian and there is no other Indian party; therefore I vote for D.L.P.' 'We like D.L.P., we do not like P.N.M., there are too many Negroes.' 'Negroes can not govern, they have education, but they are just not the type of people who can govern.'

Obviously here party loyalty is identical with loyalty to the ethnic group. The subcultural division between Negroes and East Indians leads them to identify themselves with their own in-groups. Antipathy towards each other forces them back to their own in-groups. Party, then, becomes more than mere political organization.

VI

Constitutional Reforms, Political Ideology, and the D.L.P.

SINCE its organization the D.L.P. leadership faced two highly complex questions. One of them related to its attitude towards the issue of constitutional reforms in Trinidad and its role as a party representing the minority interests. The second one was how to attract other minority groups in order to become a broad-based multi-ethnic mass organization. To achieve this objective the D.L.P. needed a secular orientation.

Constitutional Reforms

It is noteworthy that the demand for constitutional reforms always came from the Creoles. This time, too, the P.N.M., the Creole party, came out with a demand for far-reaching constitutional reforms. The P.N.M. leadership under Dr. Williams was striving for the establishment of Cabinet government in Trinidad on the British pattern. Williams had suggested in 1955 that, 'The time has come when the British Constitution, suitably modified, can be applied to Trinidad and Tobago.'[1]

When the P.N.M. won the election in 1956, Williams had the opportunity to suggest constitutional reforms on the basis of his previously expressed ideas. In September 1957, the P.N.M. Government made the following recommendations for constitutional reforms:

(1) Introduction of Cabinet government under which the Governor was to nominate the leader of the majority party as the Prime Minister.
(2) Distribution of portfolios on the recommendations of the Prime Minister.
(3) The Prime Minister should preside over the meetings of the Cabinet.

The Government also suggested that the Chief Minister should be known as the Prime Minister, the Colonial Secretary as the

---

[1] Eric Williams, *Constitutional Reforms in Trinidad and Tobago* (published by the author, 17 Lady Chancellor Road, Port of Spain, 1955), p. 30.

Chief Secretary, and the Governor's Executive Council as the Cabinet. The Attorney-General and the Chief Secretary could remain as *ex officio* members of the Cabinet but would be deprived of the right to vote, because they were not political appointees. The P.N.M. Government demanded the creation of an independent Police Service Commission and a Public Service Commission. It suggested that certain limitations should be placed on the discretionary powers of the Governor.[1]

In 1958, it made further additions to these reform proposals and demanded that the number of ministers should be raised from seven to nine and a new ministry, headed by a Home Minister, responsible for police, immigration, and domestic affairs should be created. These proposals were sent to the Secretary of State for Colonies for his approval.

The D.L.P., as a party of the minority ethnic group, seems to have been on the defensive concerning the reform proposals. Its criticism clearly showed that it was not in favour of far-reaching constitutional changes because it feared the rise of Negroes to a position of power with the implementation of these reforms. The D.L.P. also held that these reform proposals would greatly enhance the authority of a government which had come to power with only 38 per cent of the votes. The D.L.P. opposed the transfer of the control of the police to the Home Minister without providing certain legal safeguards for the minorities. The D.L.P. made it clear that it would not oppose internal self-rule but it would demand certain safeguards for protecting the rights of individual citizens.[2]

Furthermore, the D.L.P. argued that unless the Trinidad Legislature was made a truly representative body, the powers and responsibilities of the Executive Council should not be increased. It held that there could not be any wholesale application of the British parliamentary practices in Trinidad, as Trinidad lacked the basic conditions which made parliamentary democracy a success in England. It pointed out that with an increased number of ministers, parliamentary secretaries, speakers, and deputy speakers, almost everyone on the P.N.M. side in the Legislature would be holding one or the other office.

The D.L.P. sent a four-man delegation to London to present its

---

[1] Spackman, op. cit., pp. 291–3. [2] *Trinidad Guardian* (12 July 1959).

K

case before the Secretary of State for Colonies. Most of the objections raised by the D.L.P. were overruled by the Colonial Office, and the recommendations of the P.N.M. Government were embodied in the Order in Council of 1959. On 8 July 1959, the Cabinet system of government was inaugurated in Trinidad with the power to exercise control over the police.[1]

Immediately after the introduction of the new constitutional reforms, the P.N.M. Government sent another delegation to the United Kingdom for constitutional talks. The Government suggested the creation of a bicameral legislature, consisting of a House of Representatives (elective) and a Senate (nominated in place of the existing unicameral legislature). The Government recommended that the number of elected members of the House should be raised from twenty-four to thirty.[2] It also urged the revision of the electoral districts[3] and suggested that the Trinidad Parliament and its members should enjoy the same powers, privileges, and immunities as those enjoyed by members of the British Parliament.[4] It held that the post of Attorney-General should become a political post subject to appointment like other Ministers on the advice of the Prime Minister.[5] The P.N.M. also raised and discussed the question of granting complete independence to Trinidad.

B. S. Maraj, the then leader of the D.L.P., asserted that after its defeats in the federal election of 1958 and subsequent county council election, the P.N.M. had no mandate from the people to introduce far-reaching constitutional reforms in the country.[6] The D.L.P. strongly objected to the revision of the boundaries of the electoral districts, and it also opposed an increase in the number of seats in the House from twenty-four to thirty. The D.L.P. Executive issued a resolution demanding that elections should be held on the basis of the existing twenty-four electoral districts.[7]

B. S. Maraj held that the P.N.M. was seeking additional seats in order to consolidate its position. He said that these extra seats should be created only after the election.[8]

During this period the D.L.P. boycotted legislative delibera-

---

[1] *Trinidad Guardian* (9 July 1959).   [2] Ibid. (25 October 1959).
[3] Ibid. (7 November 1959).   [4] Ibid. (5 August 1959).
[5] Ibid. (25 October 1959).   [6] Ibid. (20 October 1959).
[7] Ibid. (1 November 1959).   [8] Ibid. (8 November 1959).

tions on the constitutional reforms, refused to submit its memorandum to the Legislative Select Committee appointed to examine
the question of constitutional reforms, and never made its position
clear regarding its objectives.[1] The D.L.P. strategy at this stage
seemed to be negative, but in a way it reflected its orientation
towards the emerging political structure in Trinidad. The D.L.P.
leadership had a feeling of alienation towards the whole issue of
change in the political system, and its attitude, feelings, and
evaluations of the far-reaching changes were unfavourable. It
tended to favour maintenance of the *status quo* rather than any
basic change in the existing structure. While in London, the
D.L.P. leaders made several pronouncements on the question of
constitutional reforms. They said that they were not opposed to
self-government and had no objection to constitutional reforms,
provided a general election was held before the introduction of
constitutional reforms, on the basis of twenty-four electoral
districts.[2] Subsequently, they withdrew their opposition to the
addition of seats on two conditions: an independent Boundaries
Commission should be created; Tobago (a Negro majority area)
should be treated as a single electoral district rather than two.[3]
The D.L.P. also opposed the creation of a bicameral legislature
before the general election.[4]

However, the Colonial Office agreed to the P.N.M. Government's request for thirty seats and to hold an election on that basis
rather than twenty-four. But the Colonial Office also agreed to
the D.L.P.'s demand for a Boundaries Commission,[5] and to defer
the creation of a second Chamber until after the election.

The Trinidad and Tobago (Constitution) Order in Council of
1961 gave the final, formal shape to the establishment of Cabinet
government in Trinidad. It provided for a Cabinet of twelve
Ministers headed by a Prime Minister, who until this time was
known as the Chief Minister. The post of the Attorney-General
became a political post and the Governor became the formal head
of the state, required to act on the advice of the Prime Minister.

It also provided for the creation of two Chambers of the Trinidad
Parliament—a House of Representatives and a Senate. The
Senate was to consist of twenty-one members. The Governor was

[1] *Trinidad Guardian* (29 October 1959).
[2] Ibid. (31 October 1959).   [3] Ibid. (18 November 1959).
[4] Ibid. (29 November 1959).   [5] Ibid. (19 November 1959).

to appoint twelve members on the advice of the Prime Minister and two members on the advice of the Leader of the Opposition. The rest of the members (seven) were to be appointed by the Governor, in consultation with the Prime Minister, from among persons representing special interests.[1] The House of Representatives was to be elected for five years. The Governor was given the power to summon, prorogue, and dissolve the House on the advice of the Prime Minister.

The new constitutional system came into force immediately after the election of 1961. The next step was the attainment of full independence.[2] Thus some of the demands of the D.L.P. were conceded. The right of the Leader of the Opposition to nominate two members of the Senate was the P.N.M. Government's step to remove some of the grievances of the D.L.P.

The Independence Constitution

After the general election of 1961, the D.L.P. faced two major problems: the question of the independence of Trinidad, and the future institutional structure of the country. The D.L.P. could not oppose the demand for independence, but it fought to modify the institutional structure proposed by the P.N.M. Government for an independent Trinidad. At this stage the D.L.P. tried to play a dual role; in one role it tried to get constitutionally built-in safeguards for the minority ethnic group, the East Indians; and in the other role, it made efforts to see that adequate provisions were made for the successful working of a democratic constitution in Trinidad.

The D.L.P. leadership also attacked the legitimacy of the P.N.M. Government. It held that the P.N.M. won the election through organized 'fraud', and unless elections were held again through ballot boxes, the P.N.M. Government should not be allowed to frame a constitution for an independent Trinidad. The charges were ignored by the Government and the Secretary of State for the Colonies.

A 64-page draft of the Trinidad and Tobago Constitution (known as the Trinidad and Tobago (Constitution) Order in Council 1962) was published on 19 February 1962. The draft of the independence constitution was prepared by the Cabinet; the Opposition was not consulted. About 1800 copies were distributed

[1] *Trinidad Guardian* (3 December 1961).   [2] Ibid. (5 December 1961).

in Trinidad and Tobago, and individuals and organizations were invited to give their comments.

The draft was modelled on the existing political institutions, but it also contained provisions concerning fundamental rights, the office of a Governor-General with limited powers, the organization of judicial and civil services, and the amending process. It made no provision for holding new elections by regular paper ballots instead of voting machines, as had been demanded by the D.L.P.[1]

The reaction of the D.L.P. was critical and adverse. A memorandum prepared by the D.L.P. Executive termed the draft of the constitution 'unsatisfactory and extremely dangerous'.[2] Before spelling out its differences with the Government on the independence constitution, it repeated the demand for holding fresh elections by ordinary ballots after dissolving the existing Parliament. It objected to the provisions regarding fundamental rights, which it found, were hedged about with numerous disguised restrictions. It also objected to the composition and position of the Senate as provided under the draft. It held that a fully-nominated Senate would serve no useful purpose. It found that the arbitrary exercise of power gave too much latitude to the Government to change the constitution. It raised strong objections to the way in which the chairman and the members of the Boundaries Commission, Public Service Commission, and the Judicial and Legal Service Commission were to be appointed by the Governor-General on the advice of the Prime Minister. The D.L.P. Executive observed, 'Generally we find that the powers of the Prime Minister are so extensive that the country would under this constitution be virtually governed by the Prime Minister alone.'[3]

The D.L.P. instead demanded that the Leader of the Opposition and the Director of Prosecutions, on the pattern of the Jamaican constitution, should be given some share in the executive powers of the state. It suggested that the constitution should provide that in making all major appointments the Prime Minister should consult with the Leader of the Opposition. For the supervision of election arrangements and conduct of impartial elections, the D.L.P. suggested the creation of an independent Election Commission, on the pattern existing in India. At the same time it demanded

[1] *The Statesman* (23 February 1962), p. 1.
[2] *Trinidad Guardian* (13 April 1962).   [3] Ibid.

that voting machines should be abandoned in favour of paper ballots. It also recommended some important modifications in the provisions concerning fundamental rights and demanded that a provision should be made for a guarantee of the writ of habeas corpus on the British pattern.[1]

The D.L.P. placed special emphasis on the modification of the powers of the Prime Minister and the Cabinet. It advocated greater rigidity in the procedure for amending the constitution, so that no party in power could change it arbitrarily. The D.L.P. looked to the constitutions of Jamaica and Kenya as models for the constitution of Trinidad and Tobago.[2] Prime Minister Williams justified the position and powers of the Prime Minister and the Cabinet on the basis of the constitutions of Nigeria and Sierra Leone.[3] The D.L.P. criticisms were quite constructive and suggested that the D.L.P. was eager to place legitimate checks on the powers of the Prime Minister. Believing that Williams and many of his associates were great admirers of Ghana's former dictator Kwame Nkrumah, the D.L.P. leaders felt justified in pleading for restrictions on the powers of a Prime Minister in order to arrest any possibility of the rise of dictatorship. The D.L.P. leadership also charged that the draft constitution was not a bipartisan product, as East Indian leaders were not consulted.

Williams dismissed the D.L.P. charge as absurd and argued that it was the duty of the Government to present something tangible to the people for their comments and suggestions. The D.L.P. responded that the formation of a constitution was a national issue and the Opposition, representing about 40 per cent of the population, should have been consulted while the fundamentals of the constitution were being laid and not when the Government had already made up its mind and presented the Opposition with a finished draft for its comments. In view of the racial tension existing in the society, the unilateral formulation of the constitutional draft by the party in power was bound to create misapprehensions in the minds of the leaders of the minority ethnic group. Perhaps to meet this criticism the Government finally created a bipartisan select committee of the members of the House

[1] *Trinidad Guardian* (13 April 1962).

[2] *The Statesman* (6 April 1962), pp. 1–2.

[3] 'Report by the Premier on the Draft Independence Constitution' (mimeographed radio broadcast, 8 April 1962), p. 10.

of Representatives to discuss the draft. All the members of the D.L.P. except Jamadar, Ramdeen, and S. N. Capildeo, were made members of the committee.[1]

The Prime Minister also called a national conference of all the individuals and organizations[2] who had submitted comments and memoranda on the draft for a final round of discussions. The D.L.P. delegation, headed by Dr. Capildeo, decided to participate. The conference was held from 25 April to 27 April, and it was attended by two hundred citizens representing different interests and organizations. Prime Minister Williams presided. Every speaker was given five minutes, and each organization was represented by one speaker.[3] The D.L.P. clashed with the Government from the start. It objected to the procedure of the conference being dictated by the Government. Rather, the conference should appoint a steering committee from the assembly which should report back to the House within fifteen minutes with the rules of procedure. The Government rejected the suggestion.[4] There were certain other fundamental differences between the position of the D.L.P. and that of the P.N.M. Government. The D.L.P. objected to the strict control of the agenda by the Government. It charged that the Government wanted to confine discussion to the draft of the constitution as prepared by the Government. It asserted that the Government had already made up its mind on the fundamentals of the constitution and wanted to use this conference as a forum for its propaganda instead of discussing the fundamental issues. The D.L.P. wanted to raise questions concerning the future foreign policy of the country, the republican character of the Government, the position of fundamental rights in the constitution, and other matters. The D.L.P. also objected to the exclusion of the Press and the public from the conference and the fact that the conference hall was heavily guarded by the police.[5]

The objections were overruled and the Prime Minister 'invited

---

[1] *Trinidad Guardian* (17 April 1962).

[2] It was announced that the Government received 432 pages of comments from 84 organizations and 52 memoranda from individuals signed by 723 persons. *Trinidad Guardian* (9 April 1962).

[3] Ibid. (27 April 1962).

[4] *Verbatim Notes of Meeting on Draft Constitution Held at Queen's Hall* (Port of Spain, 1962, publisher missing), p. 12.

[5] *The Statesman* (27 April 1962), p. 1.

those who did not want to follow the procedure to get out, to take their exit from the Queen's Hall'.[1] The D.L.P. called the conference a fraud and walked out, followed by the delegations of the Indian Association, headed by H. P. Singh, and the County Council Association, headed by Ram Persad Bholai and M. G. Singh, all East Indians.[2]

Even the *Trinidad Guardian* (which by this time had become distinctly pro-P.N.M. due to its change of ownership from local hands to a Canadian firm) conceded that there were shortcomings in the procedure and said, 'The Government could have been more flexible in its handling of the arrangements.'[3]

The P.N.M. Government and the D.L.P. failed to reach any agreement even in the Select Committee of the Parliament. Peter Farquhar, speaking before the House, said that he was afraid that the Government had not even looked into the memorandum submitted by the Opposition.

Tajmool Hosein, considered to be the outstanding lawyer member of the D.L.P., put the case of the D.L.P. on the draft constitution before the House. He demanded that the Opposition be given equal seats with the party in power on the Boundaries Commission, and attacked the position and role of a nominated Senate in the new constitutional structure. He said it could have some independence only if the seats in the Senate were divided on party lines. He stated that the D.L.P. was opposed to the two-third majority provision for amending the constitution, and suggested that it should be increased to a three-fourth majority. In cases involving amendment of constitutional provisions concerning fundamental rights, he proposed the institution of a referendum. He also criticized the provisions concerning the declaration of an emergency. The draft should be changed so as to make the declaration of an emergency a little more difficult.

The Opposition also sought to increase the discretionary powers of the Governor-General. In view of the unequal ethnic composition of the population of the island, the Opposition expected greater impartiality from a non-elected official than from the elected officials. Tajmool Hosein declared that the Select Committee 'achieved very little by way of narrowing down the differences which existed between them in these fundamental points'.[4]

---

[1] *The Statesman* (27 April 1962).   [2] *Trinidad Guardian* (26 April 1962).
[3] Ibid. (27 April 1962).   [4] Ibid. (12 May 1962).

The Minority Report submitted by the D.L.P. also declared that the area of disagreement between the Government and the Opposition remained substantially the same.[1]

A. S. Sinanan, who was acting as Leader of the Opposition in the absence of Capildeo, also expressed his general dissatisfaction with the Government's handling of the whole issue of constitution-making. He said that from the very beginning the cart was put before the horse; without consultation with the Opposition, the constitution was prepared and put before them. He asserted: 'The allegations had been made against the Government that it was merely a substitute for the imperialist power, that it was taking the place of the British Government. He could be a hypocrite if he did not state quite candidly that there was some evidence to support that allegation.'

He declared that the country was ridden with 'fear, mistrust and suspicion'[2] and urged the Government to tackle the racial problem as being the most urgent problem. At the same time, he repeated the D.L.P. demand for elections with the use of the ballot box before independence was achieved. However, the suggestions put up by the Opposition were rejected and the Government motion for the adoption of the draft of the constitution was passed by a 16 to 9 vote.[3]

The next stage in the struggle over the independence constitution was the Independence Conference held at Marlborough House in London, from 28 May to 8 June 1962. The D.L.P. delegation was led by Dr. R. N. Capildeo. Ashford Sinanan and Tajmool Hosein were the other members and L. F. Seukeran, Peter Farquhar, and Stephen C. Maharaj were advisers.[4]

Two separate delegations, one from the Indian Association and another from the *Maha Sabha*, also went to London to protest against the independence constitution.

In London the D.L.P. delegation increased the number of its demands. It demanded now a moratorium on independence for Trinidad and Tobago for a period of five years, proportionate representation for East Indians in the police force, a constitutional

---

[1] Trinidad and Tobago. *Report from the Joint Select Committee to Consider Proposals for an Independence Constitution for Trinidad and Tobago* (Port of Spain, Government Printing Office, 1962), Appendix III.

[2] *Trinidad Guardian* (12 May 1962).

[3] Ibid.   [4] Ibid. (15 May 1962).

provision for consultation between the Prime Minister and the Leader of the Opposition on major appointments and on all issues of national importance, a larger share for the D.L.P. in the appointment of Senate members, and a provision for a two-third majority for adopting any legislative measure in the Senate.[1]

Dr. Capildeo declared that the existing police force was predominantly Negro, and was therefore one-sided and partisan. Proportionate recruitment of East Indians was essential in order to avoid discrimination against Indians.[2]

At this stage the Indian Association, which represented an influential section of the East Indian community, declared that if adequate safeguards were not provided for East Indians, and if there was no provision for proportional representation and parity between East Indians and Negroes in the civil services, police force, and the Cabinet, then, the country should be partitioned into Negro and East Indian states.[3] The D.L.P. leadership hesitated to support publicly these demands since it claimed to be a multiracial party.

Many of the demands of the D.L.P. such as pre-independence election, removal of the voting machines, and constitutional provision for consultation between the Prime Minister and the Leader of the Opposition, were rejected outright not only by the P.N.M. Government but even by the Colonial Office.[4] The P.N.M. held that there could not be any government by the Opposition, and therefore there could be no explicit constitutional provision for consultations between the Prime Minister and the Leader of the Opposition. However, the P.N.M. was not opposed to the development of this as a conventional practice.[5]

When the Conference was almost deadlocked, Dr. Williams, during the Conference break, went to Dr. Capildeo and told him that he would make a statement which he hoped would remove their misapprehensions and doubts. The two leaders finally reached an understanding, and Williams went back and assured the Conference that concerted efforts would be made to remove racial tension and declared that the Government would hold

---

[1] *Trinidad Guardian* (5 and 6 June 1962).   [2] Ibid.

[3] Singh, *Hour of Decision*, pp. 9–10, and also *Memorandum of the East Indian Association*, pp. 11–12.

[4] *Trinidad Guardian* (6 June 1962).

[5] *The Nation* (Trinidad, 15 June 1962).

bipartisan discussions on affairs of national importance. A national integration committee would also be formed to promote national solidarity. Dr. Capildeo, to the surprise of the Secretary of State for the Colonies, accepted the statement made by Williams and withdrew his opposition to the date of independence,[1] which was fixed for 31 August.

Although the gains of the D.L.P. from the London Conference were not spectacular, it would be wrong to say, as the political correspondent of *Trinidad Guardian* put it, that the Opposition virtually capitulated as most of their demands were either withdrawn or rejected.[2] The East Indian leadership of the D.L.P. certainly did not get everything which it demanded; still it did obtain certain important concessions. The D.L.P. was interested in increasing the rigidity of many of the important provisions of the constitution called 'entrenched provisions': ordinary entrenched provisions, and specifically entrenched provisions. Under the agreement made at the London Conference, their number was considerably increased. Ordinary entrenched provisions included fundamental rights and freedom, abrogation of Parliament, appointments, dismissals, and control of judicial officials. Their amendment required a two-third majority vote in both the House of Representatives and the Senate.

Specifically entrenched provisions related to the office of the Governor-General, the composition of the Senate and the House of Representatives, the Boundaries Commission, general election, appeal to Her Majesty's Privy Council, universal suffrage, and the Election Commission.[3] They could be amended with a three-fourth majority vote in the House of Representatives and a two-third majority in the Senate. The composition of the Senate was also changed; under the new arrangements, the Opposition could nominate four members instead of two, the Government was given thirteen members to nominate, and seven members were to be independents.[4]

On the issue of consultations between the Prime Minister and the Leader of the Opposition, the Report of the London Conference incorporated the following paragraph:

The Conference agreed that it was a matter of great importance to honour the convention whereby the Prime Minister consults the

---

[1] *The Nation* (Trinidad, 19 July 1962). [2] *Trinidad Guardian* (9 June 1962).
[3] Ibid. (23 June 1962). [4] Ibid. (11 June 1962).

Leader of the Opposition on all appropriate occasions, in particular on all matters of national concern, including appointments to suitable offices of a national character—for example the chairmanship of the Election and Boundaries Commissions.[1]

Thus the D.L.P. gained some important concessions. It seems that there was a realization both in P.N.M. and D.L.P. circles that if some type of workable compromise was not achieved, the result might be widespread bloodshed and violence. Some of the D.L.P. leaders praised Dr. Capildeo and said that by agreeing to these compromise arrangements he had saved the country from racial war. The D.L.P. leadership also recognized that they had no other alternative. They said that the attitude of the British Government was basically hostile towards the people of Indian origin whom it did not want to see in power. The British Government was eager to please the Negro middle class through which it was hoped to retain control over the economy of the island. Also the D.L.P. did not push the system of proportional representation for Trinidad because it could have weakened the position of Jagan in British Guiana.

Under these conditions, the D.L.P. asserted that the main issue was to save the lives and limbs of the Indian community in Trinidad. They said that 90 per cent of the police were Negroes and East Indian masses were unarmed. Had violence erupted in the island, it was the Indian community which would have suffered heavily both in life and property.

After his return from London, Capildeo said that, 'At the start of the London Independence Conference, the decision confronting the leaders of the D.L.P. was whether they should plunge the country into chaos with civil commotions and strife or try to explore whatever reasonable avenue may be presented as the Conference developed.'[2] He said that the D.L.P. could have achieved more, but it had to struggle against the history of its past leadership and its internal conflicts.

However, the D.L.P. had failed to get any special safeguard or any substantial concessions in the form of proportionate representation for the minority ethnic group which it claimed to represent.

After the London Conference, both parties pledged to improve the relations between the two ethnic groups. The East Indian

---

[1] Spackman, op. cit., p. 310.   [2] *Trinidad Guardian* (20 August 1962).

leadership declared that the D.L.P. along with the P.N.M. Government, would make a concerted effort to wipe out racialism from the island. The P.N.M. also extended the hand of friendship to the D.L.P. Consultations between the leaders of the two parties increased. But on the basis of the public pronouncements of the leaders, it would be an oversimplification to conclude that a genuine change of heart had taken place on both sides. The complexity of the situation hardly warranted such a conclusion.

Efforts Towards Ideological Orientation

On 31 August 1962, Trinidad and Tobago became independent. The racial tension subsided, and at least on the surface race relations assumed a normal form. There was an acute sense of frustration among East Indian leaders and the masses born out of political defeat. Until this time the East Indian leadership had put up a united front against what was termed as an effort to impose Negro rule over East Indians. Now that the majority ethnic group had become the ruling *élite*, the unity within the D.L.P. leadership started to decline. The first to leave the political scene was no less than the D.L.P. leader. Dr. Capildeo, failing in his bid to capture political power and faced with certain financial difficulties[1] in the beginning of 1963, accepted a teaching position at the University of London. But to everybody's surprise, he resigned neither the leadership of the Opposition nor the leadership of his party, but decided to run the affairs of the party from London. It was only during the recess periods, when the University was closed, that he would pay visits to Trinidad to look after his party and to attend the sessions of Parliament as Leader of the Opposition. This caused considerable discontent in the top stratum of the D.L.P. Many senior party leaders started questioning the propriety of holding two positions simultaneously and collecting the salary of Leader of the Opposition without performing the job.[2] He was, however, granted a special leave of absence by the Speaker, and was also permitted to hold his seat

[1] Mr. Stephen C. Maharaj, one time Deputy Leader of the D.L.P., wrote that Dr. Capildeo was paid a salary of TT$1,000 per month as head of the D.L.P. But once he was elected to the House in 1961 the thousand dollars stopped and he received only TT$600 as Leader of the official Opposition. Stephen C. Maharaj, 'Trinidad and Tobago Politics 1950–1965', p. 6.

[2] *Daily Mirror* (3 January 1964).

in the House of Representatives even while being absent from the House for more than six months.

After independence, Dr. Capildeo decided to give his party some kind of ideological orientation. We have seen that the D.L.P. did not have any clear set of policies and programmes when it entered the electoral fight in 1961. In March 1963, Capildeo gave some indication of changing the policy and programme of his party and adopting 'democratic socialism' as its official creed in order to broaden the base of the D.L.P. and to move it away from its ethnic-oriented outlook. He asserted that democratic socialism was the only policy which could save the country from communism and racialism.

There is no doubt that Capildeo was forcing a new creed on the party which was originally founded on an anti-socialist programme. He was trying to arm his party with an alternate programme, mindful of the fact that the D.L.P., as an alternate government party, should offer something concrete and distinctive. This put the non-East Indian conservative element on the alert. This section of the party consisted mainly of the businessmen and merchants of Port of Spain who dominated the party Executive and had earlier rallied round the D.L.P. in fear of the P.N.M. radicalism.

Dr. Capildeo's long absence from the island and his radical pronouncements now finally forced the party Executive to ask him either to stay in Trinidad or to quit the leadership of the party.

Until this time the party did not have a constitution of its own; it had only an appointed Executive rather than an elected one. The only elected official was Capildeo, who was nominated and elected leader at the party convention of 1960. Capildeo, therefore, paid little attention to the Executive. When he visited Trinidad during the Christmas recess of 1963, he did not call a meeting of the party Executive. Instead, he called a meeting of the D.L.P. parliamentarians where, on his suggestion, Stephen C. Maharaj was elected Leader of the Opposition.[1] Thus he gave up his position of Leader of the Opposition but retained the leadership of his party, a key position in the politics of East Indians in Trinidad.

Although all sections of the party were not satisfied with his solution, Capildeo could claim it as a compromise solution

[1] *Daily Mirror* (31 December 1963).

whereby he could answer the critics of his absentee leadership in the House while at the same time keep his hold on the party organization. Dr. Capildeo also announced that he would call the party convention in July 1964, to adopt the new policy of democratic socialism and frame a new constitution. He said that the convention would provide an opportunity for all those who wanted the party leadership to put up their claims, which would of course remove a grave source of dissension.

Capildeo told me that he nominated Stephen Maharaj as his successor for two reasons: first, that he was the least controversial among the D.L.P. parliamentarians and, secondly, Capildeo thought he would not betray him by trying to take over the leadership of the party. Stephen C. Maharaj, a druggist-chemist from Princes' Town of South Trinidad, is known for his personal integrity, but he did not have the formal education or experience to keep the D.L.P. parliamentarians under control. From the beginning he had to face, if not open hostility, thinly disguised unfriendliness and indifference from many of his colleagues. The senior members of the party, like Ashford Sinanan, S. N. Capildeo, and L. F. Seukeran showed scant respect for the new Leader of the Opposition.

Decline of Cohesion within the D.L.P.

With the selection of Stephen Maharaj as the acting leader, the difficulties of the D.L.P. were not over. The Executive of the party was not satisfied with this arrangement, and after Dr. Capildeo's departure from the political scene of Trinidad, it demanded his resignation and pressed Stephen Maharaj to accept the leadership of the party both in and outside the House. It seems that Stephen Maharaj was willing to accept but was reluctant to betray Capildeo. Therefore, he phoned him in London. Capildeo dismissed the entire Executive and threatened Maharaj that he would not remain leader of the party for two days. Stephen Maharaj decided to side with his leader rather than with the Executive. No member of the Executive had a mass following among the East Indians and therefore none could challenge Dr. Capildeo's action. They accepted their dismissal.

When Capildeo was asked whether he was not overstepping his constitutional powers, he was reported to have replied, 'Certainly not. I am the leader of the D.L.P. and every member of the

Executive is a nominated and not an elected member. Either they accept my instructions or the Democratic Labour Party will be finished.'[1]

With the dismissal of the Executive, the D.L.P. lost not only the main source of its financial support, but also whatever non-East Indian following it had enjoyed so far. The majority of the members of the Executive were from the conservative section of the business community, and no doubt they resented the imposition of the new ideology of democratic socialism on the party, but they also equally resented the prolonged absence of Capildeo from the island.

Capildeo and his faction, on the other hand, made no effort to win the support of other sections of non-East Indians to offset the loss caused by the dismissal of the Executive. The dismissal set the disintegration of the party in motion. The first group of resignations included the secretary of the party and some of the former D.L.P. candidates for House seats. Much more serious and damaging were the resignations of the three D.L.P. Members of the House of Representatives: on 13 January 1964, M. A. Forrester (chairman of the D.L.P.), Peter Farquhar, and Tajmool Hosein resigned from the party on account of the continuous absence of Dr. Capildeo from the island. They found it difficult to associate with a party whose leader was sitting four thousand miles away from the actual political arena. There was also a realization among the dissidents, as Farquhar told me in an interview, that after the election of 1961 Capildeo had drawn the conclusion that it was impossible for the D.L.P. with East Indian leadership to win elections and capture power. Therefore he changed his political strategy. He stopped opposing the Government and his object became to get concessions for the leadership or for the members of the East Indian community. The long leave of absence granted to him was cited as an example of such concessions, which, according to Farquhar, blunted the criticism of the Opposition and placed limitations on its freedom. Many D.L.P. Members went abroad on behalf of the P.N.M. Government; even Dr. Capildeo toured Israel on behalf of the Prime Minister. Thus, according to this section, the D.L.P. had given up its controlling goal of seeking power, and it was fruitless to be associated with it if one desired political power. Peter Farquhar and his associates also differed

---

[1] *Trinidad Guardian* (4 January 1964).

with Dr. Capildeo on his ideology of democratic socialism. They believed in a pragmatic rather than an ideologically-oriented party.

Peter Farquhar and other dissident former D.L.P. Members finally founded the Liberal party of Trinidad and Tobago in March 1964. Thus the split within the D.L.P. leadership led to the formation of the third party of the island. D.L.P. Members in the House of Representatives were reduced from ten to seven. Both Negro M.P.s elected on the D.L.P. ticket walked out of the party; the East Indian *élite* had failed to retain the non-East Indian element.

Supporters of Dr. Capildeo held that Farquhar and Forrester had resigned because it was difficult for Negro intellectuals to work under East Indian leadership. They could not tolerate an East Indian leader even though both of them were elected from East Indian majority areas. Dr. Capildeo held that the function of the Opposition in Trinidad was not the same as that of the Opposition in the British Parliament. In a society like Trinidad where there was no homogeneity and where the two parties derived their support from two different ethnic groups, the basic conditions for the working of parliamentary government were absent. How then could the D.L.P. perform like the Opposition in the House of Commons? The performance of the functions of an official opposition in Trinidad was a highly difficult goal to achieve. Dr. Capildeo held that it was in order to achieve this goal that he insisted on the adoption of an alternate ideology. Therefore, in spite of the defections, he and his associates went ahead with the re-organization of the party on the basis of his previous declarations.

The long-promised D.L.P. convention was finally held on 12 and 13 July in the Naparima Bowl of San Fernando, and was distinctly pro-Dr. Capildeo. He presented his programme of democratic socialism with a declaration that if it was rejected, they would have to find somebody else to lead the party. He said that the D.L.P. contested the 1961 election without a policy or programme. He held that the only thing D.L.P. Members had in common was that: 'We are against the People's National Movement.'[1] Dr. Capildeo added that what took place in 1961 was a racial election and something had to be done to remove racialism

[1] Ibid. (13 July 1964).

from the island, 'otherwise sooner or later the position which exists in British Guiana would have been attained here'.[1] Obviously, an effort was being made by Capildeo to modify the purely East Indian character of the D.L.P. and adjust its strategy to the changed conditions since independence.

Defining his concept of democratic socialism, he declared, 'The central idea of democratic socialism is the brotherhood of man and its purpose is to make this a reality everywhere. Accordingly it rejects discrimination on the grounds of race, colour or creed, and holds that men should accord to one another equal consideration and status in recognition of the fundamental dignity of man.'[2] He rejected capitalism because capitalism was based upon the creed of acquisitiveness; whereas democratic socialism aimed to build a society on the ideals of fellowship, co-operation, and service. Under the new programme, he promised, the D.L.P. would place emphasis on a co-operative movement rather than on state ownership of property. Due to a dearth of trained technicians, he said, nationalization of such basic industries as oil and sugar was out of the question. He advocated the adoption of a labour code providing for the regulation of wages, equal rewards, employment insurance, and social insurance for the families. He also advocated freedom of organization for workers and said that the D.L.P. would actively encourage the trade union movement. In many of his earlier articles in *The Statesman*, the D.L.P. organ, he had advocated increased spending on public education and welfare activities and had promised elimination of unemployment from the island. He also advocated the introduction of a co-operative movement in agriculture and democracy in industries.[3]

T. Bleasdell, the public relations officer of the party, said, 'When we of the D.L.P. speak of Democratic Socialism, we mean the socialism as enunciated by the British Labour Party, with modifications of course to suit our own local conditions.'[4]

With the adoption of his programme by the party convention, Dr. Capildeo declared that the D.L.P. now possessed an ideology of which anyone would be proud. It is significant, however, that the D.L.P. leadership did not have any trade union experience.

[1] *Trinidad Guardian* (13 July 1964).   [2] Ibid.
[3] *The Statesman* (issues of 7, 14, 21, 28 February, 3 and 17 April 1964, contain detailed articles on the new party programme).
[4] Ibid. (21 February 1964).

None of the top parliamentarians of the D.L.P. were ever actively associated with the socialist movement or had the opportunity of leading a left-wing labour organization. None of them was ever a socialist intellectual like Nehru or J. P. Narayan of India. Dr. Capildeo himself had no association with the labour movement either in England or in Trinidad. He also had no intellectual background in socialism. Thus the D.L.P. leadership lacked all those attributes which are normally associated with the colonial socialists. The bulk of the D.L.P. supporters who overwhelmingly voted for the party's candidates were motivated by common ethnicity rather than by ideology. Any superimposition of a socialist ideology on such a party could not change its basic character. Although this ideological change might not have been very deep, the traditionalist element of the East Indians, led by B. S. Maraj, strongly denounced the new creed and demanded the resignation of the ten D.L.P. parliamentarians and its leadership.

The new ideology which was claimed to be an alternative to the policies and programme of the P.N.M. was not in essence different. Everything stated in the new D.L.P. programme could also be found in one form or the other in the P.N.M.'s election platform. Thus, even after adopting the new ideology, the D.L.P. failed to present any meaningful alternative to the P.N.M.

In order to capture power, political parties must organize an effective machinery which constantly remains in touch with the electorate and makes efforts to win over new adherents. Until this time, the D.L.P. had not had any party constitution. However, in 1964, its leadership tightened the formal structural organization, adopting a new constitution. It created an elaborate mass party structure headed by a Leader (called 'Political Leader') assisted by a Deputy Leader. It also provided for a National Council, a party convention, a Central Executive, a Shadow Cabinet, a number of subcommittees and divisional and constituency committees. For running the affairs of the parliamentary wing of the party, it provided a Parliamentary Committee headed by the Political Leader himself.[1] Even the organizational structure of the D.L.P. was modelled on the party constitution of the P.N.M. Much of this party structure, however, exists only on paper. Many of the institutions provided in the constitution either do not exist at all

[1] 'The Democratic Labour Party: Constitution and Rules' (Mimeographed, Port of Spain, D.L.P. Office, 1964).

or, if they exist, do not perform the functions assigned to them. The knowledgeable sources in the party told us that the party Executive, the main functioning organ of the D.L.P., was unable to exercise any real control over the D.L.P. parliamentarians, who mainly acted independently. In organizational matters, it seems that the real power rests with the Political Leader and the party Executive. It is the Political Leader and the party Executive who rule who should attend the party convention, thus deciding the composition of the party convention and the National Council. Because of his mass popularity among East Indians, the Political Leader of the D.L.P. wields far more power than any other member or even group of members of the Executive.

The party headquarters was unable to give us any exact figure of the local party units. A few existed in East Indian majority areas but how well they worked under the control of the central party organization, it was difficult to say. In a later internal party conflict, some of the constituency organizations switched their support from one faction to another. Up to then, they had played no role in the selection of the D.L.P. candidates for Parliament. In 1965, Dr. Capildeo declared that the constituency organizations would sponsor the candidates for the election. However, as compared with the constituency organizations of the P.N.M. the D.L.P. party units are much less in number, and they also do not seem very active.

In spite of its efforts to present an organization on the basis of a formal constitution, the D.L.P. leadership has not been able to build an efficient structural machinery capable of mobilizing the electorate through active propaganda and constant communications with the masses.

Failure to Develop a Polyethnic Following

Tightening of the structural organization and adoption of democratic socialism as the party's official ideology could not turn the D.L.P. into a broad-based, multiracial mass party. Stephen Maharaj found it difficult to hold the party together and run it on the basis of its officially accepted ideology. He was in no position to enforce discipline among his parliamentary colleagues. The new party policy was highly distasteful to L. F. Seukeran and Ashford Sinanan, and they more or less followed independent policies. Both of them are also known to have a relationship with the island's sugar manufacturers. Maharaj was getting lukewarm support from S. N. Capildeo and Vernon Jamadar. Many of the officials and members of the party Executive frankly conceded that they had little understanding of the new party ideology and only Dr. Capildeo knew what he meant by democratic socialism.

The D.L.P. leadership, by adopting the ideology of democratic socialism, asserted that the party would move away from its old ethnic orientation. However, it soon faced a test which proved that there was no genuine change in the party's basic orientation. In 1965 the D.L.P. leadership had an opportunity to make the D.L.P. a genuine multiracial party based on secular-rational political ideology. The P.N.M. had been steadily losing ground among the Negro industrial workers since the general election of 1961. Leadership of many important trade unions—especially that of the oilfield workers, one of the island's most powerful labour unions—became outspoken in its criticism of the policies of the P.N.M. Government. Since the two major industries of the country—oil and sugar—were controlled by foreigners, the workers thought that the P.N.M. leadership had been bought by big business. In order to maintain industrial peace, the Government was following more and more anti-strike and pro-industry policies which led to the disenchantment of working-class Negroes with Dr. Williams' government.

Leadership of the oilfield workers passed into the hands of George Weekes, an anti-P.N.M. Negro trade union leader with strong political ambitions. In the sugar belt, Bhadase Sagan Maraj's leadership came to be challenged by a young East Indian leftist leader, Krishna Gowandan. Gowandan organized the Freedom Fighters among the sugar workers and challenged Maraj to face election in his All-Trinidad Sugar Estate and Factory Workers Union. (B. S. Maraj was never elected to the position of president general by the rank and file of the union.)

Fifteen thousand sugar workers went on strike in March 1965, which led to the closing down of five sugar factories, including Caroni Ltd., the island's biggest sugar manufacturers. This led to the declaration of an emergency by the Government in the sugar belt against the advice of Stephen C. Maharaj, the Leader of the Opposition. With the declaration of emergency the Government assumed virtually absolute power over citizens and their movements in the area.[1] Meetings and demonstrations were banned and the police were empowered to carry out searches without warrants for explosive materials and subversive literature.

This action of the Government brought out the Negro-dominated Trade Union Congress in support of the sugar workers. George Weekes, president of the T.U.C., and Eugene Joseph, its secretary general, both Negroes, successfully got a resolution passed by the Executive in support of the sugar workers asking for an end to the emergency condition in the sugar belt. Thus for the first time since the late 1930s, a coalition between Negro oilfield workers and East Indian sugar workers became feasible. This does not mean that the T.U.C. did not face opposition from other Negro-dominated trade unions. The Seaman's Union, one of the most powerful unions of the island, withdrew from the T.U.C. in opposition to its decision. But unmistakably a powerful section of the Negro trade union was working towards the formation of a close alliance with the East Indian sugar workers. From the standpoint of the island's politics, the situation was becoming fluid, and possibilities for new political alliances were developing. An imaginative and bold leadership would not have failed to make use of this opportunity.

The Negro-dominated trade unions were further alienated from the P.N.M. when on 12 March 1965, the Government introduced a bill in the House of Representatives prohibiting strikes in public services and imposing strong curbs on strikes and lock-outs in general in all industries. In accordance with the proposed Industrial Stabilization Bill, the strikes or lock-outs could take place only after the Minister of Labour had been given advance notice. The bill also provided for the establishment of an industrial court.

The D.L.P. leadership had now an opportunity to act as the champion of the working class. Also, it could, by its opposition to the bill, prove the genuineness of its adherence to the newly-adopted ideology of democratic socialism. However, in the absence of a dedicated leader and with no commitment to a secular-rational ideology, the D.L.P. leadership became deeply divided on the controversial bill. Maharaj, acting chief of the party, issued instructions to his colleagues asking them to vote against the bill, but two D.L.P. Members voted for it. Similarly,

[1] *Trinidad Guardian* (10 March 1965).

in the Senate, all the D.L.P. nominees, including Thomas Bleas-dell, the public relations officer of the party, and Mrs. Lucky Samaroo, the treasurer, voted for the bill in violation of the party chief's directives.[1] It may be noted that both Seukeran and Sinanan, the D.L.P. Members of the House, because of their relations with the sugar manufacturers, could less easily vote against the bill. Similarly, Mrs. Samaroo, an industrialist and cinema proprietor, wholeheartedly supported it. The bill would have passed without the D.L.P. assistance, but the majority of the D.L.P. parliamentarians went all out to second it.

Maharaj decided to take disciplinary action against the rebels and he took the case before the Central Executive of the party which referred it to the Disciplinary Committee. The rebels claimed that Maharaj had not given any directions at the meeting of the party caucus, but had given them a free-conscience vote. So, they voted as their consciences dictated.

Maharaj had some pro-labour leanings because of his past association with Butler. At this stage, he was much influenced by East Indian leftist friends like Dr. M. J. Dube and A. C. Rienzi. They encouraged him to broaden the base of the D.L.P. by bringing in the discontented Negro element. A. C. Rienzi is an old-guard politician who once was associated with Captain Cipriani and his Trinidad Labour Party. Subsequently he left politics and joined the government service; at the age of sixty he wanted to stage a comeback into politics. A highly polished and mild-mannered gentleman, he could have provided excellent modernizing and secular leadership for East Indians. However, like several other political East Indian leaders, he left politics for a civil service career. Now he thought that there existed an excellent opportunity for uniting the oilfield workers and sugar workers under the D.L.P. if certain important changes were brought about in the party.

Another highly significant development took place in the politics of Trinidad and Tobago. C. L. R. James, a former friend and adviser of Dr. Williams and ex-editor of the P.N.M. weekly, *The Nation*, returned to Trinidad after a two-year stay in England. The 64 years old James, a staunch Marxist and a great admirer of Lenin (although he rejects Stalinist communism) is regarded as one of the great West Indian intellectuals. Like Williams, James

[1] Ibid. (20 March 1965).

spent a number of years in the United States then went to England where he became a member of the British Labour Party and was associated with George Padmore, another Trinidadian Marxist, who later on became Kwame Nkrumah's adviser. James himself was once a great admirer of Nkrumah, but became disenchanted with him because of Nkrumah's abolition of the independence of the judiciary. In 1956, when Williams came to power in Trinidad, he invited James to help him in organizing the P.N.M. and running *The Nation*. In 1958, James came to Trinidad and became associated with the People's National Movement. In 1960, in disagreement with Williams, he resigned from the editorship of *The Nation* and went back to England. He came back to Trinidad in 1963 and at the request of many Negro leftist leaders decided to stay and go into politics.

Knowing that the D.L.P. had a strong East Indian mass base and had the potential of making a strong and powerful party, leftist leaders like James, Weekes (Negroes), Rienzi, and Jack Kelshal (a former adviser of Jagan) sought places in the D.L.P. and advised Maharaj to press the issue of violation of the party directions in the case of the Industrial Stabilization Bill and to throw out the conservative element. It can be argued that Maharaj, who was already alienated from many of his colleagues, was being manipulated by this group so that they might secure a place in the top leadership of a party of which none was even a member.

Soon the struggle for leadership developed into Maharaj versus the D.L.P. Executive, dominated by the middle-class East Indians. They became aware of Maharaj's move and the men behind it, closed ranks, and turned against him.

The Disciplinary Committee, headed by Vernon Jamadar, found the four senators and the two Members of the House of Representatives innocent and declared that no clear directions had been given to the party Members of the House on the Industrial Stabilization Bill, and therefore, no action could be taken against any of them. The findings of the Disciplinary Committee were accepted by the Executive by nine to seven votes.

Maharaj was reported to have tendered an oral resignation and walked out. Politics in Trinidad are not always run solely on an ideological basis; Rienzi and James were not only fighting for a political base but they were also interested in getting seats in the

Senate. The resignation of Maharaj would not have served their purpose. On the advice of his friends, Maharaj announced that he had not actually tendered his resignation and would do so only after the arrival of Capildeo.[1]

With this announcement a determined struggle to capture the D.L.P. began. By this time the D.L.P. leadership came to be divided into three distinct groups. The first one could be termed as left-oriented and pro-labour, led by S. C. Maharaj. It believed in broadening the base of the D.L.P. by forming an alliance with the Negro-dominated labour unions.

There was a centrist group led by Vernon Jamadar and supported by middle-class D.L.P. professionals. They opposed the Industrial Stabilization Bill and believed in a limited leftist orientation of the D.L.P., but were highly cautious in their approach to the discontented Negro element. They pointed out that the D.L.P. had been opposed by organized Negro labour on a racial basis in the 1961 election. Now when they were getting kicks from their own leadership, they were turning to the D.L.P. The centrists held that the leftist orientation of the D.L.P. should not result in the complete control of the party by outsiders. For them, Rienzi and James were both outsiders; they would not have opposed Rienzi's joining their ranks, but were highly suspicious of C. L. R. James. They believed that the East Indian leadership had to be very careful in pursuing its pro-labour policies, because they feared that in case of labour unrest, the Government would throw the entire blame on East Indians and declare an emergency in the East Indian majority areas as it had done in the sugar belt. They held that they would not let the East Indian masses be exploited by the Negro leftists.

There was the realization among the East Indian leaders that the Negro middle class was getting maximum benefits from the P.N.M. Government and that in order to keep its hold on political power, it could create racial tension and win elections on a racial basis. The Negro leftist leaders under such conditions would not be able to retain the support of the Negro masses for the D.L.P., the centrists argued, let them come to the D.L.P.; why should the D.L.P. go begging to them? Hence they rejected the move, whereby, they said, Maharaj was trying to put the D.L.P. at the disposal of the Negro radicals. This group represented, in fact, the

[1] *Sunday Mirror* (20 June 1965).

point of view of a majority of educated and enlightened East Indians. For them the first consideration is loyalty to their own in-group; ideological considerations come afterwards. There is a deep-rooted suspicion of outsiders—especially of the former supporters of the P.N.M.

The rightist group led by Ashford Sinanan and L. F. Seukaran was opposed to democratic socialism and believed that the adoption of such an ideology by the D.L.P. was its greatest blunder. Not only did they vote for the Industrial Stabilization Bill, but they actively supported the Government and its stand on the Act. They termed the opponents of the bill as subversive elements and communists.

The balancing factor was the centrist group and Maharaj, in his efforts to bring new elements such as the Negro trade union leaders into the party, was banking on its support. But the centrist group aligned itself with the conservatives and thus was successful in isolating Maharaj in his efforts to take action against the party rebels.

Although rejected by the Executive, Maharaj still claimed to be the chief of the party and the Leader of the Opposition in the House. Capildeo was maintaining an ambiguous stand on the issue of disciplinary action against the party rebels. Both groups claimed to have his support. He declared his opposition to the Industrial Stabilization Act but remained non-committal about enforcing discipline among his fellow party men.

Under the constitution of Trinidad the Leader of the Opposition could nominate and recall the four senators nominated to the Senate. In order to seat his friends, C. L. R. James and A. C. Rienzi, in the Senate, Maharaj decided to exercise his constitutional power and recommended to the Governor-General the removal of four D.L.P. senators. In their places he recommended the nomination of only three men: James, Rienzi, and Clive Phil. As noted, Rienzi and James were not even members of the D.L.P.

The Governor-General, Sir Soloman Hochey, instead of complying with Maharaj's request, dismissed him as Leader of the Opposition. At the time Hochey had received these recommendations from Maharaj, he had also received a letter from the four D.L.P. parliamentarians stating that they no longer recognized Maharaj as their leader. The Executive then appointed S. N.

Capildeo as the acting Leader of the Opposition, subject to the subsequent approval of the D.L.P. parliamentarians in the House.[1]

How different factions, organized around personalities, conspired and planned their strategies against each other is apparent from the incidents reported within the party. Ashford Sinanan, a master strategist whose brother, Dr. A. Sinanan, was one of the senators to be dismissed, anticipated Maharaj's action. He prepared and got endorsed a letter from his party colleagues to the Governor-General, expressing their lack of confidence in Maharaj before the leader's departure for England to report to Dr. Capildeo in May 1965. He had instructed his party to send the letter to the Governor-General as soon as they learned of Maharaj's attempt to unseat the senators. Thus, long before Maharaj took action, the D.L.P. parliamentarians had agreed among themselves to get him dismissed as the Leader of the Opposition. This pact was kept confidential, and Maharaj knew nothing about it. After the dismissal of Maharaj, the Executive Committee met in an emergency session until he walked into the meeting and adjourned it. But as soon as Maharaj left the place, the meeting was reconvened under the chairmanship of Alloy Lecquany, the party secretary, and it 'accepted' the verbal resignation of Maharaj from the D.L.P. Maharaj, however, continued to assert that he was still a member and the leader of the D.L.P., and that the meeting of the Committee was unconstitutional.

During the struggle, Maharaj asserted, time and time again, that he had the backing of Capildeo and was constantly in touch with him. Dr. Capildeo, the absentee party chief, on the other hand, was playing an unclear role. In a statement from his London office, he said that while he regretted Maharaj's resignation and pledged that he would do his best to bring him back into the D.L.P., he had always worked for the conditions in which everybody in the party could speak and act freely.[2] Evidently Capildeo was trying to please both factions by making such vague and non-commital statements.

With its commitment to democratic socialism, the leftist faction believed that Capildeo would support it in its drive against the rebels. But Capildeo failed to support Maharaj and rejected outright any alliance with the Negro radicals. When he returned to

[1] *Trinidad Guardian* (24 June 1965).   [2] *Daily Mirror* (19 June 1965).

Trinidad in July, he denounced the Industrial Stabilization Act and pledged to fight against it. He also expressed his delight at the way in which, for the first time, a discussion was taking place in the country on issues and not on personalities. But within two days of his arrival he accused his brother, S. N. Capildeo, of being the main source of trouble in the D.L.P. He publicly charged that his brother had sent a hired killer after him. In some circles it was thought that he attempted to create a sensation and tried to hide his own weakness under the cover of family feuds. At the same time he paid high tribute to the Government and pointed out that 'the People don't understand how much has been gained in this country. They do not seem to understand the change that has taken place from one regime (colonialism) to another (independence).'[1] He said that people could walk the streets in peace. There is still an independent judiciary and 'we still have law and order'. He remarked, 'The Government must be congratulated on this. It has not been an easy job for them.'[2] Thus, publicly, Dr. Capildeo, the Leader of the Opposition, was all praise for the Government, though privately he bitterly criticized it as being inimical to the interests of East Indians.

In a private meeting with Stephen Maharaj and his supporters, Dr. Capildeo pledged to fight in his party against the Industrial Stabilization Act and assured Jack Kelshell, James, Rienzi, and Maharaj that he would ask six of his party men who had voted for the I.S.A. to publish an immediate retraction of their stand and to undertake to support the D.L.P. in its fight against the Act. He found it inadvisable to dismiss them because this would have resulted in the loss of his leadership of the Opposition.[3]

But the next day he publicly accused James, Maharaj, and Rienzi of hatching a plot and attempting to make a deal with him by offering him the prime ministership of the country. This was no crime, since by virtue of his leadership of the party, he would have become Prime Minister had it won the election. He seems to have been deliberately misrepresenting the whole issue. Actually, as seen above, Maharaj and his associates were thinking of making a broad-based alliance with Negro labour to strengthen the D.L.P. in order to capture political power, but Capildeo and his associates did not seem to be willing to change the ethnic-oriented character

[1] *Trinidad Guardian* (30 July 1965).   [2] Ibid.
[3] Ibid. (23 August 1965).

of the D.L.P. He slammed the door of the D.L.P. in the face of C. L. R. James by declaring that there was no room in his party for men like him, who, in his opinion, was internationally known as an extremist. In spite of his declared creed of democratic socialism, Dr. Capildeo basically stood close to the centrist group which, guided by East Indian middle-class instinct, considered Negro radicals as outsiders. He agreed with them that East Indians and the D.L.P. should not become tools in their hands.

The whole socio-economic background of the East Indian leaders makes them highly ethnic-oriented and precludes any possibility of the formation of a bold and imaginative alliance with the Negro working classes. Confident of the ethnic solidarity of their own followers and hoping to get the East Indian block vote, the D.L.P. leadership believed that the formation of any party based upon an alliance with Negro leaders would hurt the P.N.M. and not the D.L.P. Ultimately such a party would be looked upon by East Indian masses as a Negro party. Therefore, Dr. Capildeo and his top D.L.P. colleagues were not worried when Maharaj, C. L. R. James, and their Negro labour friends founded a party of their own—the Workers and Farmers Party.

The first post-independence election in Trinidad was held in November 1966. The number of seats was increased from 24 to 36. Four political parties—the P.N.M., the D.L.P., the Liberals, and the W.F.P.—and a number of independents contested the election. All the parties put up multiracial slates; the Liberals and the W.F.P. claimed to be non-racial parties and accused the P.N.M. and the D.L.P. of practicing racialism. The election results once against confirmed the supreme importance of ethnicity in determining the voting behaviour of the masses. The Liberal party and the W.F.P., which put up experienced East Indian parliamentarians, such as S. N. Capildeo and S. C. Maharaj, and such Negro leaders as Peter Farquhar and C. L. R. James, were unable to capture a single seat. The P.N.M. won 24 seats in Negro majority areas. The East Indian leaders, such as Bhadase and Seukeran, who sought election to the legislature from the electoral districts with East Indian majorities, were badly beaten by the East Indian D.L.P. candidates.

Most of the victorious D.L.P. candidates had little political experience, all of them were young—either in their late thirties or forties—without any independent political base of their own. A

look at the list of candidates shows that Dr. Capildeo was careful to select candidates who could not challenge his leadership,
if he decided to leave the island. 'Such stalwarts of the D.L.P. as
S. N. Capildeo and Bhadase Maraj, who could have challenged
the absentee leadership of Dr. Capildeo, were either forced out
of the party or denied party ticket.'[1]

Again Dr. Capildeo attributed the defeat of his party to the
working of the voting machines, and he termed the election a big
fraud.[2] The election results confirmed the stand of Dr. Capildeo
and his conservative followers, who had earlier precluded the formation of any alliance with the Negro working-class leaders,
believing that only the D.L.P. could get the East Indian vote.

After the election of 1966 the D.L.P. leadership for some time
followed a negative policy of 'maintaining silence' in Parliament
to express its discontent with the electoral process and the policies
of the P.N.M. Government. East Indians have been effectively
excluded from political decision-making, as the new P.N.M.
Government included only two East Indians (one Muslim and one
Indian Christian) out of a Cabinet of 18 members. The country is
faced with a serious economic crisis due to a high rate of unemployment, a decline in the oil reserve of the island, and a general
shortage of capital. East Indian leadership of the D.L.P., however, continues to follow a policy of drift and isolation. Contrary to
the expectations of his followers, Dr. Capildeo asked for a leave of
absence, which was sanctioned by the Executive of the D.L.P., and
he left the country. His seat in the House was declared vacant by
the Speaker due to his prolonged absence from the sessions of
Parliament. As the leader of independent P.D.P., Bhadase contested elections from Dr. Capildeo's constituency and was returned

[1] *Trinidad Guardian* (28 September 1966).

[2] Since the general election of 1966 there has been increased criticism of the
use of the voting machines in particular and the electoral process in general.
Not only the three Opposition parties have denounced the use of the voting
machines. Even the newspapers and the government-appointed Senators have
criticized their use. Henry Pain, a correspondent of *Trinidad Guardian*, wrote:
'I am convinced that well over 50% of the population of the country thinks
that the voting machines were used dishonestly during the last elections.'
Trinidad Guardian (20 December 1966). Senators Conrad O'Brien and Jeffrey
Stollmeyer, in their speeches before the Senate, demanded scrapping of the
voting machines and a return to the ballot boxes. They expressed strong
dissatisfaction with the conduct of the 1966 general election. *Trinidad Guardian*
(9 August 1967).

to the House. Vernon Jamadar became the Leader of the Opposition in place of Dr. Capildeo though Capildeo continues to claim the position of Political Leader—the leader of the mass party organization.

In spite of repeated assertions by the D.L.P. that it would boycott all future elections unless the voting machines were replaced by ballot boxes, the D.L.P. contested the County Councils election in June 1968, and was able to capture only 23 seats with 73 going to the P.N.M. and four being won by independents. There was an extremely low turn-out of voters with only 30 per cent of eligible voters participating in the election.[1] The election results once again demonstrated that the D.L.P.'s support was confined to the East Indian majority areas, and that it was unable to draw support from other sections of the society.

In spite of an official ideology and its profession of faith in multiracialism, the D.L.P. continues to be a party of East Indians. Due to its lack of internal cohesion, ideological confusion, inexperienced leadership, and narrow ethnic orientation, the D.L.P. is still unable to offer any alternative to the party in power.

[1] *Trinidad Guardian* (25 June 1968).

VII

Assessment and Conclusion

THIS investigation into the role of East Indians in the politics of Trinidad makes it evident that in plural societies such as Trinidad, where the population is divided on ethnic and cultural bases, the struggle for political power accentuates the divisions existing within the society. During the colonial period these deep cleavages were dormant. When the country started moving towards independence, the prospect of a majority ethnic group becoming the ruling *élite* tended to widen the gulf existing between the different groups. The organization of a party in such a situation is the result not only of desire to capture political power to ward off the domination of a hostile majority rule but also the result of a strong desire to maintain cultural and ethnic identities. The political struggle does not tend to revolve around issues of alternative policy or programme. Speaking of such societies, Lucian W. Pye observed 'that the fundamental framework of non-Western politics is a communal one, and all the political behaviour is strongly coloured by consideration of communal identification. . .'[1]

In the absence of intimate social relations and because of the existence of strong ethnic and cultural pride, the non-intimate political relations between different groups become vitiated with distrust and hostility. There is an absence of common values and goals as the different groups living within the society have different world views.

Cultural and Institutional Factors in the Political Failure of the East Indian Leadership

Political parties or other types of political activities in plural societies will represent and reflect the subculture of a sub-society to be found within the system. Therefore, the failure of the East Indian leadership to build a multi-ethnic mass party can be understood in the context of the East Indian subculture and the general environmental factors. Since they came to Trinidad, the East Indians have been living in a world of their own. This

[1] Lucian W. Pye, *Politics, Personality and Nation Building* (New Haven, Yale University Press, 1962), pp. 16–17.

tendency still persists. In the absence of primary relations between East Indians and members of other ethnic groups, there always exists a condition of latent hostility and suspicion. At the early stage of their stay in Trinidad society, they participated in India's fight for freedom. Therefore the rise of local nationalism was left to the initiative of the local Creole. The East Indians, with a few exceptions, feared the rise of a Creole-dominated nationalist movement and the movement for constitutional reform. As a minority group they sought shelter either in continuous colonial rule or through communal representation. Their fear of the Creole-dominated nationalism was genuine, as Cipriani, the father of Trinidad nationalism, sought to deprive the East Indian masses of their right to vote through the introduction of an English language test requirement. Furthermore, Captain Cipriani was supported in his move by most of the Creole and local white leaders, including Albert Gomes, Fred Grant, and H. Robinson.[1] Subsequently, the East Indians supported the demand for self-government as a tactical move to oppose the popular demand for the creation of a Federation of the British West Indies, in which they thought they would be hopelessly outnumbered by the Negroes.[2] With the introduction of constitutional reforms, the East Indian *élite*, as leaders of the minority, could not come forward in support of self-government. Self-government in Trinidad without any protection for East Indians meant domination by the majority ethnic group. Therefore, the initiative for the organization of a militant movement in favour of complete self-government came from the Negroes. The P.N.M., in the eyes of the East Indian leaders and East Indian masses, was a 'People's Nigger Movement' to take over Trinidad and to dominate them. It was taken as a threat to their security and East Indians opposed it. Thus, East Indians did not actually participate in Trinidad's movement for self-government. As we have seen, there flourished in Trinidad an East Indian nationalism distinct from the West Indian nationalism, which was led by the Negro middle class.

The political independence of Trinidad was not a highly desired goal of Trinidad East Indians; their nationalism, therefore, fed upon a religious revival. In the 1950s East Indian nationalism

[1] Kirpalani, *et al.*, op. cit., p. 109.
[2] J. H. Proctor, 'East Indians and the Federation of the British West Indies', *India Quarterly* (July-September 1961), p. 399.

found expression in the building of schools, temples, mosques and in the organization of various religious bodies such as the *Sanatan Dharma Maha Sabha, Sunnat-ul-Jamait*, and others. The religious and cultural revival led to the further strengthening of the isolative tendencies of the East Indian leaders, and slowed down the process of acculturation.

Lack of Cohesion within the D.L.P.

Excepting a few occasions, the D.L.P. was rarely in a position to present itself as a cohesive force before the electorate. Even during the most crucial periods the in-group fighting, personal wrangling, and mutual mud-slinging went on unabated among the D.L.P. leaders. Whatever organizational cohesion it achieved in the 1958–61 period was gradually lost. The D.L.P. came to be organized around powerful and independent personalities. That is not unusual in politics. The P.N.M. is organized around Dr. Williams. In British Guiana, both the P.P.P. and P.N.C. (People's National Congress) heavily rely on the strong central leadership of Jagan and Burnham.[1] The D.L.P. came into existence as a result of an alliance formed by a few powerful politicians against their common enemy, the P.N.M. Most of these politicians seemed to have their own independent power bases and thus all of them were leaders in their own right. For instance, Albert Gomes, who joined the D.L.P. in 1957, was formerly the leader of the P.O.P.P.G. and drew his support from the upper stratum of Trinidad whites. Similarly, Bhadase Maraj built his popularity and power on the basis of his leadership of the *Maha Sabha*. Most of the D.L.P. leaders have their own factions organized around them. Morton Klass, as we have seen, refers to the *praja* relationship, which is based upon the recognition of inferior and superior status of two persons. These relations are found on an island-wide basis among East Indians of Trinidad, where an East Indian politician help his clientele by way of distribution of patronage only to his followers. Most of these 'spoils-seeking' politicians, having their independent power bases, vie with each other for capturing the party leadership or the key positions in the party organization. These intense personal rivalries in the top stratum of the D.L.P. leadership seriously weaken the cohesion within the party.

[1] Bradley, op. cit., p. 353.

Personal rivalries, in-group fighting, and wrangling are also the result of mutual jealousies nurtured in East Indian society.

East Indian society in Trinidad is too small. Most of the leaders know each other intimately; they meet frequently at social functions, such as weddings, betrothals, festivals, and other religious or family celebrations. They know each others' family histories. In this type of face-to-face relation and closed society, they are intensely jealous and distrust each other. Family feuds and conflicts on the division of joint properties are reflected in public lives. We have seen that the East Indian social structure is based upon what Banfield calls an 'amoral familism', which breeds exclusiveness and strong feelings of distrust of outsiders and makes organization of effective leadership quite difficult.[1]

There is another reason for the decline of cohesion within the D.L.P. The East Indian community in Trinidad is not a cohesive group, it is not a solidly united ethnic block. It is divided into religious and caste groups, and East Indians have strong subgroup loyalties. Although the traditional antagonism between Hindus and Muslims is not as tense as it would be in India, by no means is it altogether absent. In spite of the efforts of the D.L.P. leaders, there are still many Muslims who regard the D.L.P. as predominantly a Hindu party. The very fact that there are Muslim Ministers in the P.N.M. Government makes it clear that some sections of Muslims have aligned themselves with the P.N.M. The close identification of the D.L.P. leaders with the *Maha Sabha* made the D.L.P. suspect even in the eyes of Indian Christians.

The Hindu society is further divided into caste groups. The East Indian leadership is of high-caste origin; all top D.L.P. leaders are Brahmins. It also contains a highly caste-conscious group of individuals who believe in ascriptive values. The East Indian leadership of the D.L.P., therefore, has been lacking in equalitarian outlook. In order to keep its hold on the low-caste East Indian masses, its appeal has always been to common ethnicity rather than based upon equalitarian political ideology. Klass noted that in Felicity, the village which he studied, among the low castes the D.L.P. was known as the Maharaj party[2]—the party of Brahmins and high castes. In the 1956 election the votes were split on caste basis—the low caste voting for the *Vaish*

---

[1] Banfield, op. cit., p. 89.
[2] Klass, *East Indians in Trinidad*, p. 225.

(middle caste) candidates and high caste voting for the Brahmin candidates.[1] Although in the election of 1961, with increased racial antagonism and under the leadership of Dr. Capildeo (more respected for his academic achievements than for his Brahmin origin), the caste differences were played down, still, the upper stratum of the D.L.P. is not free from caste prejudices. Thus divisions existing within the East Indian society play a divisive role, and do not lead to the development of the D.L.P. as a well-organized, cohesive force.

Absence of a Secularly-Oriented Leadership and a Party Organization

Although the East Indian community in Trinidad has been successful in producing outstanding business leaders, lawyers, and professionals, it has failed to provide a competent and intellectually mature political leadership. Dr. Capildeo lacked the political experience and temperament to organize a mass party and to mobilize mass support for electoral victories. Failing in his bid to capture political power, he decided to leave the country even if he was still officially Leader of the Opposition. His prolonged absence from the island contributed to the gradual decline of cohesion within the East Indian leadership. The East Indian community, on the other hand, could not find any competent substitute for Capildeo.

The socio-economic background of the East Indian leadership tended to push it towards a conformist and sectarian role. The top East Indian leadership lacked any secular-rational orientation, almost all of the members coming from well-to-do families. Most of them equated socialism with communism and opposed all types of innovations. They held contradictory and confusing views on the role and functions of the State in a modern society and were unable to present any alternate and clear-cut programme or policy to attract mass support from all sections of the society. Because of their parochial and kinship-oriented social structure, East Indians favour a patriarchial or, what has been termed a village headmanship type of leadership, based more on personal and informal relations than on well-organized party mechanism. This explains why the D.L.P. had no constitution until 1964 and why it could never develop an effective organizational structure with clear boundaries between different sections of the party. The most

---

[1] Klass, *East Indians in Trinidad*, p. 225.

important informal unit has always been a personal clique around the leader.

Failure to Ally with Non-East Indian Elements

The absence of ideological and nationalist orientations rendered the D.L.P. incapable of aggregating a majority. But unlike some of the minority parties elsewhere,[1] the D.L.P. constitution does not bar non-East Indians from becoming members. We can ask why in a pluralistic society like Trinidad, where numerous minority groups exist, the East Indian leadership could not form a broad-based alliance with the other groups to capture political power. Recently in British Guiana, where Negroes are in the minority, the P.N.C. (The People's National Congress), a Negro-dominated party, has been successful in forming a non-East Indian front with the local whites.[2] Because of the isolative tendencies of the East Indian leaders and the cultural exclusiveness of East Indians, the non-East Indian element of the island finds it difficult to associate with East Indians in politics. The Negro is not culturally different from the island's other miscellaneous non-East Indian elements, but there is a cultural gap between East Indian and non-East Indian elements of Trinidad society. Commenting on the relations between Negroes and whites, M. G. Smith says, 'Despite the racial and cultural polarities within this Negro-White amalgam, mis-cegenation, acculturation, and assimilation have established a single continuum in racial, cultural, and social terms.'[3]

The primary group relations of East Indian *élites* outside their own ethnic group are very limited—almost non-existent in the case of political leaders—as only 7 per cent of the political leaders go to any racially mixed clubs. In the absence of informal social relations between East Indians and non-East Indians, the East Indian leadership of the D.L.P. has not been successful in winning the confidence of non-East Indians on a large scale. Another factor is its conservative and conformist attitude. The East Indian leadership of the D.L.P. could attract only the discredited non-East Indian element, the element which did not have mass support.

---

[1] Theodore P. Wright, Jr., 'The Muslim League in South India since Independence: A Study in Minority Group Strategies', *The American Political Science Review* (September 1966), p. 598.
[2] Despres, *Cultural Pluralism and Nationalist Politics in British Guiana*, p. 266.
[3] M. G. Smith, *The Plural Society in the British West Indies*, p. 13.

And when the D.L.P. got an opportunity to form an alliance with the working-class leaders, its ethnic-oriented and conservative middle-class leadership shunned it. The Negro element which the D.L.P. recruited in 1961, for instance, Dr. Forrester, Peter Farquhar, and others, complained that they always remained on the outer fringes of the party. Finally, finding the D.L.P. leadership too sectarian in its outlook, they left the party. Thus, whatever non-East Indian element came within the fold of the D.L.P. remained unintegrated and unassimilated with the East Indian leadership and did not promote cohesion within the D.L.P.

The Minority Complex of the Leadership

The D.L.P. leadership also suffers from a minority complex. We have seen that after the 1961 election Dr. Capildeo came to the conclusion that any party with Indian leadership would not win because East Indians are the minority. He said that if the D.L.P. had won the election, it would not have been able to run the Government; hostile Negro police and Civil Servants would have made it impossible. Many other East Indian leaders concurred with these views. They added that had the D.L.P. won, there would have been widespread bloodshed and the Negroes would have destroyed East Indian property and raped East Indian women. As a result, Dr. Capildeo concluded that if the P.N.M. was successful in maintaining law and order and could save the necks of the East Indians, he would not mind if the P.N.M. continued to hold power for the next twenty-five years.

It is also because of this attitude that the D.L.P. leadership was hesitant to form any alliance with the disgruntled Negro element. They feel that by co-operating with the P.N.M. Government or at least by abstaining from an openly hostile attitude towards it, they might get more concessions for their community. They feel that non-East Indian elements—Negro labour leaders or the local white business community—want to use them against the P.N.M. Government for their own interests. They suspect everyone and feel that no one can be trusted; everyone would betray East Indians.

Decline of the Threat from the P.N.M.

Another factor which led to the increasing decline of cohesion within the D.L.P. was that the P.N.M. was less feared. At the initial stage of the formation of the D.L.P., and later, the attitude of the P.N.M. leadership was extremely hostile. In spite of their assertion that opposition was an essential part of democracy, by their actions and behaviour the P.N.M. leaders showed scant tolerance for the D.L.P. On the other hand, the D.L.P. leadership was not ready to concede the legitimacy of the P.N.M. Government. But after the London Independence Conference, when ultimate control over political power in Trinidad was in sight, the P.N.M. sought a *rapprochement* with the D.L.P. in order to promote racial harmony in the island. As a first step in this direction, it stopped making direct attacks on the East Indian leadership. Later on, it started making minor concessions to the Opposition by accommodating its leaders on various Government delegations going abroad.

This so-called 'spirit of Marlborough House' lessened the racial tension which had reached its peak in the 1961 election. An important and subtle change also took place in the attitude of the leadership of the majority ethnic group towards the cultural and institutional structures of the East Indians. The Negro leadership of the P.N.M., which earlier recognized only the Creole culture as the genuine West Indian culture, and was intolerant of the cultural exclusiveness of East Indians and strongly disapproved the East Indian cultural revival, now reversed its policy and started encouraging the revival of East Indian music, dance, and drama. The Prime Minister himself encouraged the existence of cultural pluralism by associating with the cultural activities of East Indians. This lessened the apprehension of many of the East Indians who earlier feared a forced creolization by the P.N.M.

Until the 1961 election, some sections of the business community feared the radicalism of the P.N.M. and were afraid that the P.N.M. might disregard their interests and introduce socialism. However, when firmly in office, the P.N.M. modified many of its radical policies and succeeded in winning back the confidence of the business community. With the relaxation of this tension, many of the leading East Indian businessmen turned to the P.N.M. to win official support and favour. Those East Indian business interests which were still with the D.L.P. became apprehensive and finally withdrew their support.

With the decline of the fear of the P.N.M., the unity achieved within the East Indian community in the 1961 election declined and internal divisions, based on religion, became sharp. In the absence of an external threat to its existence, the sectarian and communal interests within the East Indian social structure always assume greater importance.[1] In British Guiana, in almost the same situation, a threat of the rise of Negroes to power kept the East Indians united. The threat from without kept the internal division of East Indian sub-society to a minimum. Jagan's P.P.P. can be described as what Apter calls a 'Party of Solidarity' wherein 'diverse groups are held together by a unifying ideal, such as independence, personalized in the figure of a heroic leader'.[2] Jagan's party has been performing the role for East Indians in British Guiana which the P.N.M. has performed for Negroes in Trinidad. Jagan is a charismatic hero to the East Indians as Dr. Eric Williams is in Trinidad. Thus, many of the weaknesses of the D.L.P., no doubt, spring from the certain special characteristics of the East Indian subculture, such as the lack of cohesion within the East Indian community, amoral familism, strong subgroup loyalties, the presence of ascriptive values, tradition-oriented masses, and an incompetent political leadership.

Conclusion

This case study demonstrates that a cultural-ethnic minority, even though in a position to win political power with the support of other minority groups, cannot succeed in doing so as long as it maintains cultural and social segregation. Also, social and cultural pluralism in a society presents serious problems in the creation of a national identity and in the management of political conflicts. The political struggle continues to be a struggle between two different ways of life, and the incumbent majority does not hesitate to take steps to prevent its replacement. Though temporarily the tension subsides, the potentials for the recurrence of acute tension and serious conflicts are still present in the society.

[1] Morris, who studied Indians in Uganda, found that there were 'unending rivalries within the Indian community on religious, caste and sectarian basis', and observed that the 'structural units that significantly guide the lives of Indians are their caste and sectarian communities'. H. S. Morris, 'Communal Rivalry Among Indians in Uganda', *British Journal of Sociology* (Vol. 8, No. 4, December 1957), p. 316.

[2] David E. Apter, *The Politics of Modernization* (Chicago, The University of Chicago Press, 1965), p. 197.

In the continued absence of intimate social relations between the rival groups, with the increased expectations and demands of the masses, and with the limited capacity of the political system to meet these demands, the problems of managing political tension are likely to increase.

Appendix

Questionnaire Used for Interviewing the Élites
Socio-Economic Variables
Life Sketch

1. What is your name: ....
2. Age .... Caste.................. Sex ....
3. When did your parents migrate to Trinidad? ....
4. What is your religion? ....
   Hindu   Muslim   Catholic   Protestant
   Kabir Panth   None
   Others specify:
5. Were you born into: A joint family, a single family, or an extended family? ....
6. How much do you think your family has played a role in your career? ....

Caste Organization and Religious Association

1. How much importance do you give to your caste origin?
   None   A little   Very much
2. Do you think that the caste system is:

   in the interests of East Indian community?
   against the interest of the country?
   stands in the way of social assimilation?

3. Do you approve the following:

   (a) inter-caste marriage   (b) inter-religious marriage
   (c) inter-racial marriage

4. Are you a member of any one of the following religious organizations?
   The *Arya Samaj*, The *Sanathan Dharma Sabha*, The Muslim League, The *Hindu Maha Sabha*. If any other, specify:
5. Have you held or are you holding any office in these organizations? Give the name of the office and the period:
   ....
6. Were you holding this office at the time of your election or were you elected to this office after your election to the Council?
   ....
7. Are you holding any office in any educational organization of the East Indian Community? ....

8. If Yes, what do you think should be the educational policies of such organizations? ....
Should they place more emphasis on: Westernization, Indianization, Compromise?

9. Hindu Muslim differences have important bearings on social life in India. How important are they in Trinidad?
....

10. If not, what are the reasons? ....
....

11. Do they affect the political affiliation of Hindu–Muslim groups?
....

12. If yes, how? ....
....

13. If not, why not? Specify: ....
....

Educational and Cultural

1. How many years of formal education have you had?
....
(If you attended a secondary school)

2. What secondary school did you attend? ....
Is it public school or private? ....

3. If private, who runs it? ....
If you attended college or university:

4. What college or university did you attend? ....

5. What college or university degree do you hold? ....
....

6. What is your mother tongue? ....

7. Do you know Hindi or Urdu? ....

8. If yes, how did you learn these languages? ....
....

9. What books have you read on India? Give names:
....

10. What new points of admiration do you find in independent India?
....

11. What do you think about the situation in British Guiana?
....

12. Have you published any book or article, if yes, give name, place, and date of publication. ....
....

13. Do you belong to any cultural organization such as The India Club, The West India Club, The Country Club, The Rotary Club, etc.? Give the name of club to which you belong. ....
....

14. Who are, normally, the members of these clubs?

....

Economic

1. In what kind of business or organization are you employed? Give the name: ....

2. If you are a businessman or industrialist, usually how many people are employed by you? ....

3. What was your father's occupation during your youth?

....

4. What is your approximate income? ....

5. Do you belong to any professional or business organization? If yes, give the name: ....

6. What is the ethnic composition of these organizations? East Indian .... Mixed ....

7. Do you hold office in any of these organizations? .... If yes, what is the nature of this office? ....

....

Trade Union Leaders

Name of office: ....   Name of the Union: ....

Period of office held ....   Mixed or East Indian ....

Election and Political Office
(old and present members)

1. When were you first elected to the Legislative Council?

....

2. How long have you been a member of the Council? ....

....

3. Who proposed your name for election? ....

....

4. How did you conduct your campaign for election?
By personal canvassing ....   By party machines..................
By hiring canvassers ....   By all these ....

5. How much help were you given in your election by such organizations as The Arya Samaj, The Sanatan Dharma, The Muslim League; if any other specify: ....

6. What role did organized labour or trade unions play in your elections? ....

....

7. Referring to the main ethnic groups in your constituency for whom did they vote and in what proportion? Also, why? ....

....

....

8. What do you consider was the main reason of your victory in election? ....
....

9. What would you consider the main reason of the defeat of your major opponent?..
....

Government Office

10. Have you ever held any government office? If yes, specify the office in the successive order: ....
....

11. What do you think are the reasons of the poor showing of the D.L.P. in the election of 1961? Specify: ....
....

12. Do you think the D.L.P. succeeded in mobilizing the East Indian Support? ....

13. When and why did you join the D.L.P.? ....
....

14. What do you think the D.L.P. should do in order to win the next election? ....
....

15. Do you think that the D.L.P. will in the near future be able to capture office? ....

16. If not, what are the reasons? ....
....

17. If yes, what may be the reasons of optimism? ....
....
....

Top Élite

1. Which five East Indian civic, political or business leaders appeal to the general public and have the largest following? ....
....
....

2. What are the bases of their popularity? ....
....
....
....

Opinion on Current Issues

1. Considering the present political, economic and social conditions in Trinidad, what type of leaders do you think Trinidad needs most? ....

2. Do you consider that the existing government's policies towards East Indians are: Too harsh, conciliatory, or just right?   ....
....

3. What do you think is the solution of the racial problems of Trinidad?..

4. Do you think that Jagan and his P.P.P. in British Guiana can be a model for the D.L.P. and its leadership?   ....
....

   If not, why not? Give reasons: ....
....

5. Do you think that the policies of the P.N.M. Government endanger any one of the following: Welfare of the community; National solidarity; or Welfare of the East Indian Community?   ....
....

6. What important changes do you think will occur in Trinidad during the next 10 years? ....
....
....
....

Select Bibliography

Official Documents, Memoranda, and Government Publications

Great Britain

Trinidad and Tobago, The Making of a Nation. New York, British Information Service, 1962.

Colonial Office. *Annual Report on Trinidad and Tobago.* London, H.M.S.O., 1946.

Report of the Committee on Emigration from India to the Crown Colonies and Protectorates (Known also as the Sanderson Report). Cmd. 5193 and 5194. London, H.M.S.O., 1910.

Report of the Government of India on the Conditions of Indian Immigrants in Four British Colonies and Surinam (Known as the Chaman lal Report). Part I, Cmd. 7744. London, H.M.S.O., 1915.

Report by the Hon. E. F. L. Wood on His Visit to the West Indies and British Guiana, 1921–1922. Cmd. 1679. London, H.M.S.O., 1922

Trinidad and Tobago Independence Act. London, H.M.S.O., 1962.

The West Indian Royal Commission Report. Cmd. 6607. London, H.M.S.O., 1945.

The West Indian Royal Commission Recommendations, 1938–1939. London, H.M.S.O., 1940.

Report of the Commission on Trinidad and Tobago Disturbances, 1937. London, H.M.S.O., 1938.

Trinidad and Tobago

Memorandum Submitted by the Indian Association of Trinidad and Tobago on the Draft Trinidad and Tobago Constitution. St. Clair, Port of Spain, 1962.

Report of Inter-colonial Conference on Indian Immigration. M.P.N. 3304. Trinidad Archives.

Rural Development in Trinidad and Tobago (Classified Confidential). Port of Spain, UNESCO Regional Office, 1964.

Annual Statistical Digest (No. 13). Port of Spain, Central Statistical Office, 1963.

Census of 1960, Bulletin No. 1. Port of Spain, Central Statistical Office, Population Census Division.

Economic Development of the Independent West Indies. Port of Spain, Government Printing Office, 1960.

Hansard (Parliamentary Debates) Session 1961–1962. Port of Spain, Government Printing Office, 1964.

Report of the Electoral District Boundaries Commission to the Legislative Council with a Minority Report by Hon. S. C. Maharaj. Port of Spain, Government Printing Office, 1961.

Report from the Joint Select Committee to Consider Proposals for an Independence Constitution for Trinidad and Tobago. Port of Spain, Government Printing Office, 1962.

Report of the Commission of Inquiry into Subversive Activities in Trinidad and Tobago (House Paper No. 2 of 1965). Port of Spain, Government Printing Office, 1965.

Report on the Legislative Council General Elections 1956. Port of Spain, Government Printing Office, 1958.

Report on the General Elections of 1961. Prepared by the Supervisor of Elections, Port of Spain, 1965.

Representation of People's Ordinance 1961. Port of Spain, Government Printing Office, 1961.

What Independence Means to You. Port of Spain, Government Printing Office, 1962.

Verbatim Notes of Meeting on Draft Constitution Held at Queen's Hall. Port of Spain (Publisher not given), 1962.

Trinidad and Tobago Year Book 1964–1965. Port of Spain, Yuille's Printeries Ltd., 1964.

Tyson, J. D., *Memorandum of Evidence for the Royal Commission to the West Indies.* Port of Spain, Yuille's Printeries Ltd., 1939.

The U.N. Statistical Year Book 1965. New York, Statistical Office of the U.N., Department of Economic and Social Affairs, 1966.

Mimeographed and Unpublished Material

'Arthur Calder Marshal's Memorandum on Trinidad (1938) to the West Indian Royal Commission, 1938–1939.' Trinidad Archives.

'Governor's Dispatch to the Secretary of State for Colonies, dated November 21, 1921.' Trinidad Archives.

Governor's Dispatch to L. S. Amery, 5 March 1928. Trinidad Archives.

'The Hammer and the Anvil: The Indian Case for Proportionate Representation in Trinidad and Tobago' (mimeographed pamphlet). Port of Spain, Indian Association of Trinidad and Tobago, 1962.

Letter of the Protector of Immigrants, 30 January 1928. Trinidad Archives.

'The Memorial of the East Indian National Congress of Trinidad,' submitted to Mr. E. F. L. Wood signed by Rev. H. H. Imam Shah (Secretary), dated 3 February 1922. Trinidad Archives.

'Report by the Premier on the Draft Independence Constitution' (mimeographed radio broadcast), 8 April 1962.

Party Publications and Documents

'The Democratic Labour Party: Constitution and Rules' (mimeographed). Port of Spain, D.L.P. Office, 1964.

Federal Elections Manifesto of the Democratic Labour Party (of the West Indies). Tunapuna, Trinidad, Printed by Gem Printery, 1958.

For the Sake of Trinidad and Tobago Vote D.L.P. Printed at San Fernando, Rahman's Printery, for the D.L.P., 1961.

A Guide to Policy. Democratic Labour Party, Port of Spain, Tricolor Printery, Ltd., 1961.

Know Your Party. Democratic Labour Party, Port of Spain, Rahman's Printery, 1961.

The Party in Independence. The P.N.M.'s General Council Research Committee, Port of Spain, P.N.M. Publishing Co. (No year of publication.)

People's National Movement Election Manifesto 1956. Port of Spain, printed for the P.N.M. by the College Press, 1956.

People's National Movement Election Manifesto General Elections, 1961. Port of Spain, P.N.M. Publishing Co., 1961.

Books

Ahsan, Syed Reza. 'East Indian Agricultural Settlements in Trinidad: A Study in Cultural Geography.' An unpublished Ph.D. dissertation. Gainesville, University of Florida, 1963.

Almond, Gabriel A. *et al.* (eds.). *The Politics of the Developing Areas.* Princeton, Princeton University Press, 1961.

Apter, David E. *The Politics of Modernization.* Chicago, The University of Chicago Press, 1965.

——'Political Religion in New Nations,' in Clifford Giertz (ed.). *Old Societies and New States.* Glencoe, Illinois, The Free Press, 1963.

Bahadoorsingh, Krishna. *Trinidad Electoral Politics: The Persistence of the Race Factor.* Institute of Race Relations, Special Series, 1968.

Banfield, Edward C. *The Moral Basis of a Backward Society.* Glencoe, The Free Press, 1958.

Bell, Wendell. *Jamaican Leaders, Political Attitudes in a New Nation.* Berkeley, University of California Press, 1964.

Bell, Wendell and Ivar Oxaal. *Decisions of Nationhood, Political and Social Development in British Caribbean.* Social Science Foundation, University of Denver Press, 1964.

Benedict, B. *Maurituis: The Problems of a Plural Society.* London. Pall Mall, 1965.

Blowers, Charles William. 'The Industrial Development of Trinidad—1952–62.' An unpublished Master's thesis. Gainesville, University of Florida, 1964.

Carmichael, G. *The History of the West Indian Islands of Trinidad and Tobago, 1498–1900.* London, A. Redman, 1961.

Craig, Hewan, *The Legislative Council of Trinidad and Tobago*. London, Faber and Faber, 1951.

Cumper, George. *Social Structure of the British Caribbean* (excluding Jamaica), Part III. Mona, Extra-Mural Department, University College of the West Indies, 1949.

Cumpston, I. M. *Indian Overseas in British Territories, 1834–1854*. London, Oxford University Press, 1953.

Dahl, Robert A. *Political Opposition in Western Democracies*. New Haven, Yale University Press, 1966.

Dally, F. W. *Trade Union Organization and Industrial Relations in Trinidad*. London, H.M.S.O., 1949.

Davis, J. M. *The East Indian Church in Trinidad*. New York, International Missionary Council, 1942.

Despres, Leo A. *Cultural Pluralism and Nationalist Politics in British Guiana*. Chicago, Rand McNally and Co., 1967.

Duverger, Maurice. *Political Parties: Their Organization and Activities in the Modern State*. New York, John Wiley and Sons, 1954.

Easton, David. *A System Analysis of Political Life*. New York, John Wiley and Sons, 1965.

Eldersveld, Samuel J. *Political Parties: A Behavioral Analysis*. Chicago, Rand MacNally and Co., 1964.

Freilich, Morris. *Cultural Diversity Among Trinidadian Peasants*. Unpublished Ph.D. dissertation. Ann Arbor, University Microfilm, Inc., 1961.

Furnivall, J. S. *Colonial Policy and Practice*. London, Cambridge University Press, 1948.

——*Netherland Indies*. London, Cambridge University Press, 1939.

Gangulee, N. *Indians in the Empire Overseas*. London, New India Publishing House, 1947.

Gordon, M. M. 'Social Structure and Goals in Group Relations,' in M. Berger (ed.). *Freedom and Social Control in Modern Society*. New York, D. Van Nostrand and Co., 1959.

Grant, K. G. *My Missionary Memories*. Halifax, N. S., The Imperial Publishing Co., 1923.

Herskovits, M. and Frances S. Herskovits. *Trinidad Village*. New York, Alfred A. Knopf, 1947.

Hoetink, H. *Two Variants in Caribbean Race Relations: A Contribution to the Sociology of Segmented Societies*. London, Oxford University Press for the I.R.R., 1967.

Hopkins, L. G. *West Indian Census 1946, General Report on the Census Population*, 9 April 1946. Kingston, Jamaica, Government Printing Office.

Ifill, Max B. *The Solomon Affairs: A Tale of Immorality in Trinidad*. Published by the author, Port of Spain, 22 Jerningham Avenue, Belmont, 1962.

James, C. L. R. *Party Politics in the West Indies*. San Juan, Trinidad, Vedic Enterprises, 1962.
—— *Federation: 'We Failed Miserably,' How and Why*. Published by the author, Tunapuna, Trinidad, 1 Ward Street, 1960.
—— *West Indians of East Indian Descent*. Port of Spain, IBIS Publication Co., 1965.
Kirpalani, Murli J., *et al. Indian Centenary Review*. Guardian Commercial Printery, Port of Spain, Trinidad, 1945.
Klass, Morton. *East Indians in Trinidad: A Study of Cultural Persistence*. New York, Columbia University Press, 1961.
Klass, Sheila Solomon. *Everybody in this House Makes Babies*. New York, Doubleday, 1964
Kondapi, C. *Indians Overseas, 1938–1948*. New Delhi, Indian Council of World Affairs, 1951.
Knowles, William H. *Trade Union Development and Industrial Relations in the British West Indies*. Berkeley, University of California Press, 1959.
Lasswell, Harold, *et al. The Comparative Study of Elites: An Introduction and Bibliography*. Stanford, Stanford University Press, 1952.
Mahar, John Lindsay. 'Trinidad Under British Rule, 1797–1950' (Microfilm). Ann Arbor, University Microfilm, Inc., 1956.
Matthews, Don Basil. *Crisis in the West Indian Family*. Port of Spain, Trinidad, Government Printing Press, 1953.
Mayer, Adrian E. *Peasants in the Pacific: A Study of Fiji Indian Rural Society*, London, Routledge and Kegan Paul, 1961.
Michels, Robert, *Political Parties*. Glencoe, Illinois, The Free Press, 1949.
Mohammed, K. *Unifying Our Cosmopolitan Community*. Port of Spain, P.N.M. Publishing Co., 1960.
Morton, Sarah, E. *John Morton of Trinidad*. Toronto, Westminster Co., 1916.
Moosai, Maharaj S. 'Problems of Race and Language in the British Caribbean,' in P. A. Lockwood (ed.). *Canada and the West Indies Federation*. Sakville, N. B., Mt. Allison University Publication No. 2, 1957.
Naipaul, V. S. *A House for Mr. Biswas*. London, André Deutsch, 1961.
—— *The Middle Passage*. London, André Deutsch, 1962.
—— *The Suffrage of Elvira*. London, André Deutsch, 1958.
Neehal, R. G. 'Presbyterianism in Trinidad,' (A Study of the Impact of Presbyterianism in the Island of Trinidad in the 19th Century). An unpublished M.A. thesis submitted to Union Theological Seminary, New York City, 1958.
Niehoff, Arthur and Juanita. *East Indians in the West Indies*. Milwaukee, Milwaukee Public Museum Publications in Anthropology, 1960.

Ottley, C. R. *Spanish Trinidad*. Port of Spain, College Press, 1955.

Oxaal, Ivar, *West Indian Intellectuals in Power*. Davis, University of California, 1963.

—— *Black Intellectuals Come to Power*. Cambridge, Schenkman Publishing Co., Inc., 1968.

Parsons, Talcott. *The Social System*. Glencoe, Illinois, The Free Press, 1951.

Parsons, Talcott, and Edward Shils. *Toward a General Theory of Action*. Cambridge, Harvard University Press, 1951.

Proudfoot, M. *Britain and the United States in the Caribbean*. New York, Praeger, 1953.

Pye, Lucian W. *Politics, Personality and Nation Building*. New Haven, Yale University Press, 1962.

Rajkumar, N. V. *Indians Outside India*. New Delhi, All-India Congress Committee, 1950.

Reis, Charles. *The Government of Trinidad and Tobago. Law of the Constitution 1797–1947*. Port of Spain, Trinidad, Yuille's Printeries, 1947.

Richardson, E. C. *P.N.M. and Its Agricultural Policy*. Printed by the Vedic Enterprise, Ltd., for Dr. Richardson, 19 Springbank Avenue, Cascade, Trinidad. (No year of publication given.)

Ross, Aileen D. *The Hindu Family in Its Urban Settings*. Toronto, University of Toronto Press, 1961.

Ryan, Selwyn. 'Transition to Nationhood in Trinidad and Tobago, 1797–1962.' Unpublished Ph.D. dissertation, Cornell University, 1966.

Schattschneider, E. E. *Party Government*. New York, Rinehart and Co., 1942.

Schwartz, Barton M. *Caste in Overseas Indian Communities*. San Francisco, Chandler Publishing Co., 1967.

Singh, H. P. *Another Congo?* Port of Spain, Trinidad, 91 Queen Street, 1962.

—— *Hour of Decision*. Port of Spain, Trinidad, 91 Queen Street, 1962.

—— *The Indian Enigma*. Port of Spain, Trinidad, 91 Queen Street, 1964.

Smith, L. S. *The British Caribbean: Who, What, Why, 1955–56*. Glasgow, Bell and Bain, Ltd., 1957.

Smith, M. G. *The Plural Society in the British West Indies*. Berkeley, University of California Press, 1965.

—— *West Indian Family Structure*. Seattle, University of Washington Press, 1962.

Smith, Robert Jack. 'Muslim East Indians in Trinidad: Retention of Identity Under Acculturation Conditions.' Unpublished Ph.D. dissertation. Ann Arbor, University Microfilm, Inc., 1963.

Smith, R. T. *British Guiana*. London, Oxford University Press, 1962.
—— *That Unitary State*. Port of Spain, Trinidad, 91 Queen Street, 1962.
Verba, Sidney, 'Comparative Political Culture,' in Lucian W. Pye and Sidney Verba (eds.). *Political Culture and Political Development*. Princeton, Princeton University Press, 1965.
Weller, Judith A. *The East Indians Indenture in Trinidad*. P.R. Institute of Caribbean Studies, 1968.
Williams, Eric. *British Historians and the West Indies*. Port of Spain, P.N.M. Publishing Co., 1964.
—— *Capitalism and Slavery*. Chapel Hill, University of North Carolina Press, 1944.
—— *The Case for Party Politics in Trinidad and Tobago*. Published by the author, 17 Lady Chancellor Road, Port of Spain, 1955.
—— *Constitutional Reforms in Trinidad and Tobago*. Published by the author, 17 Lady Chancellor Road, Port of Spain, 1955.
—— *Documents of West Indian History*, Vol. 1, 1942. Port of Spain, Todd and Fogarty, 1963.
—— *The Future of the West Indies and Guyana*. Port of Spain, Government Printing Office, 1963.
—— *History of the People of Trinidad and Tobago*. New York, Frederick A. Praeger, 1962.
—— *Massa Day Done*. Port of Spain, P.N.M. Publishing Co., 1961.
—— *My Relations with the Caribbean Commission*. Published by the author, 17 Lady Chancellor Road, Port of Spain, 1955.
—— *Our Fourth Anniversary*. Port of Spain, P.N.M. Publishing Co., 1960.
—— *Prospective for Our Party*. Port of Spain, P.N.M. Publishing Co., 1958.
—— *Prospective for the West Indies*. Port of Spain, P.N.M. Publishing Co., 1960.
—— 'Race Relations in the Caribbean Society,' in Vera Rubin (ed.). *Caribbean Study: A Symposium*. Seattle, University of Washington Press, 1960.

Articles

Akzin, Benjamin. 'Political Problems of Poly-Ethnic Society' (mimeographed). Paris, International Political Science Association, 1961.
Apter, David. 'Some Reflections on the Role of Political Opposition in New Nations', *Comparative Studies in Society and History* (Vol. IV, June 1962).
Augelli, John P. and Harry W. Taylor. 'Race and Population Patterns in Trinidad', *Annals of the Association of American Geographers* (1960).
Ayearst, Morley, 'A Note on Some Characteristics of West Indian Political Parties', *Social and Economic Studies* (Vol. III, No. 3, September 1954).

Benedict, B. 'Social Stratification in Plural Societies', *American Anthropologist* (Vol. 64, 1962).

Bradley, C. Paul. 'Party Politics in British Guiana', *Western Political Quarterly* (Vol. XVI, No. 2, June 1963).

Braithwaite, Lloyd. 'Social Stratification and Cultural Pluralism', *Annals of the New York Academy of Sciences* (Vol. 83, January 1960).

—— 'The Problem of Cultural Integration in Trinidad', *Social and Economic Studies* (Vol. III, No. 1, June 1954).

—— 'Social Stratification in Trinidad', *Social and Economic Studies* (Vol. II, Nos. 2 and 3, October 1953).

Cameron, Pearl. 'New Democratic Party Upholds People's Rights', *Trinidad Guardian* (5 June 1957).

Collins, B. A. N. 'The End of a Colony', *The Political Quarterly* (October–December 1965).

Comitas, Lambros. 'Metropolitan Influence in the Caribbean: The West Indies', *Annals of the New York Academy of Sciences* (Vol. 83, January 1960).

Cross, Malcolm. 'Cultural Pluralism and Sociological Theory', *Social and Economic Studies* (Vol. 17, December 1968).

Crowley, D. J. 'Plural and Differential Acculturation in Trinidad', *American Anthropologist* (Vol. 59, No. 5, 1957).

Davids, Leo. 'The East Indian Family Overseas', *Social and Economic Studies* (Vol. 13, No. 3, September 1964).

Despres, Leo A. 'The Implications of Nationalist Politics in British Guiana for the Development of a Cultural Theory', *American Anthropologist* (Vol. 66, No. 5, 1964).

Dey, Mukul. 'The Indian Population in Trinidad and Tobago', *International Journal of Comparative Sociology* (Vol. 3, No. 2, December 1964).

Ehrensaft, Phillip. 'Authentic Planning or Afro-Asian Appalachia?' *American Behavioral Scientist* (Vol. XII, No. 2, November–December 1968).

Erickson, Edger L. 'The Introduction of East Indian Coolies into the British West Indies', *Journal of Modern History* (Vol. VI, No. 2, June 1934).

Ferkiss, Victor and Barbara. 'Race and Politics in Trinidad and Guyana'. Mimeographed paper presented at the 1969 annual convention of the American Political Science Association, New York.

Firth, Raymond, *et al.* 'Factions in Indian and Overseas Indian Society', *British Journal of Sociology* (Vol. 8, 1957).

Gomes, Albert. 'Race and Independence in Trinidad', *New Society* (27 August 1964).

Green, Helen B. 'Values of Negroes and East Indian Children in Trinidad', *Social and Economic Studies* (Vol. 14, No. 2, June 1965)

Harewood, Jack. 'Population Growth of Trinidad and Tobago in the 20th Century', *Social and Economic Studies* (Vol. II, No. 4, December 1962).

Haug, Maria. 'Social and Cultural Pluralism as a Concept in Social System Analysis', *The American Journal of Sociology* (Vol. 73, No. 3, November 1967).

Hyde, Douglas. 'Communism in Guiana', *Commonwealth* (2 February 1962).

James, C. L. R. 'A. A. Cipriani: The Greatest of All British West Indian Leaders', Independence Supplement, *Sunday Guardian* (26 August 1962).

Klass, Morton. 'East and West Indians: Cultural Complexity in Trinidad', *Annals of the New York Academy of Sciences* (Vol. 83, January 1960).

Lall, G. B. 'A Brief Survey of the Arya Samaj Movement in Trinidad', *The Arya-Samaj Brochure* (Vol. 1, No. 1, February 1945).

Laurence, K. O. 'Colonialism in Trinidad and Tobago', *Caribbean Quarterly* (Vol. 9, No. 3, September 1963).

Lewis, Gordon K. 'The Trinidad and Tobago General Elections of 1961', *Caribbean Studies* (Vol. II, No. 2, July 1962).

Madan, T. N. 'The Joint Family: A Terminology Clarification', *International Journal of Comparative Sociology* (Vol. III, No. 1, September 1962).

Maharaj, Stephen C. 'Trinidad and Tobago Politics 1950–1965', *We the People* (Vol. I, No. 15, October 1965).

—— 'Trinidad and Tobago Politics 1950–1965', (II), *We the People* (Vol. I, No. 19, 29 October 1965).

McKenzie, H. I. 'The Plural Society Debate, Some Comments on Recent Contributions', *Social and Economic Studies* (Vol. 15, 1966).

Morris, H. S. 'Communal Rivalry Among Indians in Uganda', *British Journal of Sociology* (Vol. 8, No. 4, December 1957).

Morris, Stephen. 'Indians in East Africa: A Study in Plural Society', *British Journal of Sociology* (Vol. VIII, No. 3, September 1950).

Moskos, Charles E. and Wendell, Bell. 'West Indian Nationalism'. *New Society* (23 January 1964).

Nadel, S. F. 'The Concept of Social Elite', *International Social Science Bulletin* (Vol. VIII, No. 3, 1956).

Niehoff, A. 'The Survival of Hindu Institutions in an Alien Environment', *Eastern Anthropologist* (Vol. XII, No. 3, March–May 1959).

Oxaal, Ivar. 'C. L. R. James and Eric Williams: The Formative Years', *Trinidad and Tobago Index* (Vol. I, No. 2, Fall 1965).

Proctor, J. H. 'East Indians and the Federation of the British West Indies', *India Quarterly* (July–September 1961).

—— 'The Functional Approach to Political Union: Lessons from the Efforts to Federate the British Caribbean Territories', *International Organization* (February 1956).

Ramphal, S. S. 'Federal Constitution Making in the British West Indies', *International Comparative Law Quarterly* (2 April 1953).

Rex, John. 'The Plural Society in Sociological Theory', *British Journal of Sociology* (Vol. X, No. 2, June 1959).

Richmond, A. H. 'Theoretical Orientations in Studies of Ethnic Group Relations in Britain', *Man* (Vol. 57, August 1957).

Rubin, Vera. 'Discussion on Smith's Social and Cultural Pluralism', *Annals of the New York Academy of Sciences* (Vol. 83, January 1960).

—— (ed.) *Caribbean Studies: A Symposium*, Jamaica, the University of the West Indies (1957).

—— 'Approaches to the Study of National Characteristics in a Multiracial Society', *International Journal of Social Psychiatry* (1959).

—— 'Culture, Politics and Race Relations', *Social and Economic Studies* (Vol. XI, 1962).

Schwartz, Barton M. 'Caste and Endogamy in Trinidad', *Southwestern Journal of Anthropology* (Vol. 20, No. 1, 1964).

—— 'Pattern of East Indian Family Organization in Trinidad', *Caribbean Studies* (Vol. 5, No. 1, April 1965).

—— 'Ritual Aspects of Caste in Trinidad', *Anthropology Quarterly* (Vol. 37, No. 1, January 1964).

Sherlock, Philip. 'The Story of Trinidad', Independence Supplement, *Sunday Guardian* (26 August 1962).

Shils, Edward. 'The New States', *Comparative Studies in Society and History* (Vol. II, No. 4, July 1960).

—— 'Political Development in the New State', *Comparative Studies in Society and History* (Vol. II, No. 3, April 1960).

Sires, Ronald V. 'Government in the British West Indies: An Historical Outline', in H. D. Huggins (ed.). *Federation of the West Indies*. Institute of Social and Economic Research, Jamaica, University of West Indies, B.W.I. (1958).

Smith, M. G. 'Social and Cultural Pluralism', *Annals of the New York Academy of Sciences* (Vol. 83, January 1960).

Smith, R. T. 'Review of Social and Cultural Pluralism in the Caribbean', *American Anthropologist* (Vol. 63, 1961).

Spackman, Ann. 'Constitutional Development in Trinidad and Tobago', *Social and Economic Studies* (Vol. 14, No. 4, December 1965).

Speckman, J. D. 'The Indian Group in the Segmented Society of Surinam', *Caribbean Studies* (Vol. 3, No. 1, April 1963).

Vieira, Phil. 'The Human Mosaic: That is Trinidad. Life and Times of Early Immigrants', Independence Supplement, *Sunday Guardian* (23 August 1962).

Wooding, H. O. B. 'The Constitutional History of Trinidad and Tobago', *Caribbean Quarterly* (Vol. VI, Nos. 3 and 4, May 1960).

Wright, Theodore P. 'The Muslim League in South India since Independence: A Study in Minority Group Strategies', *The American Political Science Review* (September 1966).

Newspapers and Weeklies

Andhra Patrika (Madras), 1927.

Bombay Chronical, 1927.

Daily Express (Madras), 1927.

Daily Mirror, 1964–5.

East Indian Weekly, 1929.

East Indian Herald, 1925.

East Indian Patriot, 1922.

Forward (Calcutta), 1927.

Nation (Trinidad), 1958–65.

Port of Spain Gazette, 1930.

Statesman, 1961–5.

Sunday Guardian, 1950–65.

Sunday Mirror, 1964–5.

The Times (London), Supplement on Trinidad and Tobago (25 January 1966).

Trinidad Guardian, 1950–66.

We the People, 1965.

Index

Abidh, C. E., 75
Achong, Carlton, 97
Adams, G., 89
African National Congress, 120
African religions, survival in Trinidad, 7; *Dahomea, Shango, Yoruba*, 7, 8
Africanism, revival, 8
Africans, 17; embrace Christianity, 7; retention of cultural heritage, 7 n. 3; cultural maturity, 8; associated with primitiveness, 8 *see also* Negroes
Agriculture, E.I. majority occupation, 12, 13, 17, 45
Ahmed, Aziza, visits Ayub Khan, 36
Ahsan, Seyed Reza, and E.I. cultural ambitions, 15
All-Trinidad Sugar Estates and Factories' Workers' Trade Union, general strikes (1954), 85 (1965), 149; loses its identity, 86; Bhadase and, 118, 149; and 1961 election, 119
Almond, Gabriel A., on political socialization, 26 and n.
America *see* United States
Americans, industrial and banking ownership, 11; alleged distrust of Indians, 66–7
Amerindians ('Caribs'), virtual extinction, 6
'Amoral familism', Bancroft's concept, 29, 163
Anglicans, percentage of Trinidad population, 6, 38; social prestige of Church, 7
Anglo-American Caribbean Commission, Williams and, 90
Apter, David, his 'political religion', 25 and n.; Party of Solidarity, 168
Arabs, 6, 12, 116
Arya Pritinidhi Sabha, rival factions, 32
Arya Samat, Hindu reformist sect, xi, xiii, 47, 48; rich, high-caste follow-

ing, 32; brought by missionaries, 32; internal dissensions, 50
Ayub Khan, President of Pakistan, 36

Bahadoorsingh, Krishna, and voting in 1961 election, 121 and n. 1
Bahamas, immigrant population, 5
Banfield, Edward C., concept of 'amoral familism', 29, 163
Banks, ownership, 11
Barbados, statistics, xi n.; immigrant population, 5; leadership, 89
Bholai, Ram Persad, 136
Bleasdell, T., 151; on Democratic Socialism, 146
Boodoosingh, L. D., 72
Boundaries Commission, 131, 133
Brahmins, 11, 31, 33–4, 78; rejection of rituals by Kabir, 32; subdivisions 41 n. 2; and political leadership, 47, 163; and intercaste marriage, 56
Braithwaite, Lloyd, and revival of Africanism, 8 and n. 4; and subcultural expectations, 24
Brassington, F. E., and D.L.P., 105
Brazil, African affiliations, 7 n. 3
British, industrial and banking ownership, 11; and situation in British Guiana, 65; alleged distrust of Indians, 66–7
British Empire Workers' and Citizens' Home Rule Party (Butler's Party), 81, 82
British Government, and Trinidad Legislative Council, 69–70; and her political reform, 73, 74, 75, 129–30, 131; and D.L.P. demands, 138, 140
British Guiana, 32; suggested partition, 32; position of Negroes, 63, 165; Negro–E.I. conflict, 63, 168; E.I. *élite* and, 63–8; United Force party, 88; demand for self-government, 108; election broadcasts, 118; formation of broad-based alliance, 165 *see also* Jagan